FOR PROS BY PROS® BUILDER-TESTED | CODE APPROVED

Building Decks

EDITORS OF

FineHomebuilding

The Taunton Press

The Taunton Press
Inspiration for hands-on living®

The Taunton Press, Inc., 63 South Main Street, PO Box 5506, Newtown, CT 06470-5506
e-mail: tp@taunton.com

Editor: Christina Glennon
Copy editor: Diane Sinitsky
Indexer: Jay Kreider
Interior design: Carol Singer
Layout: Susan Lampe-Wilson
Cover photographer: Charles Bickford, courtesy of *Fine Homebuilding,* © The Taunton Press, Inc.

Fine Homebuilding® is a trademark of The Taunton Press, Inc., registered in the U.S. Patent and Trademark Office.

The following names/manufacturers appearing in *All New Building Decks* are trademarks: 3M™; Accoya®; American Dry Deck™; AridDek™; Azek®; Behr®; Bigfoot Systems®; Bostitch® Strapshot™; Cali Bamboo® BamDeck®; CAMO™; CertainTeed®; ChoiceDek®; Clubhouse® Decking; CopperMoon®; Cortex®; Deckorators®; Dek Drain®; Dekor™; Diablo®; DockSider®; DryJoist™; DrySnap®; DrySpace™; DuraLife™; Earthwood Evolutions®; EB-TY®; Endeck®; Enduris®; EverGrain®; Evolve®; Exterior Fire-X®; Fairway®; FastenMaster®; Fiberon®; Freud®; FRX®; Genovations®; GeoDeck™; GeoLam®; Grace Ice & Water Shield®; Heatcon®; HIDfast®; Invisi-Fast™; InvisiDeck®; Kichler® Lighting; Last-Deck®; Latitudes® Intrepid™; LedgerLOK®; LockDry®; Lumberock®; Maine Ornamental®; ModernView™; MoistureShield®; Moonlight Decks™; NextDeck®; NyloDeck®; Olympic®; Penofin®; Pro Plug®; ProWood Dura Color®; RailEasy™; RainEscape®; ReliaBoard®; Resysta®; Ridgid®; Rubberall®; Rust-Oleum®; Scotch-Weld™; Simpson Strong-Tie®; Speed® Square; Square Foot™; Strong-Drive®; Superdeck®; TeeJet®; TerraDeck®; ThruLOK®; Tiger Claw™; TimberLOK®; TimberSIL®; TimberTech®; Transcend®; Trex®; TUFboard®; TwinFinish®; UltraDeck®; UltraShield®; UnderDeck™; Unique Lighting Systems®; VEKAdeck™; Veranda®; Versadeck™; Vulcan Vent™; Vycor®; Wagner®; Wolman™ CopperCoat™; WP Fail-Safe Form Fitter™; YouTube℠; Zuri™

Library of Congress Cataloging-in-Publication Data

Building decks (Taunton Press)
  All new building decks / editors of Fine Homebuilding.
    pages cm
  Revised edition of: Building decks. 2011.
  Includes index.
  ISBN 978-1-63186-328-8
1. Decks (Architecture, Domestic) I. Taunton Press. II. Fine Homebuilding. III. Title. IV. Title: Building decks.
  TH4970.B8523 2015
  690'.893--dc23

                      2015026360

PRINTED IN THE UNITED STATES OF AMERICA
10 9 8 7 6 5 4 3 2 1

ABOUT YOUR SAFETY: Construction is inherently dangerous. Using hand or power tools improperly or ignoring safety practices can lead to permanent injury or even death. Don't try to perform operations you learn about here (or elsewhere) unless you're certain they are safe for you. If something about an operation doesn't feel right, don't do it. Look for another way. We want you to enjoy working on your home, so please keep safety foremost in your mind.

ACKNOWLEDGMENTS

Special thanks to the authors, editors, art directors, copy editors, and other staff members of *Fine Homebuilding* who contributed to the development of the articles in this book.

Contents

2   Introduction

PART 1: TOOLS AND MATERIALS

5   A Plank for Every Deck

14 A Buyer's Guide to Deck Hardware

21 Choosing the Best Deck Finish

PART 2: DECK DESIGN AND PLANNING

27 Design a Better Deck

31 Improve Your Deck's View

35 Designing a Small but Elegant Deck

39 Designing a Porch with a Rooftop Deck

42 Bending Decking for Decorative Inlays

51 Bright Ideas for a Well-Lit Deck

57 A Homeowner's Guide to Deck Permits

PART 3: DECK FRAMING

66 Deck Loads

69 Frost Heave

72 Sizing Deck Footings

80 Deck Footings Done Right

83 Framing a Grade-Level Deck

91 Framing a Deck with Steel

101 Top 10 Deck-Building Mistakes

109 Make an Old Deck Safe

PART 4: DECKING

118 Decks That Stand Up to Wildfire

126 Site-Built Deck Drainage

130 Decking over a Roof

138 Deck Refinishing

PART 5: RAILINGS AND STAIRS

147 Manufactured Railing Systems

156 Railing Retrofit

164 2 Ideas for Custom Railings

169 Mounting Deck Stairs

PART 6: COMPLETE DECK GUIDES

178 A Low, Curvy Deck

199 A Raised Deck with a
     Custom Railing

220 A Grade-Level Deck with a
     Decorative Border

245 Contributors

246 Credits

248 Index

Decks are wonderful outdoor spaces that can foster lifetime memories of friends and family. And they are a ton of fun to build, with a simple structure and plenty of opportunities for customization. But I also see a lot of decks that are poorly—even unsafely—built. That happens for several reasons. While we've been building houses for millennia, decks are a relatively new feature. New features always incur a learning curve, and in construction, that often means building things one way and then changing methods when the first ones fail. That's why it's taken 50 years or so for deck building to mature.

I've been involved with decks for about 30 of those 50 years. When I became a carpenter in 1986, some of my first jobs were building decks for a tract builder. At first, he didn't even supply pressure-treated lumber for the framing or lag bolts for attaching the decks to the house—two items that are now considered critical in building safe decks. In those early decks, I simply nailed the decking to the joists, an attachment method that's long been supplanted by deck screws because screws don't back out the way nails do. And I'd rather not talk about how that builder wanted me to attach the railings. Let's just leave it that we know better today. Much better.

Another reason for poorly built decks is that, although their structure is simple, some of those simple things are not obvious at a glance once the deck is complete. If you try to figure out how to build your deck by looking at your neighbor's, you might not notice critical details such as the flashing that keeps water out from between the deck and the house. Do that flashing wrong, or skip it, and your house framing will eventually rot.

No one should build decks today the way they were built when I started out, and no one should build a deck without an expert demonstrating the critical nuances that hide below the surface. That's what this book provides. *Fine Homebuilding* magazine, the source of the chapters in this book, doesn't hire professional writers to create its articles. *Fine Homebuilding* authors are professionals who are experts in their field, whether they're carpenters, masons, or designers. And the *Fine Homebuilding* editors who turn these authors' manuscripts into articles have construction backgrounds themselves, enabling them to vet the authors' information with real-world experience.

Whether you're a DIYer or a pro who simply wants the best, most up-to-date information on deck building, this is the book you need. I only wish it had been available in 1986.

Build well,

Andy Engel, Senior Editor, *Fine Homebuilding*

PART 1

Tools and Materials

5   A PLANK FOR EVERY DECK

14 A BUYER'S GUIDE TO DECK HARDWARE

21 CHOOSING THE BEST DECK FINISH

A Plank for Every Deck

BY SCOTT GIBSON

Trex® turned the decking business on its ear in the mid-1990s with a composite lumber made from finely ground wood and discarded plastic bags. Now, 20 years later, there are plenty of other makers of synthetic decking and many more sophisticated products to choose from.

The fundamentals remain unchanged, however: Wood owns most of the market, and the alternatives are all scrambling for the remaining slice of the pie, offering products that need less maintenance but cost more. Whether buyers want to stay with wood or sample one of the many synthetics, there are plenty of choices.

Builders will find no less variety in the kinds of fasteners on the market. Some carpenters still prefer to drive screws, or even nails, through the face of the decking, but most manufacturers of synthetic decking offer boards with grooved edges that are designed to work with hidden fasteners. When installation is complete, no fastener heads are visible, and deck boards are spaced evenly apart.

Hidden fasteners come in a number of variations, including clip systems such as Tiger Claw®, EB-TY®, or Invisi-Fast™; brackets that accept fasteners from below; and pneumatic fastening systems such as those made by HIDfast® and InvisiDeck®.

Other options include CAMO™, a guide for driving screws at an angle into the edge of a board, and Cortex® fasteners for face-screwing deck boards, which come with color-matched plugs. Plugs are made for a number of decking brands.

Treated or Untreated, Wood Is Still Great for Tight Budgets

Pressure-treated southern yellow pine wood decking still accounts for roughly three-quarters of the U.S. market. Even the least expensive wood-plastic composites cost nearly 4 times as much, and some types of plastic decking cost 10 times as much.

Despite the advertising budgets and the attention being paid to synthetic decking, the wood-decking market now offers an expansive menu of choices.

In addition to the pressure-treated pine and Douglas fir that have been the mainstays of the market, imported species that come with the blessing of the Forest Stewardship Council are now more widely available. In addition to the exotics, three new kinds of wood decking have found their way into the U.S. market: thermally modified, acetylated, and color-infused pressure-treated lumber.

WOOD. It's hard to beat the beauty of natural wood. This Tigerwood (goncalo alves) deck will also stand up to bugs and rot without preservatives.

Naturally Hardy Varieties

Certain species of wood—cedar and redwood, for example—have long been popular decking choices because of their natural resistance to insects and rot. Provided the decking is milled from heartwood and not sapwood, both cedar and redwood will provide many years of service. Both fade to gray unless they are stained or clear-coated, and because they are relatively soft, they gouge easily.

Species such as ipé, cumaru, and goncalo alves (sold as Tigerwood) are among the better-known tropical hardwoods that offer long-term protection against bugs and rot without the use of preservatives. They're dark and rich in color when new, fading to a silvery gray in the weather, and they are far harder and denser than cedar, pine, and Douglas fir.

Advantage Lumber, which carries all three species, says these South American hardwoods can last as long as 60 years. Look for decking that carries the Forest Stewardship Council (FSC) label, which certifies that the wood has been harvested responsibly. (Unlabeled wood carries no guarantee of having been harvested responsibly.) It's worth noting that supplies of certified material can fluctuate up and down.

Pressure-Treated Wood

Pressure-treated decking is available at most big-box stores and lumberyards. The newer copper-based preservatives are free of arsenic, and they guard the wood against termites and moisture-induced decay.

Although it shouldn't rot for a long time, pressure-treated decking is famous for twisting and checking. While applying a stain or preservative will help, these coatings have to be renewed as often as every year or two.

PRESSURE-TREATED WOOD. Pressure-treated wood has the natural look many people are looking for in a deck, but it is notorious for twisting and checking.

Universal Forest Products has introduced ProWood Dura Color®, a color-infused pressure-treated lumber. The company guarantees the product against fading for two years and offers a lifetime warranty against termites and rot.

Alternative Preservatives

Two relative newcomers to the wood-decking category in the United States are acetylated lumber and thermally modified lumber. Both offer long-term resistance to rot and insect damage without relying on conventional preservatives.

Acetylation induces a chemical change in the wood with acetic acid. Similar in concept to pickling food, acetylation makes the wood more dimensionally stable, less likely to absorb water, and far less appetizing to insects, according to manufacturers. Acetylated lumber marketed under the Accoya® label, for example, is guaranteed for 50 years above ground and 25 years in the ground.

Thermally modified wood has been available in Europe for years but has only recently started to make its way into the United States. The wood is heated in a kiln at temperatures up to 500°F. The heat removes sugars and forces other changes in the structure of the wood, resulting in greater dimensional stability and improved resistance to rot and moisture. One drawback is that the process makes wood harder and more brittle, so count on drilling pilot holes during installation.

Among the brands of thermally modified wood that are available in the United States are EcoDeck (made by EcoVantage) and Arbor Wood. A variety of wood species are used. For example, EcoDeck uses No. 1 southern-yellow-pine decking, while Arbor Wood uses ash and red-oak decking. Neither EcoDeck nor Arbor Wood is recognized by the International Code Council (ICC), but Arbor Wood says it is working with other manufacturers of thermally modified wood on standards that will be recognized by ANSI. The process is approved in Europe, Arbor Wood says. Also, because thermally modified wood is still new, distribution of EcoDeck and Arbor Wood is fairly spotty.

One last type of unconventionally treated wood is a product called TimberSIL®. The company's website says its "glass wood fusion" process improves the wood's strength and fire resistance but does so while keeping the product nontoxic. It comes with a 40-year warranty. TimberSIL has had some distribution problems, and lead times may be in the six- to eight-week range, at least in the Northeast. Also, the product has recently had some widely publicized problems on projects in Massachusetts and New Orleans, so approach with caution.

Synthetic Decking Moves beyond Wood-Plastic Composites

Although high prices have limited synthetic decking to a relatively small slice of the overall decking market, the products are continually improving in performance and aesthetics. Composites are now offered with an outer shell, or cap, made of a different type of plastic to improve durability, and cellular-PVC boards are manufactured with no wood content at all. You'll even find composites made with recycled nylon carpeting or rice hulls rather than wood flour.

A number of companies have also begun to adopt a "good-better-best" strategy with their plastic and composite decking—offering a range of prices, performance characteristics, and colors.

All-Plastic Decking

Hollow, extruded-vinyl decking was the original nonwood option, preceding even wood-plastic composites such as Trex. Although it has since been eclipsed by other products, it still has its place.

"Is it a tremendous market share in terms of decking-material type? No," says CertainTeed® senior marketing manager Patti Pellock. "Is it growing? No. But it fills a niche."

Maintenance for the nonporous surface is minimal, planks are simple to install, and the product comes with a lifetime warranty, Pellock says. But colors are limited, and the surface doesn't look anything like wood.

Other companies making vinyl decking include Genova Products and Royal Building Products, and vinyl is a popular choice in places where performance trumps aesthetics, such as docks.

In response to problems with early wood-plastic composites and clamoring by the market for a low-maintenance product that looked like wood, the industry came up with cellular PVC. Its all-plastic composition meant there was nothing to rot or promote mold (other than surface contaminants). And because of the cell structure created as the PVC was foamed during manufacturing, the cured product handled and worked something like real wood.

But cellular PVC wasn't perfect, either. Because of the plastic content, it was more expensive than composites. Decking was limited to a light color palette, and there were consumer complaints of fading and discoloration.

Manufacturers responded with capped boards, just as composite makers had done. The addition of a coextruded cap made possible the dark colors that consumers liked, improved resistance to fading and scratching, and allowed advances such as the digital wood-grain printing in Royal Building Products' Zuri planks.

A number of companies manufacture cellular-PVC decking, including Gossen, CertainTeed,

WOOD-PLASTIC COMPOSITE.
This Trex Transcend® deck in
Tree House and Vintage Lantern
comes from the company's top-line
offering, which has been designed
to mimic the look of tropical
hardwoods.

Deceuninck, TimberTech®, Veka Innovations, Azek®, and Enduris®.

Aesthetically, says CertainTeed's Pellock, there was no longer much of a difference between capped-composite decking and capped-PVC decking. Cellular-PVC decking remained more expensive, but it also carried longer warranties.

"In general, wood-plastic composites won't hold for a lifetime," Pellock says. "They have wood. You can't guarantee wood's going to last a lifetime."

With the advent of capped composites, Steve Van Kouteren of Principia, a market research and consulting firm, thinks that cellular-PVC decking has lost some of its edge and will see lower demand over time because of its higher cost.

Wood-Plastic Composites

Despite early setbacks, wood-plastic composites are still thriving. The mix of low-density polyethylene plastic and wood flour that went into the original Trex composite product opened a huge marketing opportunity for the industry. But these first-generation composites didn't live up to expectations. Because the composites contained cellulose, some products came back with reports of mold, decay, and surface staining.

It was a new product with some rough edges. According to Principia's Van Kouteren, makers of uncapped composite decking have improved early formulations to make boards more resistant to color fade, mold, and mildew. Also, they're advertised as "low maintenance," not "no maintenance," so consumers have a better idea of what to expect in terms of durability.

Uncapped composites are still available, but many manufacturers have moved toward capped versions, which consist of a wood-plastic composite core and an outer shell of another type of plastic. The two materials are bound together as the boards are manufactured, a process known as coextrusion.

Capping composite boards increased stain and scratch resistance and seemed to solve other performance problems related to cellulose content. And capped decking, or capstock as it's often called, is typically less expensive than all-plastic versions such as cellular PVC.

Capped and uncapped composite decking is now made by more than a dozen companies, including Trex, AERT, Tamko, TimberTech, and Fiberon®. Most wood-plastic composites are made with polyethylene or high-density polyethylene plastic, but at least two are a mix of hardwood fiber and polypropylene: DuraLife™ and Iron Woods' Boardwalk HCX. Both have a coextruded cap of polypropylene. Although polypropylene is more expensive than polyethylene, manufacturers say that the plastic is tougher and stiffer, and that it has high stain resistance and excellent dimensional stability.

Yet even as products improve, nonwood decking still only captures 20% or so of the total market, says Van Kouteren. Some manufacturers are attempting to solve this problem and coax more customers away from wood by offering different grades of composite decking. Trex, for example, now has three lines of capped boards: Select, Enhance, and Transcend.

Adam Zambanini, Trex's vice president for marketing, says that all three options start with a 50-50 mix of low-density polyethylene and wood. The differences are in the profile of the board (Select decking is ⅞ in. thick rather than the full 1-in. thickness of typical 5/4-in. decking), the properties of the cap material, and the available colors. Transcend, the company's top-of-the-line offering, offers colors designed to mimic tropical hardwoods.

Trex isn't the only company pursuing this tiered approach. Toby Bostwick, product management director of CPG Building Products, which sells decking under both the Azek and TimberTech brands, says the company wants to offer a good-better-best lineup for its wood-plastic composites, capped composites, and all-plastic decking.

TimberTech's Earthwood Evolutions® Terrain decking, for example, is an entry-level synthetic product that aims to help consumers make the jump from wood. Tropical, at the top of the brand's line of capped products, has variegated streaking designed to mimic hardwoods like Tigerwood.

Nonwood Composites

Most composites are made with wood flour and plastic. One alternative is GeoDeck™, which is manufactured from powdered paper sludge, dried rice hulls, and polyethylene. The company says the hard rice hulls contain silica, which offers mold resistance, and very little lignin, which means better color retention.

EPS Plastic Systems' Bear Board is a mix of high-density polyethylene and minerals with a 50-year guarantee.

Cali Bamboo®'s BamDeck® is made from 60% reclaimed bamboo fibers and high-density polyethylene, a combination the company claims is three times as strong as other composites. It has a 25-year warranty.

NyloDeck®, which its manufacturer calls the "non-composite composite," is made from recycled carpet fiber and contains no wood.

Keep in mind that not all decking is available everywhere. Some brands have limited availability and may not be stocked locally.

NONWOOD COMPOSITE. Made from recycled carpet fiber, this composite deck from NyloDeck contains no wood.

ALUMINUM. This NextDeck Dakota Oak wood-grain aluminum deck from Nexan Building Products has a class-A fire rating.

Aluminum

If you want a long-lasting, rotproof deck and don't give a hoot whether it looks like wood or not, one option to consider is aluminum.

Aluminum decking is made by a number of companies, including Nexan Building Products, Versadeck™, Wahoo Decks, and Last-Deck®. Specs are similar.

Nexan Building Products' LockDry® decking, for example, comes in seven powder-coated colors, has a class-A fire rating, has been tested to loads of 240 lb. per sq. ft., and has a nonskid surface.

Once assembled, LockDry makes a waterproof barrier so that you can use the space under the deck for storage or as a patio. There is a nonwaterproof version called NextDeck®.

INDEX OF SYNTHETIC DECKING MANUFACTURERS

LISTED HERE IS A SNAPSHOT of current synthetic-decking manufacturers. Keep in mind that the decking market is very active, and companies enter and leave it at a surprising rate. Also, not all of these companies have national distribution. Most building materials, including decking, are sold through what's called two-step distribution, in which manufacturers supply a limited number of regional wholesalers who then supply lumberyards and home centers. Because of space and inventory-turnover concerns, wholesalers tend to limit the lines of decking they carry to proven profit makers. This makes it difficult for new or smaller manufacturers to find a wholesaler and gain a toehold in the national market.

PLASTIC

AZEK (www.azek.com)

BEAR BOARD (epsplasticlumber.com)

CLUBHOUSE® DECKING (www.deceuninckna.com)

ENDECK® (www.enduris.com)

EVOLVE® (www.renewplastics.com)

FIBERON (www.fiberondecking.com)

GENOVATIONS® (genovationsdeck.com)

GOSSEN (www.gossencorp.com)

KLEER DECKING (thetapcogroup.com/brands/kleer)

SHEERGRAIN (www.lbplastics.com)

TUFBOARD® (www.tufboard.net)

VEKADECK™ (vekaoutdoorliving.com)

WOLF (www.wolfhomeproducts.com)

ZURI (zuri.royalbuildingproducts.com/zuri)

WOOD-PLASTIC COMPOSITES

ARMADILLO DECK (www.armadillodeck.com)

CHOICEDEK® (www.choicedek.com)

DURALIFE (www.duralifedecking.com)

EVERGRAIN® (www.tamko.com)

FIBERON (www.fiberondecking.com)

GEOLAM® (www.geolaminc.com)

LATITUDES® (www.latitudesdeck.com)

MODERNVIEW™ (www.modernviewdecking.com)

MOISTURESHIELD® (www.moistureshield.com)

PC DECKING (www.premiumcomposites.com)

TIMBERTECH (timbertech.com)

TREX (www.trex.com)

ULTRADECK® (www.midwestmanufacturing.com)

ULTRASHIELD® (www.newtechwood.com)

VERANDA® (www.verandadeck.com)

WOLF (www.wolfhomeproducts.com)

NONWOOD COMPOSITES

GEODECK (www.greenbaydecking.com/geodeck)

LUMBEROCK® (www.lumberock.com)

NYLODECK (nyloboard.com)

RESYSTA® (www.resysta.com)

TERRADECK™ (naturescomposites.com)

ALUMINUM

ARIDDEK™ (wahoodecks.com)

LAST-DECK (www.lastdeck.com)

LOCKDRY (www.nexaninc.com)

VERSADECK (www.versadeck.com)

A Buyer's Guide to Deck Hardware

BY PATRICK MCCOMBE

I used to hear people say, "It's just a deck. Anyone can build a deck. What's the big deal?" When the deck pulls off the side of a house or when the railing gives way, though, it is a big deal. People can get hurt; they can even be killed.

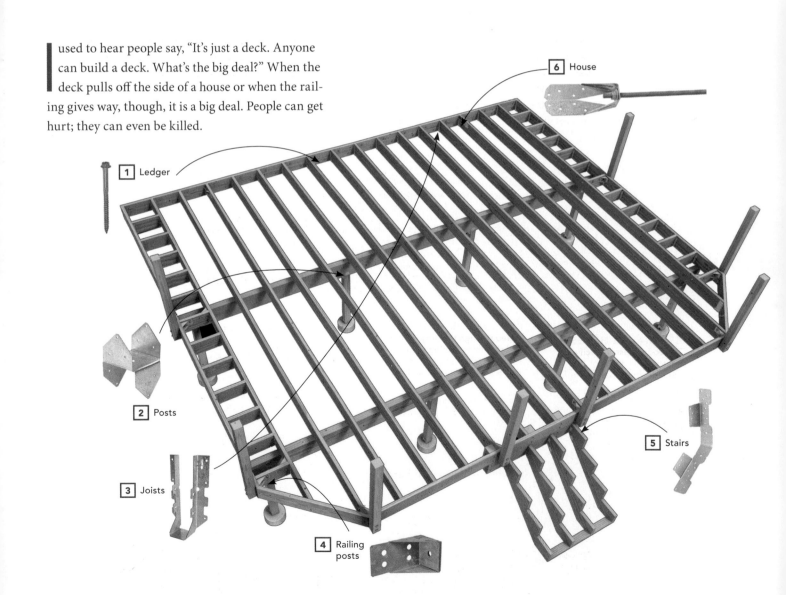

1 Ledger

2 Posts

3 Joists

4 Railing posts

5 Stairs

6 House

With tragic deck collapses mainstream news in towns all over the country, code writers and building inspectors have understandably made deck safety a priority. These deck collapses can generally be traced to failure at one of the six critical connections shown in the drawing on the facing page. Not surprisingly, hardware makers have focused their products on these same six connections.

Fortunately, the innovative fasteners and steel connectors now available are straightforward to use. Some may even save you time. More important, though, they allow any deck builder, pro or novice, to satisfy code requirements and to build a safer deck.

I. LEDGER TO RIM JOIST

WHEN A LEDGER ISN'T ADEQUATELY FASTENED to the house's rim joist, it can break free from the house, resulting in a deck that crashes to the ground. The traditional way to fasten a ledger is with ½-in.-dia. (or larger) lag screws or through bolts long enough to penetrate the house's rim joist. The number of fasteners needed depends on the length of the ledger and the anticipated load. Consult the code, your building official, or an engineer for the number of bolts or lags needed for your project. The drawing below shows proper placement.

STRUCTURAL SCREWS
Self-drilling structural screws cost more than lag screws or through bolts but can save time, as they don't require pilot or clearance holes. Some manufacturers offer screw-spacing tables; others list only technical specs and leave it up to you to calculate the spacing.

FastenMaster LedgerLok (www.fastenmaster.com)
Length: 3⅝ in. and 5 in.
Material: Coated steel

GRK RSS (www.grkfasteners.com)
Length: Many sizes
Material: Stainless steel and zinc-coated steel

Strong-Drive® SDS (www.strongtie.com)
Length: 3½ in., 4½ in., and 5 in. (¼ in. dia.)
Material: Coated steel and stainless steel

PILOT AND CLEARANCE HOLES
The code doesn't specify how to drill holes for ledger fasteners, but here are the best practices and guidelines, based on the American Wood Council's National Design Specification (NDS) for Wood Construction.

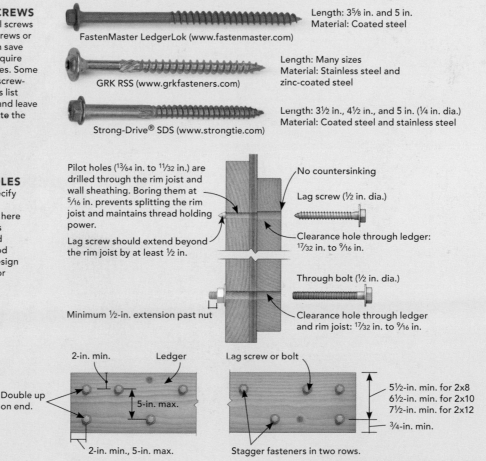

Pilot holes (¹³/₆₄ in. to ¹¹/₃₂ in.) are drilled through the rim joist and wall sheathing. Boring them at ⁵/₁₆ in. prevents splitting the rim joist and maintains thread holding power.

Lag screw should extend beyond the rim joist by at least ½ in.

No countersinking

Lag screw (½ in. dia.)

Clearance hole through ledger: ¹⁷/₃₂ in. to ⁹/₁₆ in.

Through bolt (½ in. dia.)

Minimum ½-in. extension past nut

Clearance hole through ledger and rim joist: ¹⁷/₃₂ in. to ⁹/₁₆ in.

2-in. min.   Ledger   Lag screw or bolt

Double up on end.

5-in. max.

5½-in. min. for 2x8
6½-in. min. for 2x10
7½-in. min. for 2x12

¾-in. min.

2-in. min., 5-in. max.   Stagger fasteners in two rows.

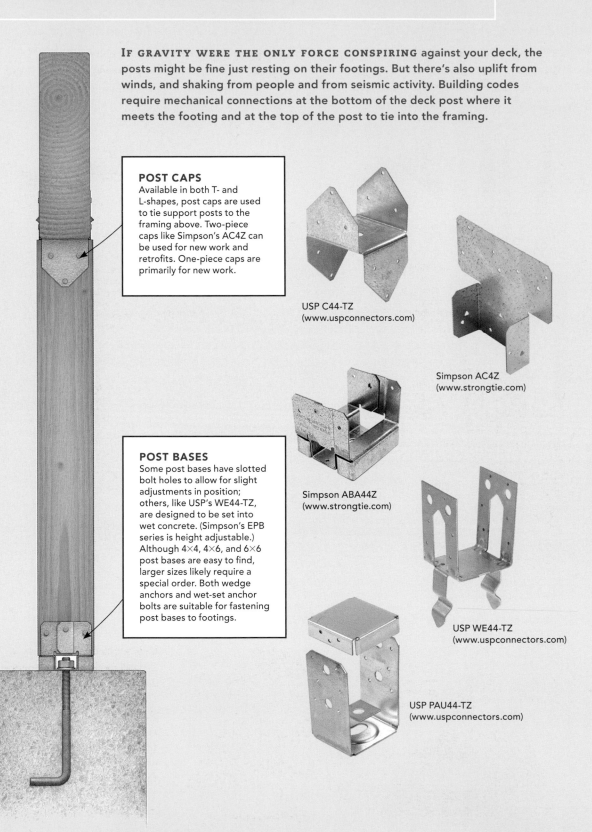

2. POSTS TO FOOTING AND FRAMING

IF GRAVITY WERE THE ONLY FORCE CONSPIRING against your deck, the posts might be fine just resting on their footings. But there's also uplift from winds, and shaking from people and from seismic activity. Building codes require mechanical connections at the bottom of the deck post where it meets the footing and at the top of the post to tie into the framing.

POST CAPS
Available in both T- and L-shapes, post caps are used to tie support posts to the framing above. Two-piece caps like Simpson's AC4Z can be used for new work and retrofits. One-piece caps are primarily for new work.

USP C44-TZ
(www.uspconnectors.com)

Simpson AC4Z
(www.strongtie.com)

POST BASES
Some post bases have slotted bolt holes to allow for slight adjustments in position; others, like USP's WE44-TZ, are designed to be set into wet concrete. (Simpson's EPB series is height adjustable.) Although 4×4, 4×6, and 6×6 post bases are easy to find, larger sizes likely require a special order. Both wedge anchors and wet-set anchor bolts are suitable for fastening post bases to footings.

Simpson ABA44Z
(www.strongtie.com)

USP WE44-TZ
(www.uspconnectors.com)

USP PAU44-TZ
(www.uspconnectors.com)

3. JOISTS TO LEDGER AND BEAMS

WHEN DECK JOISTS aren't adequately fastened to the ledger, the joists can pull away, leading to a collapse with the ledger still attached to the house. Use joist hangers to connect joists securely to the ledger and rim beams, when necessary.

Simpson LUS210Z
(www.strongtie.com)

SINGLE HANGER
Available for 2×4s to 2×12s. Follow the manufacturer's nailing schedule to achieve the designed load values.

Simpson LUS210-2Z
(www.strongtie.com)

DOUBLE HANGER
Used with double- and triple-ply joists. Use wide-flange, heavy-duty versions (with specified fasteners) for beams and heavy loads.

Simpson SUL210Z
(www.strongtie.com)

SKEWED HANGER
Skewed hangers solve a tricky connection easily. Most suppliers stock 45° hangers; other angles can be special-ordered.

CONCEALED HANGER
With internal flanges, these hangers are ideal for end joists. They also work well for solving clearance problems with lateral ties (see p. 19).

Simpson LUC26Z
(www.strongtie.com)

Bostitch®
MCN150
Strapshot™

Ridgid® Palm Nailer

CONNECTOR NAILERS. A typical deck requires hundreds of connector nails. Many nails are located in tight spaces that provide little room to swing a hammer. Make driving all those nails easier with a metal-connector nailer such as the Strapshot from Bostitch or a palm nailer such as the one from Ridgid.

THE LEVERING ACTION of railing posts can exert extreme force on the deck framing and connectors below. Testing has shown that bolts and lag screws alone aren't enough to withstand the 500-lb. force that's required by code.

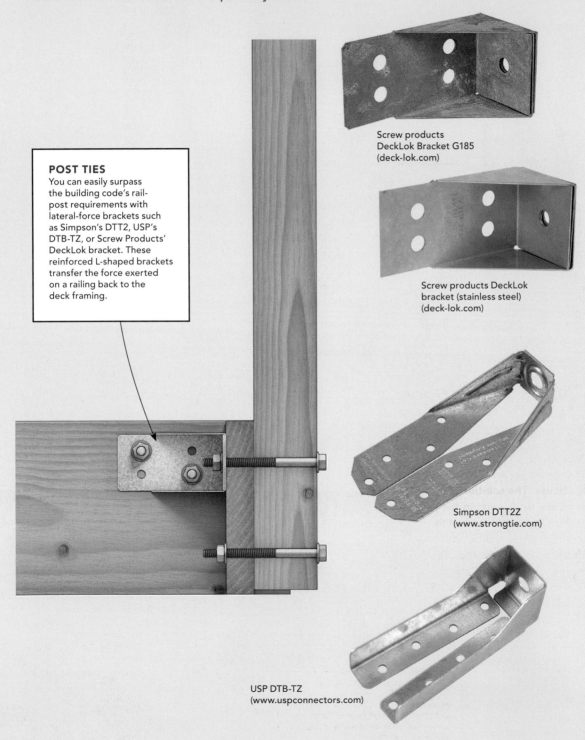

POST TIES
You can easily surpass the building code's rail-post requirements with lateral-force brackets such as Simpson's DTT2, USP's DTB-TZ, or Screw Products' DeckLok bracket. These reinforced L-shaped brackets transfer the force exerted on a railing back to the deck framing.

Screw products DeckLok Bracket G185 (deck-lok.com)

Screw products DeckLok bracket (stainless steel) (deck-lok.com)

Simpson DTT2Z (www.strongtie.com)

USP DTB-TZ (www.uspconnectors.com)

5. STAIRS TO HEADER

CODE NOW PROHIBITS the timeworn practice of toenails, or in code language, "nails subject to withdrawal," to fasten stair stringers to the framing.

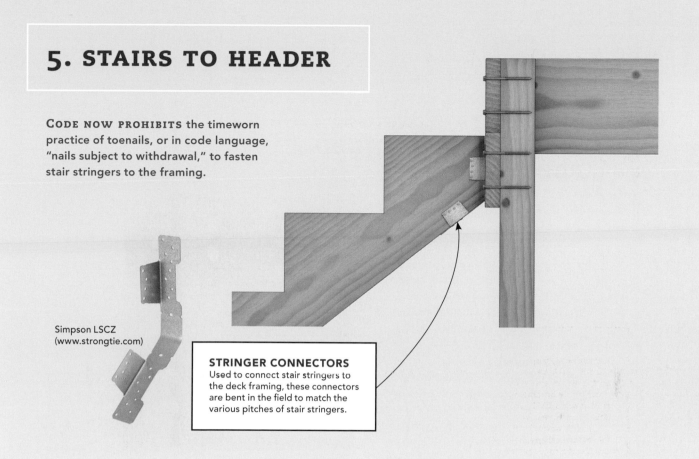

Simpson LSCZ
(www.strongtie.com)

STRINGER CONNECTORS
Used to connect stair stringers to the deck framing, these connectors are bent in the field to match the various pitches of stair stringers.

6. DECK TO HOUSE

LATERAL LOADS CAN PULL THE DECK—ledger and all—away from the house. The solution is to connect the deck joists to the house's floor joists. When used in pairs, the lateral-force brackets from Simpson Strong-Tie and USP can be used to satisfy the lateral-load attachment detail in the current code.

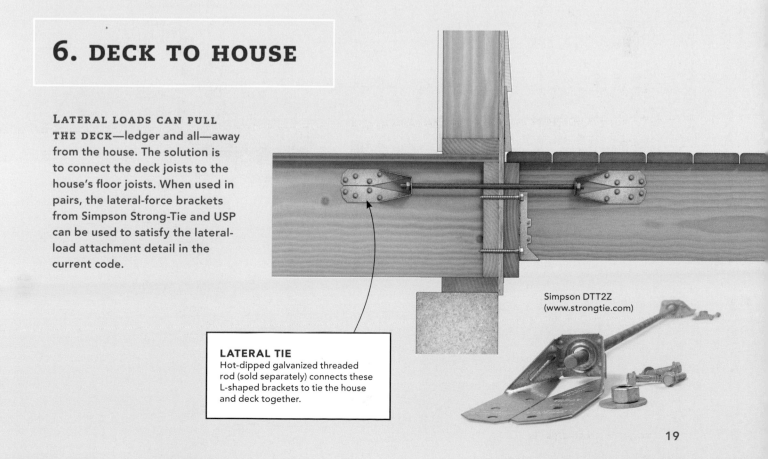

Simpson DTT2Z
(www.strongtie.com)

LATERAL TIE
Hot-dipped galvanized threaded rod (sold separately) connects these L-shaped brackets to tie the house and deck together.

19

DO FASTENERS NEED PROTECTION?

SHORTLY AFTER THE PHASE-OUT of CCA-based treatments for lumber in 2003, builders noticed that the new pressure-treating formulas were causing increased corrosion of galvanized connectors. Manufacturers responded with thicker zinc layers on their connectors, and some builders started wrapping their pressure-treated lumber to prevent contact between the treated lumber and the metal connectors. But does wrapping the lumber really help to reduce galvanic corrosion? The answer: sometimes.

In November 2008, Simpson Strong-Tie, attempting to validate research done by W.R. Grace, maker of Vycor Deck Protector (grace.com/construction/en-us), concluded that barriers can help in certain environments (see Simpson Technical Bulletin: Barrier Membranes and Preservative-Treated Wood; www.strongtie.com). Any benefit assumes that hot-dipped galvanized fasteners are used and that the membrane is installed correctly. Keep in mind that the research tested only Vycor Deck Protector, so other membranes may or may not help. *Fine Homebuilding* editorial adviser Mike Guertin thinks that wrapping pressure-treated lumber with membrane and using G185 connectors is a reasonable alternative to stainless-steel connectors in most locations, but he recommends stainless-steel hardware for decks on the coast.

Choosing the Best Deck Finish

BY JUSTIN FINK

Some species of wood deck planks will last for many years outside without a finish of any kind, but I guarantee the results won't be pretty. Sunlight and moisture take their toll, turning the delicate colors and textures of unprotected wood into something gray, checked, and fuzzy. For those of us with wood decks (still the majority of decks being built, by the way), choosing the right protective finish is crucial.

It shouldn't be too hard, right? A quick walk down the paint aisle at the home center may change your mind on that. To be fair, some manufacturers still take mercy on the consumer who's used to seeing labels that simply say "oil-based" or "water-based" deck stain. Now, though, we also have alkyd, acrylic, and alkyd/acrylic finishes, among others. There are cans that say "penetrating oil formula," but they're

on a product that can be cleaned up with soap and water. I even saw one exterior-stain product labeled as "oil-latex."

In some cases, you'll also see a complicated string of buzzwords, as on Behr®'s Premium Wood-Toned Weatherproofing Wood Finish or Olympic®'s Wood Protector Toner Waterproofing Sealant. Then, formulation aside, you also have to choose the level of opacity. This ranges from water clear to opaque, with various shades in between, each offering its own contribution to durability.

It's true that the exterior-deck-finishes market is complicated, but once you sort through the options, there are fundamental differences separating one finish from the next in terms of application, durability, and cost.

PICKING A FINISH. The options in penetrating exterior finishes may seem confusing, but there are some clues to help you choose.

Meet Your Enemies

Besides enhancing a deck's aesthetic appeal, a protective finish must defend against water and sunlight. Make no mistake that these two elements are among the most destructive forces in nature's arsenal, and in many climates, they are at work on a day-to-day basis.

SUNLIGHT

When someone talks about wood being damaged by sunlight, they're really talking about damage from ultraviolet (UV) rays. Wood is essentially a combination of cellulose fibers and lignin, the glue that holds together those fibers. UV light is especially good at destroying lignin, and as that happens, the cellulose fibers loosen and wear away. This exposes a fresh layer of fibers and lignin, and the process repeats.

To be effective, a deck finish either must reflect or absorb this harmful UV light. This applied protection, though, sits on the top layer of the wood, where it's susceptible to wear and tear. Reapplication—as often as once a year—is usually necessary. If you go without reapplication for too

long, you will be staining only the cellulose fibers that are soon to slough off. That's why lightly sanding an old deck before refinishing is best practice.

WATER

Wooden deck planks come from trees, and trees love water. They suck it up at any opportunity. As wood takes on water, it expands across its width (perpendicular to the direction of the grain). As it dries, it shrinks. The cycle will be slower in dense decking (such as ipé) than in soft decking (such as cedar).

Decks in many parts of the country are exposed to frequent wetting and drying cycles. Board ends are most susceptible to this expansion and shrinkage, which is why you often see small cracks at these areas. More cracks mean more water absorption, and the cycle continues.

Penetrating deck finishes aren't designed to waterproof a board completely, but rather to slow the wetting and drying so that the wood is less likely to develop cracks from dramatic swings in moisture content. Coating the ends of each board with finish is an essential part of sealing a deck.

The moisture level is also a factor in the growth of fungus on deck planks. Finish manufacturers typically keep this maintenance headache under control with the help of mildewcide additives.

Which Deck Finish Is Best? There's No Easy Answer

It would be nice to single out one type of deck finish as the best. Unfortunately, when it comes to preserving wood in such a torturous environment, there's no such thing as best. No matter which finish you choose, you are faced with trade-offs. It's also nearly impossible to make concrete statements about Brand X being better than Brand Y, about oil-based finishes being better than water-based, and so on. There are, however, some key points of differentiation between products and some clues to help you navigate the deck-stain market.

Formulation

Deck finishes break down into three groups: oil based, water based, and hybrid. In a perfect world, these words would be the ones you'd see on the label. In the real world, though, you're more likely to see mention of "alkyd," "acrylic," or another chemical keyword. Sometimes you don't even get this clue, just generic wording like "waterproofing wood finish," "deck and siding stain," or "waterproofer plus clear wood protector." Knowing some indicator words will help you to sort through the options. When in doubt, the cleanup instructions on the back of the can will tell you at least whether the finish is water based or solvent based.

OIL BASED

Oil finishes are the traditional option for decks, although their composition has evolved somewhat from old linseed-oil formulations. Linseed oil is still used, but it's most often combined with alkyds, a synthetic alternative that better resists yellowing. In general, oil-based finishes penetrate wood better than water-based finishes do, and they are easier to recoat. However, they carry the trade-offs of higher volatile organic compounds (VOCs) and a cleanup process that requires solvents.

HYBRID

In an effort to combine the best parts of an oil-based finish with the best parts of a water-based finish, manufacturers have focused recently on hybrid finishes. The chemistry—combining oil with water—sounds counterintuitive, but the result is a finish that has the penetration of an oil-based product with the color retention, reduced VOCs, and soap-and-water cleanup of a water-based product.

WATER BASED

Thicker, paintlike water-based deck finishes can be cleaned up with soap and water rather than solvents. Without solvents, these finishes typically don't have the same elevated VOC levels or strong odors as oil-based finishes. Acrylic and latex also are known to retain their color better than oil formulas, although

OIL BASED
AKA: oil, linseed, alkyd

HYBRID
AKA: waterborne-modified, oil/latex, acrylic/oil, acrylic/alkyd, water-reduceable

WATER BASED
AKA: acrylic, 100% acrylic, latex, silicone, waterborne

MULTIPLE FORMULA-TIONS. To comply with local VOC regulations, some companies offer the same product in different formulations. For example, though the labels are nearly identical, the Olympic Maximum Clear sold in Pennsylvania is oil based; in Alabama, it's a hybrid.

they won't absorb into wood as easily. Moreover, prepping the deck for future refinishing is more involved.

VOCs

Traditional penetrating finishes rely on a solvent, such as mineral spirits, to help deck planks absorb modified oil resins and other additives. These oil-based finishes are still widely available, but the push now is toward water-based finishes that contain lower amounts of VOCs.

The trend is due in part to stricter government regulation of VOCs, which are a principal ingredient of smog. The nationwide standard for VOCs is 550 grams per liter (g/l), but VOCs in many exterior finishes are limited further by local regulations. In many cases, a manufacturer may offer the same finish in several VOC levels, or simply not offer a product in certain markets because it's not cost-effective to reformulate products or offer multiple options. In some cases, however, you may find

multiple VOC options within the same market, leaving the decision to you. In all cases, the VOC information for a finish is listed on the label, typically near the UPC code or somewhere in the fine print on the back of the can.

Pigment

Although the terminology and number of options vary slightly from brand to brand, deck finishes typically are available in these levels of opacity: clear, toner, semitransparent, semisolid, and solid. The difference is in the amount of pigment, and it's the pigment that provides protection against UV damage.

SOLID

Solid stains offer the best protection against UV degradation, so all other factors being equal, they last the longest. They are also a good choice if you need to conceal a severely weathered deck. Pigments don't absorb into wood, though, so these stains essentially sit atop the surface of the wood, which creates a number of potential drawbacks. First, the stain is vulnerable to wear and tear from foot traffic and patio furniture. Second, the grain and the color of the underlying wood are obscured. Finally, if water gets below the finish (either from the top

CLEAR, NO UV PROTECTION   **CLEAR, WITH UV PROTECTION**

side or by being drawn up from below), there is a higher likelihood that the finish will peel. Expect warranties to range from five to ten years.

SEMISOLID AND SEMITRANSPARENT

Some companies offer both semisolid and semi-transparent options; others offer one or the other. In general, semisolids and semitransparents offer far more color options than toners, and they are the best protection you can get while still retaining some visibility of the underlying wood. These finishes also may be a good choice if you're trying to renew a weathered deck that doesn't have dramatic imperfections you're trying to hide completely. Expect warranties to range from three to six years.

TONER

Unlike the organic absorbers and stabilizers in a clear finish, toner finishes—sometimes called "wood-toned" or "tinted"—contain inorganic pigments (for example, iron oxides; transparent iron oxides, also called transoxides; and titanium dioxide) that are so finely ground that visible light essentially goes around them. The result is that the color and the grain of the wood appear virtually unaffected, but UV light is blocked. Typically, the colors in this category are wood-toned, such as browns and reds. One perk is that these stains can be matched in color to the wood substrate so that they appear nearly clear even when they're not. Expect warranties to range from two to four years.

CLEAR, TRANSPARENT, TRANSLUCENT

Low-end clear finishes, which are typically water clear or a milky white that dries clear, offer no UV protection. There are clear finishes that tend toward an amber color; they contain organic UV absorbers and stabilizers. These organic stabilizers, however, break down quickly and leave wood vulnerable to color change and surface damage. Expect warranties to range from one to four years.

Price

When it comes to paints and finishes, price often can be an indicator of quality, but this rule of thumb really applies only when comparing products from the same company. For instance, Mark Knaebe, a natural-resources specialist at the Forest Products Laboratory, says there are some $25-per-gallon finishes on the market that outperform those costing $40 or $50 per gallon. When comparing different finishes from a single manufacturer, however, price definitely counts.

Behr offers two lines (shown below), a standard and a premium, with a price difference of only about $8. Olympic says its premium clear penetrating finish, called Olympic Maximum, has better-quality ingredients than Olympic WaterGuard and costs around $20 more. It's all about what customers are willing to pay.

$37 per gallon

$29 per gallon

PART 2

Deck Design and Planning

27 DESIGN A BETTER DECK

31 IMPROVE YOUR DECK'S VIEW

35 DESIGNING A SMALL BUT ELEGANT DECK

39 DESIGNING A PORCH WITH
A ROOFTOP DECK

42 BENDING DECKING FOR
DECORATIVE INLAYS

51 BRIGHT IDEAS FOR A WELL-LIT DECK

57 A HOMEOWNER'S GUIDE TO DECK
PERMITS

Design a Better Deck

BY CHARLES MILLER

Any outdoor space is better than no outdoor space. Even the kind of deck that we call a "penalty box"—the type you've probably seen attached to one side of a house, sometimes on the second floor, with no sun protection and no way to get down to the ground—even that is better

ROOMS WITH A VIEW. The multiple levels of this expansive deck define areas for dining, sitting, and sunning. A large stone planter incorporates color and texture into the deck and further defines the separation of spaces. The cable railing keeps deck visitors safe but doesn't obstruct the view.

NO OBSTACLES. Locating the outdoor kitchen to one side of the patio doors and the dining table to the other allows for a clear path from the indoor kitchen across the deck to the yard. A retractable awning shelters the outdoor cooking area and protects the cook from blazing sun or summer showers.

than no outdoor space at all. If you're planning a new deck, though, or if you've got a penalty-box deck now and want to improve it, there are some important things to remember.

When You Think "Deck," Think "Room"

The first thing to think about when you're designing a deck is what you're going to use it for so that you can size the space accordingly. Will your deck function as a kitchen, an outdoor living room, an outdoor dining room, or some combination of

those options? If you want the new deck to be an outdoor dining room, take a look at your indoor dining room and see how you can duplicate the dimensions outside. If you're lucky enough to be able to build a deck with multiple levels, you can place individual functions on each level. Generally, three risers is enough of a change in elevation to separate different levels. Fewer risers than that can be hard to differentiate and also can create a trip hazard. Separate the levels with planters and with built-in benches. They add color and offer a place where you can sit and socialize.

Leave Some Room to Move Around

While you're planning the size of your deck, its uses, and the furniture you'll put on it, remember also to think about how traffic will move across the deck to another destination, whether it's into the house or into the yard. Don't put the path between the table and the chairs, or between the grill and the benches. It seems an obvious thing to point out, but this problem occurs over and over again. It shouldn't be an afterthought.

Control the Sun

When designing a deck, think about how you're going to deal with the sun and how best to moderate it.

One good idea is a trellis. By casting nice shadows on the deck, a trellis protects you from the sun, and it's also a pleasant structure to look at. If your deck is attached to the house, you can add a shed roof, which not only gets you out of the sun but also gives you a sense of shelter. Even a penalty-box deck can be made more comfortable with a bit of a shed roof over it.

It's important to remember that putting a roof over a portion of your deck is not the same as turning your deck into a porch. Unlike a porch, a deck has some areas that may be covered but others that are open to the sun. The idea is to give yourself the option of being in the sun (or in the rain, for that matter) or getting out of it.

An outdoor kitchen or cooking area, in particular, benefits from a little shelter. A trellis or roof will keep you out of the rain as you grill, and it provides a good place to mount lighting, also necessary for an outdoor kitchen. It's important to be particularly careful about codes when planning an outdoor kitchen (more on that later).

BLOCK THE BREEZE, NOT THE VIEW. A glass railing solves the problem of how to enjoy the view from this deck while staying sheltered from the wind blowing off the water. The multiple levels and the change in direction of the decking define the dining and sunbathing areas.

Last, a big umbrella is a great thing on a small deck. An umbrella gives a deck a sense of place. It immediately makes the deck feel festive and lets you know that it's time to sit down and have some fun.

Make Wind Work for You

Wind is another natural element worth considering when you plan a deck. Depending on the conditions where you build your deck and the general climate, you might want to block the wind, or you might want to gather it to create a pleasant breeze. Prevailing breezes can be funneled toward an outdoor space by the configuration of fences, so if you want to take advantage of a breeze, build a funnel. On the other hand, if you have a great view but there's a prevailing wind in your face that makes it uncomfortable to be on the deck, consider a glass railing. The wind will hit that and bounce over the top.

Review Codes Before It's Too Late

Decks are subject to building codes just like any construction project. Although many codes are standard, others vary from region to region. If you want to avoid headaches later, educate yourself on the codes that apply in your area before you design your deck.

I speak from experience. When building my own deck, I constructed a little gabled structure on the back half where I could put the gas grill, and I sized it so that the grill could go up against the back railing. When I had the structure inspected, my inspector was kind enough to alert me that because I had flammable materials in the deck railing, I was going to have to move the grill forward 18 in., which then put me directly in the drip line of the gable above. Instead of getting wet, I would get drenched. The lesson here: Before you add any structure to your deck, consult your local inspector—or you may end up all wet.

Use Railings for Safety and Sociability

I always recommend railings, even on a low deck. They may not be required by code, but they're still a good idea. Where I lived in Connecticut, the code height for railings was 30 in. If your deck was higher than 30 in. from the ground, you had to have a railing; if it was less than that, you didn't.

Here's the problem with that rule: People hang around on decks in the evening, and sometimes they might even have a margarita. Sometimes they get too close to the edge. If they do, 30 in. is a long way to fall.

It's not just the safety factor, though. Railings are a great place for conversations. They create gathering places. Railings are also terrific for placing boundaries on the different spaces you might have on your deck. By putting in a railing, you can separate one function from another, as well as create good places for conversation.

Illuminate Your Deck Creatively

Good lighting takes your deck design up a notch. Good lighting illuminates the pathways to and from the deck, the stairs, and the barbecue, if you have one. A first-rate deck will have all those lighting needs covered.

The rule of thumb is to illuminate the object but to hide the source of illumination. You don't want bright lightbulbs shining in your face. Put bulbs behind a sconce or some kind of shade that keeps direct light out of your eyes.

You also want to think about using lighting for decorative effect. Consider putting uplights behind a potted palm tree, or disperse some around the backyard. That way, as you look out from your deck, you can enjoy the view even when the day is over.

Improve Your Deck's View

BY RUSSELL HAMLET

A deck extends your home's living space to the outdoors, creating a backyard oasis for grilling, dining, reading, or socializing. Although building codes tell us how to build a safe deck, there's no guarantee that it will be pleasant to look at or enjoyable to use.

Shaping the view from your deck improves the experience: If there's a great view, you want to take advantage of it. If you're not overlooking a bucolic backyard, you might need to direct people's gaze away from an urban scene or shield the deck from passersby.

Deck-board patterns and railing designs have a tremendous impact on the view. Together, these features either guide your eyes outward to the landscape or focus them inward.

Choose a Focal Point

You can use the orientation of the decking to manipulate where people look when they're on the deck. Whether the wood is warm, rich ipé or utilitarian pressure-treated southern yellow pine, our eyes are drawn unconsciously along the length of each board. To direct eyes to a particular view, orient the boards in that direction. Be careful with long, narrow decks running the length of the house, however. Such decks often feel unnecessarily

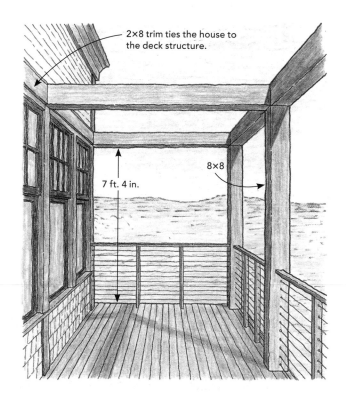

2×8 trim ties the house to the deck structure.

7 ft. 4 in.

8×8

OUTDOOR ROOMS NEED SCALE
Most people think of their deck as an outdoor room, a space that blurs the boundaries between the sights and sounds of the outdoors and the comfort and function of indoor spaces. However, there are times a deck doesn't feel comfortable because the sense of exposure is too great. Despite, or even because of, a great setting, you feel insignificant without a ceiling or surrounding walls because the horizon defines the scale. Railings that help to preserve the view, like the wire-cable version shown here, can exacerbate the problem. A post-and-beam exoskeleton preserves the view but adds human scale, a sense of enclosure, and, hence, security.

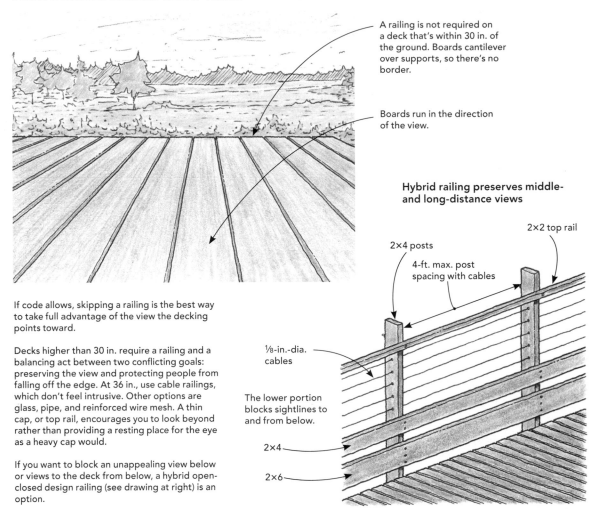

A railing is not required on a deck that's within 30 in. of the ground. Boards cantilever over supports, so there's no border.

Boards run in the direction of the view.

Hybrid railing preserves middle- and long-distance views

2×2 top rail

2×4 posts

4-ft. max. post spacing with cables

⅛-in.-dia. cables

The lower portion blocks sightlines to and from below.

2×4

2×6

If code allows, skipping a railing is the best way to take full advantage of the view the decking points toward.

Decks higher than 30 in. require a railing and a balancing act between two conflicting goals: preserving the view and protecting people from falling off the edge. At 36 in., use cable railings, which don't feel intrusive. Other options are glass, pipe, and reinforced wire mesh. A thin cap, or top rail, encourages you to look beyond rather than providing a resting place for the eye as a heavy cap would.

If you want to block an unappealing view below or views to the deck from below, a hybrid open-closed design railing (see drawing at right) is an option.

claustrophobic because the long run of each course creates a tunnel-like effect extending to the horizon (see ideas for avoiding this on p. 34).

If the view is unappealing or if you want the deck to feel smaller and roomlike, you can employ patterns to make the decking a focal point and borders to keep a person's gaze from wandering beyond the edges of the deck. Use simple patterns on smaller decks (less than 300 sq. ft.) so that they aren't visually distracting.

Decking patterns also can help to integrate the deck and house. In the Pacific Northwest, where I live, a common siding pattern alternates the exposure of each course of shingles or clapboards, creating wide and narrow bands on the wall.

Adopting alternating widths for decking boards, particularly on a ground-level deck, connects the deck to the house.

Match the Railing to the View

The railing is an opportunity to define the deck as an outdoor room by providing scale, adding boundaries, and offering a sense of security. Although I like to keep its height at the code minimum, I sometimes use the posts to support an overhead structure or trellis, adding a human scale that makes the deck more intimate.

The railing design should be determined by how you want to experience the view, something you've already considered in the decking pattern.

CREATE A FOCAL POINT WITH PATTERNS AND RAILINGS

Breaking the continuity of decking lines deemphasizes the view beyond the deck. To focus the eye inward, use a pattern to create a focal point on the deck. On small decks where a pattern might appear too busy and on low decks without a railing, a strong visual border made from a contrasting wood will catch the eye and focus it inside the deck. Railings are another way to screen views from the deck or to the deck. The traditional closed-design railing shown here effectively limits views and is easy to construct. Patterns with more depth or decorative cutouts create shadowlines that engage the eye, like the woven pattern in the drawing below.

Railings with shadowlines add visual interest.

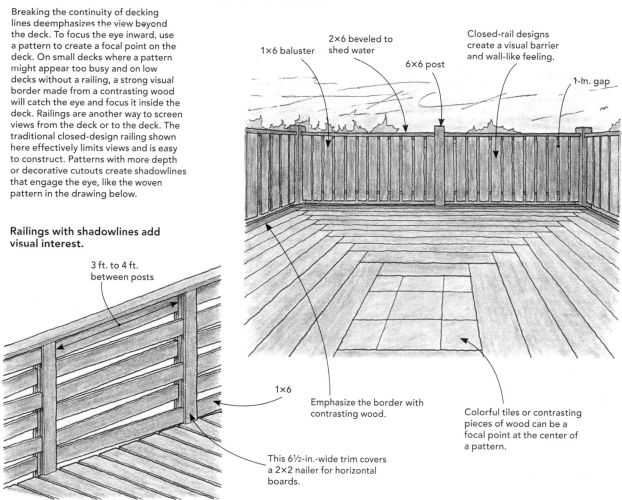

1×6 baluster

2×6 beveled to shed water

6×6 post

Closed-rail designs create a visual barrier and wall-like feeling.

1-in. gap

3 ft. to 4 ft. between posts

1×6

Emphasize the border with contrasting wood.

This 6½-in.-wide trim covers a 2×2 nailer for horizontal boards.

Colorful tiles or contrasting pieces of wood can be a focal point at the center of a pattern.

If the decking draws the eye outward, a relatively transparent, open-design guardrail takes advantage of the view. When you want to blur the end of the deck to the space beyond and the deck is within 30 in. of the ground, skip the railing (but check your local code first).

A closed-design railing with substantial elements will block the view—from inside or outside the deck—strongly defining the deck's border and serving as a privacy screen. This type of design typically relies on wide balusters with narrow spacing, but planters also can be incorporated to add privacy.

Consider Views of the Deck from the Outside Looking In

The view from the deck isn't the only design consideration. Even a small deck with a railing is likely to be the most prominent feature on a house, so it will affect views of the house.

The style of the deck needs to be congruous with the style of the house. Wide-board balusters with fanciful decorative cutouts will look out of place on a glass-and-steel modern house. If you need a closed railing for this style of house, consider panels of finished wood, metal, or obscure glass.

As you plan railing sections, take into account the location of windows and doors. Rather than falling haphazardly across the facade with posts appearing in front of windows and doors, they should frame these openings. Also, give some thought to the space under the deck. On low decks that don't require a railing, I like to define the borders with plants to block dark views underneath.

The plantings also soften the edges of the deck and tie it to the yard. If the deck is well up off the ground, stout supports look better than spindly posts that meet engineering requirements but are visually inadequate.

CHANGE THE SCALE OF NARROW DECKS

Long, narrow decks running along the length of a house can look and feel like a bowling alley. Some options for overcoming this effect on a 6-ft. by 16-ft. deck include interrupting the length of the deck with border boards (A), which emphasizes the decking joints and breaks the deck into sections. Simply orienting the decking in the shorter direction (B) deemphasizes the length of the deck in an understated way. If you want the deck to be the center of attention, designs such as a basket weave (C) or diamond pattern (D) provide visual interest and draw attention away from the long, narrow aspect of the deck.

A	B	C	D

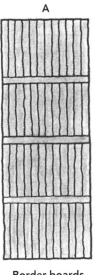

Border boards   Short orientation   Basket weave   Diamond pattern

Designing a Small but Elegant Deck

BY CLEMENS JELLEMA

A couple of years ago, I was asked to design a deck for *Fine Homebuilding*'s Project House. They were looking for a simple yet elegant design that would not be too complicated to build. It would be close to grade, accessed through a pair of French doors connected to a family room, and measure roughly 15 ft. by 12 ft. The deck would feature some built-in benches and planters, and provide a connection to the backyard.

Before I start on any design work, I always check first to see if there are any limitations. These can include slopes, setbacks, easements, and local codes or homeowners-association rules. In this project, the biggest challenge was to create a usable entertaining space while allowing access from both sides of the deck. Typically, stairs create a traffic path where furniture can't be placed, therefore limiting a deck's usable space.

The initial size limitation for this deck project also meant we only had room for a seating area. To make room for a dining set as well, I expanded the project area to include a secondary lower-level deck or a patio at ground level. In designing this deck, I used RealTime Landscaping Architect software (www. ideaspectrum.com). It is fun to work with and easy to learn, and it can create pretty much anything I can think of. It's also capable of importing models from SketchUp and produces realistic designs. The illustrations here use that software.

As I would with any client, I worked through several designs before arriving at one that satisfied us all. The process offers an instructive glimpse into developing a design for the perfect deck, no matter what the size.

Option 1

In the initial drawing (p. 36, top), the focus was on getting the overall design right, with a good traffic flow. Two stairs—one alongside the French doors and the other wrapping the opposing corner—provide two ways for moving to or from the yard. I chose a corner stair because it provides a nice, wide entrance to the deck from the patio and a strong connection between the two spaces. This deck is less than 2 ft. off the ground, so rather than a railing, I suggested enclosing the other outside corner with bench seating, using a rosewood-colored variation of the decking to add interest to the tops of the benches and to the stair treads. Because of the deck's small size, I suggested locating a dining area off to the

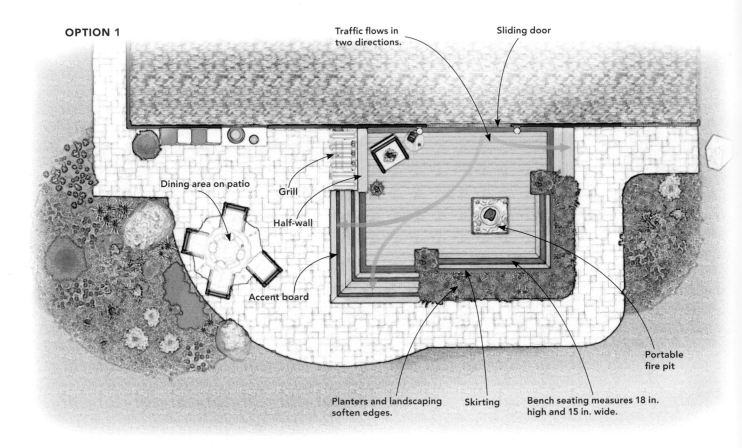

OPTION 1

Traffic flows in two directions.

Sliding door

Dining area on patio

Grill

Half-wall

Accent board

Planters and landscaping soften edges.

Skirting

Bench seating measures 18 in. high and 15 in. wide.

Portable fire pit

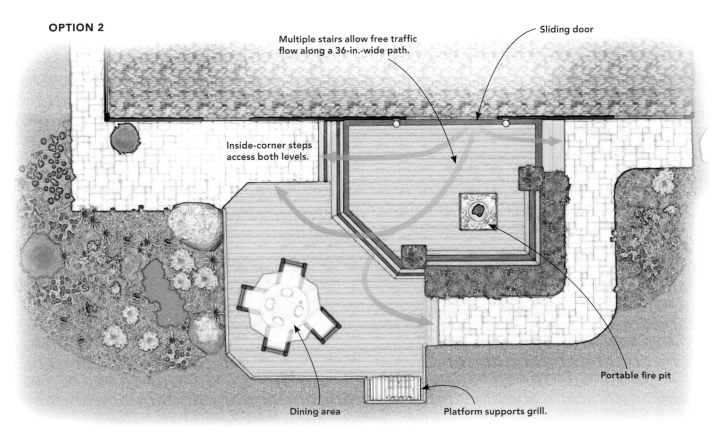

OPTION 2

Multiple stairs allow free traffic flow along a 36-in.-wide path.

Sliding door

Inside-corner steps access both levels.

Portable fire pit

Dining area

Platform supports grill.

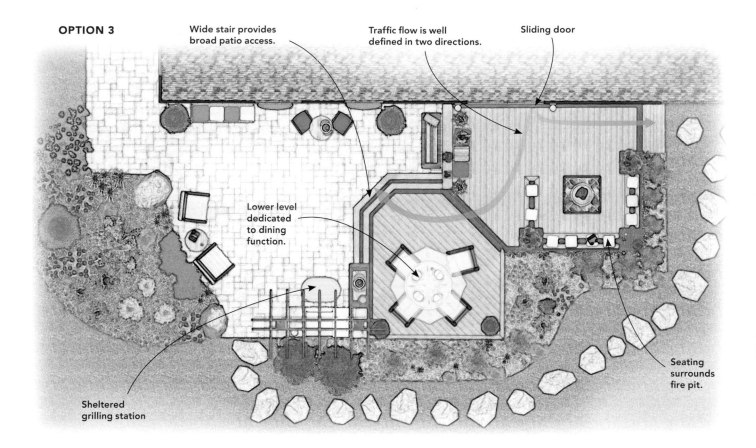

Wide stair provides broad patio access.

Traffic flow is well defined in two directions.

Sliding door

Lower level dedicated to dining function.

Sheltered grilling station

Seating surrounds fire pit.

side, on a patio that could be built in a second phase. Skirting added around the deck gives the space a more finished look when viewed from the yard.

Option 2

Although the plan had been to keep the deck simple, I also suggested this version, with a nearly grade-level platform that would accommodate the dining set. To be comfortable, a dining set needs 4 ft. of clearance all around (2 ft. for chairs and 2 ft. of open space). For example, a 4-ft.-dia. table requires a 12-ft.-wide space. A small platform extension supports the grill and keeps it out of the way. When I place a dining area on a low deck like this, I normally add 2x4s of the decking material around the perimeter to prevent chairs from sliding off the edge. Steps built into the inside corner formed by the two levels allow direct access from the patio. If budget were a concern, this project could be done in stages.

Option 3

The lower deck in this version is closer in height to the main deck and functions entirely as a dining area. To do this, I eliminated the small step on its right side and moved the grill to the patio. This creates a confined place where people can entertain out of the circulation paths. I also moved the steps to the patio so they wrap around one side of the lower deck. This provides a path from the table to the grill, which now is sheltered with a pergola. The deck is shifted to the right in this expanded design, creating a slightly wider patio and allowing me to wrap the built-in benches around the fire pit without interrupting circulation. This is a more elaborate design than the others, and it can handle more guests. If budget would allow it, this would be my favorite.

The Choice

In the end, we returned to the concept of a simple deck. We kept the positioning we had in option 1 to maximize the patio but traded the paver path for stepping stones. To make framing easier, we chose to run the decking parallel to the house, as in options 1 and 2. I should also mention here that the corner stair treads, at roughly 14½ in. wide, are suitable for seating and potted plants. This type of "stadium stair" is fine if the deck is not higher than 30 in. To dress up the deck a bit, I added a white fascia and stair risers, something that will look particularly nice with the eventual addition of white window and door trim on the house.

THE CHOICE

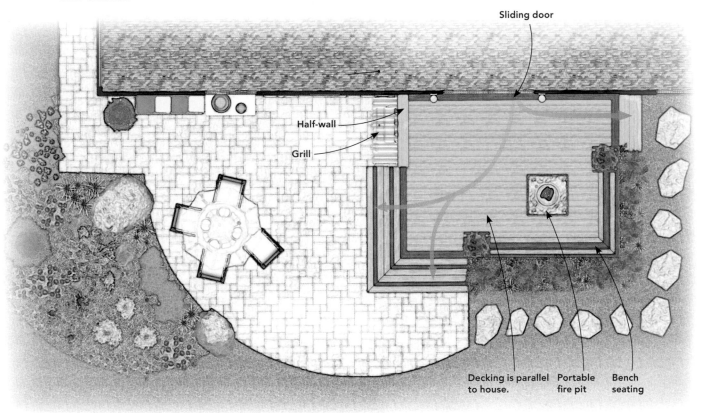

Sliding door

Half-wall

Grill

Decking is parallel to house.

Portable fire pit

Bench seating

Designing a Porch with a Rooftop Deck

BY MICHAEL MAINES

Covered porches are great places to enjoy the outdoors while being protected from the weather. The views, however, are often better from the porch roof. If built properly, the porch structure is substantial enough to support outdoor living space above, so why not take advantage of it and build a rooftop deck?

On pp. 130–137, Emanuel Silva shows how to build such a structure. Here, I show how to get the design right. To illustrate the rules of thumb I follow, I've designed a porch and deck for a one-and-a-half-story farmhouse, a home that's popular in many parts of the country. As with any other project, the ideal situation doesn't always exist, so I offer some alternatives where appropriate.

1. Layout

Long, shallow porches typically look best (see the drawing on p. 40). A depth of 8 ft. is a comfortable target. However, porches deeper than 8 ft. should be given boxy, roomlike dimensions instead—10x14 or 12x16, for example.

2. Columns: Size and Shape

Don't be afraid to use generously sized columns, but keep in mind that square columns appear wider than round columns because of their diagonal cross section. Round or turned columns usually look best with a gentle curve that narrows at the top, referred to as an entasis. Square columns can be straight, have entases, or be tapered.

3. Columns: Spacing

Place columns so that they create an opening that relates to the shape of the house. For example, a tall, narrow house looks best with closely spaced columns that create vertically oriented rectangular openings. Try to keep the columns evenly spaced and with an odd number of openings. Align these openings with windows and doors when possible.

4. Beams

The beams, more correctly called lintels, should match the width of the top of round columns. If square columns are used, the beam can overhang the columns slightly; in this case, the beam should extend beyond the columns ¾ in. on each side. In general, the face of the beam should be about one-and-a-half times as tall as the beam is wide.

5. Gutters

The roof can drain into conventionally installed gutters or concealed gutters built into the roof, or

the runoff can be allowed to spill out freely and be picked up (or not) by ground gutters. In warm climates, internal drains may work, but they're not recommended in cold climates, where they may clog with ice.

6. Posts

Railing posts should be one-half to two-thirds the width of the columns. Posts should align with the columns below and have similar or less-elaborate trim. Match square columns with square posts. If the columns are round, the posts can be round or square.

7. Pilasters

The beams supporting the roof and the deck above can be supported visually by pilasters where they meet the house (see the drawing on the facing page), or by freestanding columns placed a few inches away from the siding. Pilasters are more classically correct.

8. Roof

The roof should be sloped at least $1/4$ in. per ft. It's common to put a deck above a low-pitched shed roof. However, if the roof is deeper than 4 ft., it typically looks better to create a shallow hipped roof so that the eaves on all three sides are a consistent dimension.

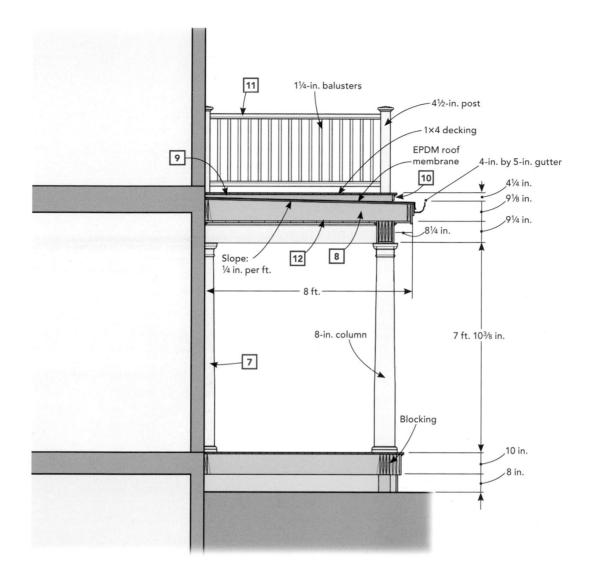

11 1¼-in. balusters

4½-in. post

1×4 decking

EPDM roof membrane

9

4-in. by 5-in. gutter

10

4¼ in.

9⅛ in.

9¼ in.

8¼ in.

Slope: ¼ in. per ft.

12 **8**

8 ft.

8-in. column

7 ft. 10⅜ in.

7

Blocking

10 in.

8 in.

9. Decking

The deck boards should be attached to pressure-treated 2x sleepers, tapered to offset the roof pitch so that the deck surface is level. If the deck boards are installed as removable panels, cleaning the surface under them is much easier.

10. Trim

A fascia board can hide the sleepers, but a ½-in. drainage gap must be maintained between the fascia and the porch roof. The outside face of the fascia should be in line with the outside face of the beam below.

11. Railings

If the porch below has railings, match them or use a scaled-down version of them above. If the porch has no railings, the deck railings should be as visually light as possible. Where the railing meets the house, there should be a wall at least as tall as the railing. The railing can terminate directly into the wall, but it looks best when it ends at a postlike pilaster or a post held 2 in. to 3 in. from the siding.

12. Ceiling

Ideally, the porch ceiling is in the same plane as the porch-roof soffit. The depth of the porch-roof overhang should match the overhang on the house or be reduced by one-third.

Bending Decking for Decorative Inlays

BY KIM KATWIJK

I t wasn't long after I started building decks full-time in 1996 that I got the opportunity to create a curve. I had designed a beautiful curved deck in cambara for a client who wanted the railing cap to follow the shape of the deck. The logical solution for most deck builders would have been to laminate thin strips of cambara into a curved rail on a bending form, but I wanted to try something completely different: Heat-form composite decking to the desired curve.

Composites are made from a mixture of wood fiber and plastic. Because these plastics are not thermally stable, it's possible to heat and bend the decking.

A Literal Learning Curve

My first attempts at board-bending were with Trex. My apparatus involved a 20-ft. by 20-in.-dia. Sonotube laid on the flat with #3 rebar shoved through the sides to suspend the decking. Two kerosene space heaters forced heated air into each end of the tube. This method produced uneven heating and more failures than successes.

Next, I tried a water-bath heater. I used a 20-ft. by 12-in. schedule-40 PVC pipe cut in half. I glued four inlets into the half-pipe, then inserted a water-tank heater into each inlet. I was able to heat the water to boiling. After an hour of boiling, I was

FRAME AND MARK THE DECK. After the deck is framed, the center of the circle is marked. Here, the centerpoint falls between joists, so we install a wooden cleat in the space. At the centerpoint, we insert a nail that stands ¼ in. proud so that a tape measure can be hooked over it. With a pencil held at the 6-ft. 9-in. mark, a circle is scribed on top of the joists to mark where the outside block-ing will go. This blocking supports the cut ends of the field boards and runs 3 in. away from both sides of the inlay. This is repeated at 5 ft. 9 in. to mark the inside blocking (the decking is 5½ in. wide). Also from the center nail, three stringlines indicate the center of the weaves that will extend to the corner and down each leg of the L.

FROM CONCEPT TO CURVE

The design for this inlay is based on a simple L-shape. Inspired by a Celtic-knot design, the pattern weaves down each leg of the L. Although complex looking, this pattern is fairly simple and uses boards bent to only two radii: 6 ft. ⅛ in. for the center circle and 6 ft. 5 in. for the weave. The curves are made of Azek PVC decking, with white for the circle, and gray and clay for the weave. A matching weave in the pergola above tops off the design.

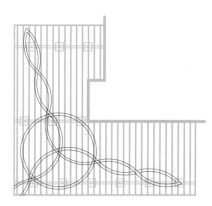

Start by overlaying the design on a deck plan with standard 12-in.-on-center joist framing.

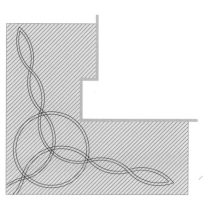

Then experiment with different board directions to get a layout that works with the design.

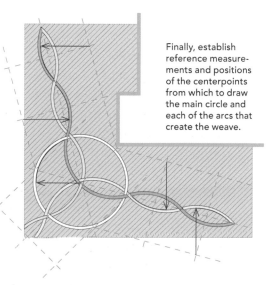

Finally, establish reference measurements and positions of the centerpoints from which to draw the main circle and each of the arcs that create the weave.

MARK THE ARCS. A 20-ft.-long 2×4 is secured 5 ft. 7 in. away from each side of each weave's centerline. Nails driven into these strips mark the centerpoints for each arc of the weave pattern. Using the measuring tape hooked over each nail, the layout lines for blocking are drawn on the tops of the joists at 7 ft. 2 in. and 6 ft. 2 in.

able to bend a 20-ft. composite board in a very large radius—about 15 ft. To get the 5-ft. radius I needed, I had to rip the 2x6 composite boards into three strips, heat them, bend them to a 5-ft. radius, and then glue and screw them back together.

On another project, I tried to get higher temperatures by insulating the pipe and capping it with rigid insulation. This succeeded so well the tank melted.

I gave up on bending deck boards until I discovered the Heatcon® bending system at a trade

BLOCK IN BULK. When blocking for an inlay, it's imperative that every deck board be supported within 3 in. of its cut end. Blocking a circle creates even more difficulties because some of the boards of the circle run parallel with the framing. This requires creative blocking to make sure there is support for all the ends of each of the deck boards and for the inlay boards that fall between the standard framing.

BUILD BENDING JIGS BEFORE HEATING THE STOCK. I lay four 16-ft. 2×12 boards on the ground 2 ft. apart and shim them level before screwing four sheets of exterior-grade ¾-in. plywood on top. I establish a pivot point that allows the arc to fall entirely on the platform. (Depending on your curve's radius, this point may be on the platform or on a 2×4 extending from it.) Using that point, I draw the radius on the plywood. I then scribe the radius on a series of 2×8 scrap boards, and cut along the line with a circular saw. The convex half of the pattern pieces is screwed down to the plywood along the layout line to form the bending jig for the boards.

show. It consists of four 8-in. by 10-ft. blankets, two control units, and two temperature probes. Working with this system, I was able to bend a flat piece of 5½-in. Azek cellular-PVC decking to a radius of 22½ in., opening the door to new levels of artistic expression.

Warranty Issues

It's worth noting that manufacturers of PVC decking have not endorsed these methods to date, although Azek worked with Heatcon to develop a heating blanket for bending trim (sidebar, p. 49) and offers a tutorial for trim-bending on its website.

According to Danny Thomas, vice president for product application/quality at Azek, some independent tests on heat-bent cellular-PVC deck boards suggest there may be a decline in some structural properties in various deck boards. Because each application and each manufacturer

AN EFFICIENT WAY TO WORK

IN A CURVED DESIGN, each piece of blocking is cut with two angles. The most efficient way to do this is for one person to take a piece of 2×6 pressure-treated board, place it vertically over the layout lines where it will be installed, scribe it, number it, and toss it to a sawyer for cutting. Using a Speed® Square, the sawyer determines the angle of the cut, sets the chopsaw, cuts both ends at the prescribed angle, brushes the cuts with preservative, and tosses the board back to be nailed into place. It took almost a week to install the blocking for this deck project.

A GARAGE FLOOR IS A GOOD PLACE FOR HEATING. We roll out the 8-in. by 10-ft. Heatcon heating blanket on top of a strip of R-13 fiberglass insulation. (I put two heating blankets end-to-end to bend a 20-ft. piece of decking.) Each blanket has lines from the control unit for the heating element and a probe that monitors the board's internal temperature. The probe is inserted in a ⅛-in. hole drilled into the side of the board. The decking is laid face down on top of the blanket; another blanket is laid on top of the board, with another layer of insulation on top.

HEAT THE BENDING STOCK SLOWLY. I select "decking," then choose a goal temperature and an internal temperature (chart, p. 50). The control box maintains the blankets at the goal temperature, and the probe monitors the plank's internal temperature. When the set internal temperature is reached, the box beeps.

USE GLOVES FOR SAFE HANDLING. With the board's temperature now at 220°F or higher, the probe is extracted, and the insulation and top blanket are removed. The decking—now the consistency of a big, hot noodle—is quickly carried to the bending jig.

is unique, he recommends checking with the manufacturer to determine if heat-bending will void the warranty.

I give my clients a five-year warranty on my work, but in 16 years of bending deck boards, I've never had a problem with this method when used with a deck board from a major manufacturer. The only physical difference that I've noticed is an expansion in the thickness of the deck board of about ¹⁄₁₆ in. after heating. This is undetectable when walking on the deck.

Boards That Bend Best

I've used both easy-to-bend cellular-PVC boards and the more dense composites in many different applications. A popular application is to ribbon the outside of a curved deck, often in a complementary or contrasting color. Inlaid deck art, like the project detailed here, is one of the most impressive ways to use curved decking. I've done many inlays,

CENTER THE SOFT BOARD ON THE JIG. Pull lightly on each end to stretch the board slightly as it forms to the jig. When bending cellular PVC, radii down to 6 ft. can be done with two people. Radii tighter than 6 ft. need an extra person to keep the center from rolling out of the pattern jig. It helps to have three when bending composite or capstock. The bending process is like a dance: It's done best when everyone knows the steps.

including compass roses, Celtic knots, and multiple deck boards woven to form artistic designs. With curved decks, the need for curved benches goes without saying, and the ability to bend deck boards takes stairs to a whole new level of expression. Even pergolas can take on new twists when you incorporate curved boards to create beautiful overhead artwork.

CHECK THE CURVE AND CLAMP AS NEEDED. Using scrap pieces of wood, the bent plank is secured with clamps at each end and, if needed, at other points around the curve. Stiffer planks need a greater number of clamps to hold them in place. The plank is smoothed out to make sure it's flat and level with the plywood foundation. If not, the board will form waves that will be noticeable when laid on the deck. It takes about 20 minutes for the board to cool and become rigid. The process is repeated with each board used in the curved design.

SECURE FIELD BOARDS ALONG INLAY EDGES. With the field decking installed, the centerpoint of the main circle is marked with a small screw on the deck surface, and the centerline for the weaves is snapped with chalk. The inlay pieces are cut and positioned on the deck. (The ³⁄₈-in. gaps between planks allow me to see the blocking.) I let the inlay ends run wild; I'll cut them later.

TRACE AND CUT. Using a carpenter's pencil held perpendicular to the board, I draw a cutline on each side of each inlay piece. The width of the carpenter's pencil allows for the proper ³⁄₈-in. gap between the main decking and the inlay pieces. I use a circular saw with a standard blade set at 1¹⁄₁₆ in. to cut the decking along the line. The cut pieces are removed, and the inlay pieces are placed and screwed to the joists.

FILLING A TIGHT SPOT. With inlays, you invariably encounter the challenge of fitting in and securing small pieces of decking to make the design work. Depending on the shape, you can attach them with stainless-steel screws through the side, or if blocking is needed, you can use fiberglass industrial grating as a support and glue in the piece.

LEAVE NO LOOSE ENDS. With the inlay boards where I want them, I secure the main deck boards along the length of the inlay to the blocking installed earlier. In keeping with the elegance of this deck design, I used the FastenMaster Cortex Concealed Fastening System. The screws self-cut a hole and set themselves at the right depth so that a plug can be placed in the hole and hammered down to become nearly invisible.

THE HEATCON SYSTEM

HEATCON HAS BEEN MANUFACTURING FLEXIBLE HEATING BLANKETS and controls for industrial-heating applications within the aerospace composite-repair industry for the past 30 years. Customers include airlines and the military.

In 2004, Azek Building Products hired the company to design a system to heat-form PVC trim. Introduced in 2005, this simple-to-use kit has become a popular tool for many builders and contractors.

Almost immediately, questions started pouring in about using the kits to heat-form synthetic decking. Heatcon responded by developing a heat-forming kit for decking based on the same heating-blanket concept as the trim-bending kit. Subsequent tests revealed the need for an internal temperature probe to monitor and regulate a slower heating process for the thicker PVC and composite deck boards.

The HC99-300 deck heat-forming kit that I use can be purchased only from Heatcon. It's pricey, but it quickly pays for itself by bringing your deck-building business to a whole new price point. With it, you can heat and bend an 8-in.-wide by 20-ft.-long deck board. The kit comes with four 8-in. by 10-ft. heating blankets, two 120v heat controllers, two thermocouples for monitoring internal board temperatures, two pairs of heat gloves, an operator's manual, and two carrying cases.

The kit is portable, light (30 lb.), and easy to transport. You also can purchase a half kit, which allows you to bend an 8-in. by 10-ft. board.

You need at least a 20-ft.-long work area and plenty of room on the side for maneuvering the deck boards in and out of the heating-blanket area. You also need access to two separate 120v, 20-amp outlets to operate the two controllers when bending any deck board more than 10 ft. long.

Even with the kit, it's important to remember that bending synthetic deck or trim materials is an art learned over time. The more you use the system and learn the tricks, the better you become at it. More information about the heat-forming kits can be found at Heatcon's website (www.heatcon.com).

WHICH BOARDS BEND BEST?

I'VE USED BOTH CELLULAR-PVC DECKING and composites in my curved designs. PVC bends most readily, but some composites can be heat-formed to a radius as tight as 10 ft. Coextruded composites (sometimes called cap-stock), in which composite material is encased in a low-maintenance plastic shell, are difficult to heat evenly. Urethane decking cannot be heat-formed. Composite railings also can be bent, but it's best to gain experience before attempting these projects.

Because the material formulas of each deck brand vary, all react differently to heat. I've compiled my observations and that of other deck benders I know in the chart below. Generally, the more plastic in a board, the easier it will bend after being heated. Color also plays a big role: The darker the color, the faster it heats up. A dark-gray PVC board may heat up in 20 minutes, while a white board of the same material will take more than 45 minutes.

DECKING TYPE	BRAND	HEAT-FORMING ABILITY	TIGHTEST RADIUS	COMMENTS
PVC INTERNAL TEMPERATURE: 220°F TO 260°F	Trex Escapes	Good	4 ft. 6 in.	Because it's 100% plastic, cellular-PVC decking bends most readily and can make the tightest curves.
	Azek XLM	Good	3 ft. 6 in.	
	Azek Harvest Collection	Excellent	3 ft.	
	Azek Arbor and Terra collections	Good	4 ft.	
COMPOSITE INTERNAL TEMPERATURE: 240°F TO 260°F	TimberTech ReliaBoard®	Fair	12 ft.	All composites will have some spring-back when taken off the mold, so bend them tighter than the radius desired. These boards are slow to heat up.
	TimberTech TwinFinish®	Fair	12 ft.	
	TimberTech DockSider®	Fair	13 ft.	
	EverGrain (Tamko) Decking	Fair	12 ft.	
CAPSTOCK INTERNAL TEMPERATURE: 240°F TO 260°F	Trex Transcend	Very poor	15 ft.	High blanket tempera-tures can melt the coating of these boards before the core is sufficiently heated. Low and slow heat is key here.
	TimberTech Earthwood Evolutions	Poor	11 ft. 6 in.	
	Fiberon Horizon	Poor	12 ft.	

Bright Ideas for a Well-Lit Deck

BY GLENN MATHEWSON

Aside from a sturdy structure and strong railings, good lighting is an outdoor deck's most important safety feature. Decks might have multiple levels, or they might be wet and slippery from nearby hot tubs and wet bars. In addition, decks can be crowded with guests unfamiliar with the layout.

Proper deck lighting is about more than just safety. The right lights in the right spots can make a deck better looking and more enjoyable. Although deck lighting can feel overwhelming with so many fixtures, brightness levels, and installation methods to choose from, the end result is worth it. After all, who wants the fun times on their deck to stop when the sun goes down?

THREE LEVELS OF LIGHT. The best deck lighting considers all three kinds of light. Essential lighting is that required by code at doors and stairs. Targeted lighting is for specific tasks, such as grilling or eating. Ambient lighting creates an inviting space and brightens dark areas.

Essential

Targeted

Ambient

51

Exterior doors

Stairways

Stairway

Essential Lighting

There are two spots on a deck where building codes require lighting. For security, the International Residential Code (IRC) requires a light near every exterior door with grade-level access. This light allows you to see visitors before you open the door. If you're installing a door adjacent to a deck that has access to grade, you'll need to include a light with a wall-mounted switch.

The code also requires that stairways be well lit; unfortunately, the IRC's language is cumbersome. In simple terms, it calls for a fixture at the top landing of every stairway and for a "means to illuminate" the whole stairway.

For a deck with stairs near the door, a single bright light may be enough to illuminate both the stairs and the entry. When the stairs are farther from the door, you'll have to light these areas separately.

Stairways must be at least 36 in. wide, so nonrecessed, post-mounted lights may create a code violation on narrow stairs. Keep in mind that according to the IRC, even a single step between two parts of a deck is a stairway and so is subject to stair-lighting requirements.

EASY ON THE EYES. Obscure glass is a better choice for fixtures where the bulb is visible. Clear glass creates a "flashbulb effect" that temporarily blinds guests with harsh light.

LIGHTING STAIRS FOR SAFETY. To prevent falls, the IRC requires a light at the top landing of every stairway. The rest of the stairway must be illuminated, too. Riser lights, post-cap lights, and post-mounted lights are all suitable options.

Food prep

Dining

Pools and hot tubs

Targeted Lighting

Many decks have lighting targeted for specific tasks. When you're making a deck-lighting plan, it's helpful to break the deck into rooms rather than approach it as one big space. Common areas include grill and food prep, dining, and pools and hot tubs.

LIGHT THE FOOD PREP AREA. A flexible grill light is a great option for lighting the grill area. It will provide direct lighting without the shadows that can be a problem with other lighting options.

FOOD PREP

Just like an indoor kitchen, a deck's food-prep area should have at least one light aimed at each workspace. To better set the mood after the cooking is done, these lights should be switched separately from general lighting. The greatest difficulty in illuminating a grill is finding a spot overhead to mount the light. One common solution is spot lighting in the home's soffit, but shadows from the chef or from the grill lid can be problematic. A better choice is flexible grill lights, which are available from several manufacturers. These lights can be mounted on a wall or installed on a guardrail.

DINING

Lighting for a deck's dining area is best installed where it can illuminate the area without shining in peoples' eyes. A logical spot is on a roof or trellis over the table, where a light can also be a decorative centerpiece. Roof or trellis mounting makes it easy to tie the lights into the house's 110v power. Using that power source also makes a ceiling fan a possibility, provided it's rated for outdoor use. For ambience, dining lights should be less bright than kitchen lights and on a dimmer. Without a trellis or a roof over the table, select a lightweight low-voltage system that hangs from an umbrella or shade frame.

LIGHT THE DINING TABLE. When you don't have a roof or trellis for a ceiling-mounted light, low-voltage umbrella lights are a good substitute.

POOLS AND HOT TUBS

Lighting is incorporated into many pools and hot tubs; when it's not, building codes affect how it's done. The IRC requires any fixtures within 5 ft. of the water's edge, including low-voltage lights, to be

Fire pit

Railing and post

Under bench

at least 12 ft. above the water. The code also requires tempered safety glass within that same distance when the glass is 5 ft. or less above a walking surface. This primarily refers to windows, but it also includes glass light fixtures.

Ambient Lighting

Compared with that of indoor spaces, a deck's ambient lighting is less intense and more dispersed. It's good for filling in where code-required and targeted lighting leave off. Ambient lights can be built into the railing, attached to balusters, or installed in the floor. Many of these lights add an attractive design element on their own.

A SOPHISTICATED CAMPFIRE. Both wood- and propane-fueled fire pits provide light and a natural gathering spot in the center of a deck, which is often tough to illuminate.

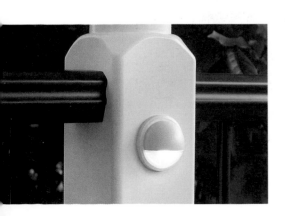

POST-MOUNTED LIGHTS. Available in many styles, post-mounted lights are a good option for ambient lighting. Some railing manufacturers offer post lights that match their rails.

LIVING SPACES

Families love sitting around indoor fireplaces, so it's no surprise that outdoor fire pits are increasingly common in deck construction. They're a great way to bring light to the center of a large deck. Just make sure that any surface surrounding the fire pit is noncombustible.

LINE VOLTAGE VS. LOW VOLTAGE

LINE-VOLTAGE OUTDOOR LIGHTS run off the same power that's used inside the house, but the fixtures and wiring methods must be approved for outdoor use. Line voltage is the right choice for switched lights near the patio door and for ceiling fans over outdoor dining tables. For other deck lighting, the conduit and watertight boxes make line voltage more difficult to install and hide.

Low-voltage lighting fixtures are more forgiving to work with, more flexible to install, and generally safer than line-voltage fixtures. Low-voltage lighting circuits start with a transformer that reduces 120v line voltage to safer and easier-to-install low voltage (12v to 30v). Many high-quality transformers have multiple taps of various voltages. Higher-voltage taps are used to prevent dimming caused by voltage drop on long runs. Transformers range from 45w home-center versions to 1,800w underground models. Many transformers are controlled by a timer or photo cell that turns the lights on and off automatically.

LINE VOLTAGE INTO LOW VOLTAGE. Transformers convert line voltage into low voltage. Products vary greatly in price and the number of fixtures they can power. Some models include timers for operating the lights on a schedule.

DINING LIGHTS SHOULD BE OVERHEAD. Porch roofs and pergolas provide the ideal location for line-voltage-connected dining fixtures and ceiling fans. The roof makes it easy to hide the wires and provides a sturdy spot for mounting the fixtures. Lighting for dining areas should be dimmer controlled to match the mood.

SOLAR

INDIVIDUALLY POWERED SOLAR LIGHTS are another lighting option. The most common are post-cap lights, which provide sufficient area for the on-board solar panel. These lights aren't bright enough for feature lighting, but they can provide low-level ambient light. However, there's little variety, and many folks find their squarish shape less attractive than other types of fixtures. The most obvious benefit of solar-powered lights is their easy installation.

SUPEREASY INSTALLATION. Powered by a small photovoltaic panel and an on-board battery, solar-powered lights are not as bright as line- and low-voltage lights. But because they don't need wires or junction boxes, installation takes minutes.

SOLAR LIGHTS ARE OFTEN POST-MOUNTED. Because they're always facing the sky, the tops of posts provide the ideal spot for solar-powered deck lighting. The on-board solar panel charges the built-in battery during the day so that the light can shine at night.

SOURCES

AURORA DECK LIGHTING
auroradecklighting.com

COPPERMOON®
coppermoon.com

DECKORATORS®
www.deckorators.com

DEKOR™
www.de-kor.com

FX LUMINAIRE
www.fxl.com

HIGHPOINT DECK LIGHTING
hpdlighting.com

HINKLEY LIGHTING
www.hinkleylighting.com

KICHLER® LIGHTING
www.kichler.com

LMT MERCER GROUP
lmtproducts.com

MAINE ORNAMENTAL® (DIVISION OF UNIVERSAL FOREST PRODUCTS)
www.postcaps.com

MOONLIGHT DECKS™
www.moonlightdecks.com

TIMBERTECH
timbertech.com

TREX
www.trex.com

UNIQUE LIGHTING SYSTEMS®
uniquelighting.com

A Homeowner's Guide to Deck Permits

BY GLENN MATHEWSON

Building a deck is a project that's within the grasp of most experienced DIYers. Decks can be enticing because not only do you end up with a pleasant outdoor space for your family, but decks also offer one of the highest returns on investment of any remodeling project. In many ways, a deck is pretty simple. Home centers sell all the materials necessary and are quick to offer encouragement and advice. There are well-defined members and hardware to connect them, and detailed instructions are widely available.

Simple as they seem, though, decks can conceal a surprising number of safety hazards. An improperly attached ledger—the structural member that joins the deck to the house—can fail, causing the deck to collapse when it's loaded with people. An improperly flashed ledger can cause the framing behind it to rot. (Flashing is the system of sheet metal and adhesive membrane that directs water away from the house.) Even with the code-required fastening, the ledger can fail and the deck collapse if the structure it's attached to isn't sound. Improper railings present obvious hazards. As a consequence of these and other risks, most jurisdictions in the United States require permits and inspections for decks. In addition to a building permit, permits for zoning, historic-district compliance, wetlands, and so forth may be required.

A permit generates project records and allows code requirements to be verified by the authority-having jurisdiction (AHJ). The AHJ is often the city where the property is located, but it may also be the county or state. Building departments are often located at the city hall or in some other prominent government location.

Permits allow an unbiased group of professional inspectors and plan reviewers to help ensure that a project is planned and completed correctly—a real benefit for DIYers. If you're hiring someone to build the deck, a permit fosters accountability in a contractor and offers you some peace of mind. Permits ensure that contractors are licensed. But permits cost money, and while skipping the permit might yield momentary cost savings, it is usually just a matter of time before that approach comes back to bite you. Property sales, tragic accidents, insurance claims, and future projects draw these skeletons from the closet. The result is often more money, time, and heartache than if a permit had been obtained in the first place.

When Is a Permit Needed?

A building permit is local-government permission for a construction project on a property. In most urban locations, the government has authority over many more construction projects than you may think. A few less obvious examples can be window, water-heater, and furnace replacements. Generally, however, anything that is "finish work" does not require a permit. Wall and floor coverings, trim molding, and interior doors come to mind. In some regions, replacing only deck boards is considered finish work, and a permit is not required. When in doubt, ask your building department.

Building permits must be applied for, reviewed, and picked up before any construction work that requires a permit begins. There is no consistency across the various jurisdictions in the United States for when decks require permits. All editions of the International Residential Code (IRC), the most widely adopted model code in the country, have language that exempts decks of certain heights and sizes, among other specifics, from requiring a permit:

2012 IRC, R105.2 Work exempt from permit, Building, #10

Decks not exceeding 200 sq. ft. in area, that are not more than 30 in. above grade at any point, are not attached to a dwelling, and do not serve the exit door required by Section R311.4.

However, local jurisdictions frequently amend the IRC prior to adopting it, so this exception may not apply where you live. Provisions that affect when permitting and inspection are required have political and economic aspects that must be evaluated for each jurisdiction; as a result, they are rarely uniform. For example, two neighboring suburbs in the Denver metro area, whose distinction can only be seen from the change in logo on the street signs, are on opposite extremes. One doesn't require permits for any deck less than 30 in. above the ground, while the other requires permits for all decks. This is nothing unusual. When planning a deck, always find out for certain if a permit is required.

It's understandable to want to get started building a deck right away, and waiting for a permit can seem like an unnecessary delay. However, when a permit is required, even demolishing an existing deck or digging holes for footings can be considered "work without a permit," something that often comes with a fine. Quite often, curious neighbors seeing or hearing any such work call the AHJ, prompting an inspector's uninvited visit. That said, some jurisdictions allow demolition to proceed and footing holes to be dug once the permit application is in. Ask your inspector; the worst answer you'll get is no.

WHICH CODE?

THAT MAY SEEM LIKE AN ODD QUESTION. The International Residential Code (IRC) applies almost everywhere, so there's no choice, right? Well, there may be. The American Wood Council, which produces the document that the IRC is largely based upon—the National Design Specification (NDS) for Wood Construction—also produces an alternative building code for decks called the Prescriptive Residential Wood Deck Construction Guide and referred to commonly as the DCA 6. It's updated periodically, and the most recent version is the DCA 6-12. It can be downloaded for free at awc.org, and many jurisdictions accept it as an alternative to the IRC.

Why bother? The IRC is a performance-based code, that is, it specifies the minimum standards a structure must adhere to. It doesn't tell you how you must achieve those standards, though, leaving design professionals a lot of leeway but also leaving DIYers with the task of figuring out how to transform code requirements into construction plans.

The DCA 6, on the other hand, is a prescriptive code. It tells you how to build the deck and provides lots of construction details. Design professionals may find that restrictive, but those details can be very useful to a builder or DIYer.

Even purchasing construction materials before obtaining a permit is a bad idea. If the plan reviewer calls for changes in your construction plans, then having purchased the wrong material may cost you a restocking fee and second delivery charge. Decks are regulated with unbelievable variety across the country, so what was right on target at your last house may be prohibited at your new one. In the worst examples, you may even find the project you planned and purchased materials for is not allowed at all, or it must be built in a manner that costs more than you budgeted. The permit process can take anywhere from a few minutes to a few weeks, depending on your jurisdiction and whether any issues arise. A stack of pressure-treated 2x10s might become a twisted and bowed mess if it sits in your driveway through a long permit delay. All of these are good reasons to avoid purchasing any material until you know exactly what will be required and have clear permission to move forward.

Who Is Responsible for Getting the Permit?

The expectation of nearly all building authorities is that the person acting as the contractor is responsible for obtaining the permit. If you're the homeowner and are doing all the work, you're the contractor. If you do no physical work but design, organize, and contract all the various pieces of the job yourself, you are still acting as the contractor, even if you are not a tradesperson.

Some homeowners have no involvement other than cutting the check. In most cases such as this, the person hired to build the deck should be responsible for permitting. If a contractor asks that the homeowner get the permit, it's often because the contractor isn't licensed. While some jurisdictions don't require contractor licensing, in others the licensing system can be a political mess. If it's regulated at the state level, then a contractor's license should be valid anywhere within that state. But licensing is often done at the municipal level, and a

contractor may build a deck perfectly legally on one side of a street but not on the other because that's a different municipality and requires a separate application and fee for yet another license.

If you as the homeowner obtain the permit on behalf of a contractor, beware of a few potential problems. Primarily, you might become responsible for any failure of the contractor's work to meet code. If the contractor isn't willing to pull a permit, it should raise questions about that person's professional standing. Does he or she have liability and workers' comp insurance, for example? Also, in many jurisdictions, unlicensed contractors cannot file liens or sue for nonpayment.

There is little consistency in this process other than the fact that, in most places, homeowners who occupy their residential property may obtain permits without being licensed contractors. The necessity of occupancy is to avoid having professional property flippers sidestep licensing requirements. Often the term *homeowner permit* is used, but that's a bit misleading. Generally, it is simply the qualifications necessary to pull a permit that are softened for homeowners. Once the permit is issued, the expectations regarding code compliance, inspections, and procedures are the same.

How Do You Get a Permit?

The permit process always begins with an application, and in some locales this may be the full extent of it. However, it will probably take a bit more effort. The application is likely generic for many types of work, and it's intended to convey the details about the property, owner, and contractor. A "work description" or "project scope" field is likely but is nothing more than a written description: "Construction of a 250-sq.-ft. composite deck with stairs" would be an example of a basic project description. The information on this application allows the person who accepts the application to enter it into the plan-review process. In some areas, the plan review is conducted by the same person

THE PERMIT PROCESS

FIRST, YOU HAVE TO GO DOWN THE HALL to the third office on the left...

I need a building permit for a deck. What? I have to go where first?

Zoning: Has to show that the proposed deck fits within the property setbacks and that it's a permitted use in that zone. May need a professionally drawn plan of the property to ensure that's so.

Planning: In some communities, the deck may have to meet appearance requirements. In towns with historic zones, may have to show that a modern structure such as a deck won't be visible from the street.

Health: In areas that rely on septic systems, may have to show that the deck won't be over the septic tank or leach fields. May need to have those systems located, if not shown on existing property plan.

Flood zones: If near water, may require a professional to prove that the project won't impact flooding or affect the ecology of wetlands.

Taxes: May need confirmation that property taxes are current.

OK, I have all the other approvals. Once the plan reviewer examines my proposal, I'll be able to get a building permit.

I got a call that my permit is ready. The fee is $299. I'll need to call for inspections at different stages.

Footings

OK, so my holes are deep and wide enough.

Framing

The framing looks good, and the ledger flashing, ledger bolts, and joists appear as on the plans.

Mechanical

I've got my GFCI outlet and the gas line for the grill.

Final

The stairs and railings meet code. I'm done!

who accepts the application; in others, it is passed to a plan reviewer or is placed in a queue for a later plan review.

Depending on the project, supporting "construction documents" must also be submitted. For a deck, that often includes a plot plan of the site as well as plan and section views of the deck that show the structural elements such as the footings, beam, joists, railing design, and ledger-attachment details. In many cases, the plans for a deck can be simple, hand-drawn renderings.

Additionally, if any electrical work or gas lines are planned, separate permits are required. Some jurisdictions that allow homeowners to obtain building permits may require licensed contractors to perform electrical or gas work. Usually, when a licensed contractor is required, that person is responsible for obtaining the permit. In that instance, the homeowner can usually drop off the permit application that the contractor has filled out and signed.

There is almost always a fee associated with any permit, and it is based on a percentage of the construction cost. However, for small jobs, a minimum fee may apply. That's why permit applications ask for the cost of the job. These fees help to offset the cost of inspectors and the supporting bureaucracy.

Getting Inspections

After a permit is obtained and the work begins, the next step is inspection. Inspections are intended to verify that the work is being done in the location, at the size, and with the materials that were approved. Inspections also visually verify that work is being performed in general accordance with the building code. It is important to understand that inspection is not intended to guarantee code compliance. Compliance is always the responsibility of the person building the project. An inspector only performs periodic inspections and can only verify what is observed. Inspections are snapshots of the process. Permitting and inspection should not be construed as quality control for a contractor's work.

For a deck, the common inspections include the footing holes before concrete is poured, a rough inspection of the framing before any portions are covered up, and a final inspection to verify such things as railing height and whether stair dimensions are within the code. In some areas and for certain designs, the framing inspection can be performed at the same time as the final. However,

LAND-USE PERMITS MAKE SURE YOUR PROJECT PLAYS NICE WITH THE NEIGHBORS

EVEN FOR A DECK, THE BUILDING PERMIT IS OFTEN THE LAST in a string of permits for which you need to apply and pay. In fact, getting the building permit can be the easiest and fastest step in the process. Here's a list of common prerequisites.

Zoning: An area's zoning laws determine whether the proposed construction is a permitted use in that area and if the planned project is within the property's building envelope. Most jurisdictions have setbacks, that is, areas within a specific distance from the property lines where building is not allowed. Setbacks vary between jurisdictions; even within the same jurisdiction, front, side, and rear setbacks usually differ. They may also depend on the neighborhood or whether a street or public property is adjacent.

You'll need to show that what you propose to build does not intrude on the setback limits, which may require a plot plan of the property that shows the relationship of the new deck to the property lines. Plot plans are usually created by surveyors, and you may have a copy in the title work for your mortgage on which you can draw the proposed deck. There may also be such a plan filed with your property records at the town hall that you can copy. When a deck is proposed well away from the setback limit, a hand-drawn plot plan may be acceptable. On the other hand, construction near the setback line may require a new survey and a professional rendering.

Planning: Housing in planned urban areas and historic districts is often regulated strictly for a consistent community appearance. Homeowners associations may have similar requirements. Style, colors, and materials may be regulated; for example, a new deck may require brick columns or a specific type of guardrail. In historic districts, you may not even be allowed to build something as modern looking as a deck if it will be visible from a public way.

Flood zones and wetlands: If your proposed deck is near water, in a flood zone, or over specific drainage channels within your property, you may have to show that it won't affect drainage. In dense housing developments, regulations require each property to work with the overall storm-drainage plan of the entire community. Any construction that could potentially disrupt this may require a review by municipal civil-engineering professionals. Also, some jurisdictions regulate any construction near wetlands to preserve the ecological and hydrological benefits they offer. These circumstances may require you to hire an engineer to provide a plan that meets regulations. This can add months to the permit process.

Taxes: Many jurisdictions will not issue a permit for new construction if property taxes are in arrears.

Health department: In areas where septic systems are used, you may have to show that your new deck isn't going to be built above the tank or in the reserve area, a spot kept open for a new leach field should the existing one fail. This usually requires a survey of your property, but that information also may be on an existing plot plan.

fixing any code-related errors to the structure is often much more costly in time and materials after the job is complete, so I encourage getting a separate framing inspection. Any electrical work, such as adding a receptacle on the deck, requires rough and final electrical inspections as well. Extending a gas pipe out to a grill or fire pit on the deck? That requires a plumbing inspection.

Although working through the bureaucracy may feel like a burden, building codes, permits, and inspections are a necessary part of urban civilization, even for work on our own homes. If you step back, history shows that construction standards are important. They have grown as a result of building failures and the injuries and lost lives resulting from those failures.

We've come to expect a certain level of safety from our houses and buildings, and government oversight of construction makes those societal expectations possible. Beyond the added safety they provide—admittedly, often with added expense—permits help with keeping property taxes properly apportioned and land records up to date. Ultimately, permitting is just a wise investment. A house is a major investment, and selling your home with good permit records is like selling a car with comprehensive maintenance records. It validates the value below the shiny wax, or in the case of decks, below the ipé decking.

PART 3

Deck Framing

DECK LOADS 66

FROST HEAVE 69

SIZING DECK FOOTINGS 72

DECK FOOTINGS DONE RIGHT 80

FRAMING A GRADE-LEVEL DECK 83

FRAMING A DECK WITH STEEL 91

TOP 10 DECK-BUILDING MISTAKES 101

MAKE AN OLD DECK SAFE 109

Deck Loads

BY DAVID GRANDPRÉ

During 20 years of investigating building and building-component failures, I've been involved with a handful of projects where individuals died or were seriously injured. Most of these incidents involved fires and construction accidents. But when you look at those cases in which some component of the structure failed and serious injuries resulted, I'd say poorly constructed residential decks are at the top of the list.

Like any other structure, a wood deck is designed to support applied loads and to transfer those loads to the ground. There are several different types of loads that come into play on a backyard deck, including gravity loads (consisting of live loads and dead loads) and lateral loads. Unless mitigated by proper construction methods, these forces conspire to make a deck collapse. Here's how it works.

Gravity Loads

Gravity, or vertical, loads fall into two categories: dead loads and live loads. In general, gravity loads are supported by the deck joists, beams, posts, footings, and the connection to the house. When designing a deck, both types need to be considered: The dead load is calculated as the actual weight of the building materials used to construct the deck; the live load must be at or above the minimum

DECK LOADS

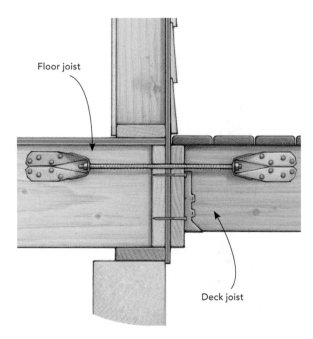

Floor joist

Deck joist

The IRC has taken wood-deck construction seriously and includes prescriptive construction details for supporting gravity loads as well as a prescriptive requirement for lateral loads.

UNDERSTANDING DECK LOADS

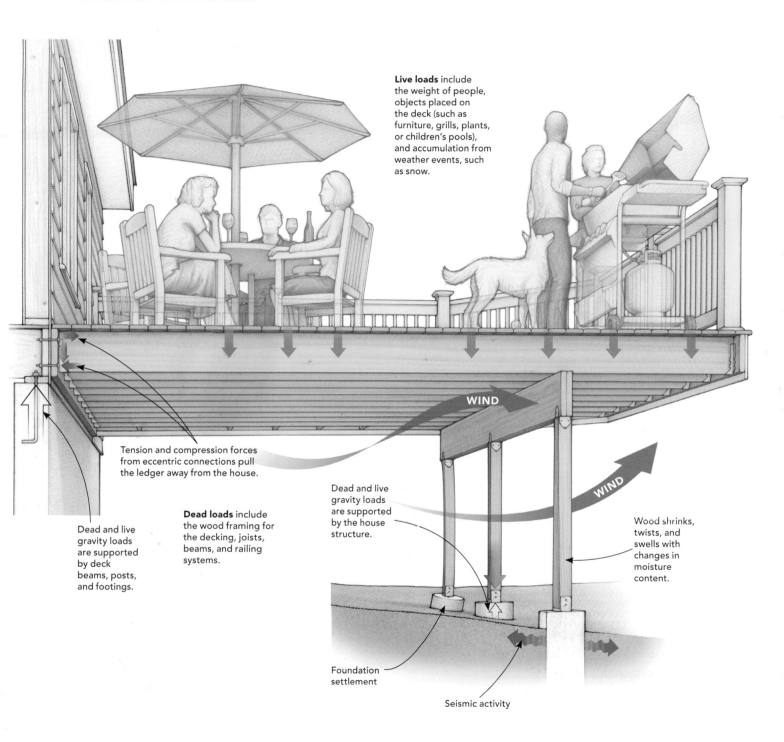

Live loads include the weight of people, objects placed on the deck (such as furniture, grills, plants, or children's pools), and accumulation from weather events, such as snow.

WIND

WIND

Tension and compression forces from eccentric connections pull the ledger away from the house.

Dead loads include the wood framing for the decking, joists, beams, and railing systems.

Dead and live gravity loads are supported by the house structure.

Dead and live gravity loads are supported by deck beams, posts, and footings.

Wood shrinks, twists, and swells with changes in moisture content.

Foundation settlement

Seismic activity

design load of 40 lb. per sq. ft. set by the IRC. Higher loads should be used if a hot tub or other heavy items are going to be placed on the deck. One awful deck failure that I investigated occurred during a cookout where friends and family were having a great time cooking, eating, and visiting, while kids played in a little swimming pool on the deck. The whole gang went tumbling down when the poorly constructed connection to the house failed. The primary force at work here was gravity, along with a lateral load component that helped to pull the ledger away from the side of the house.

Lateral Loads

Lateral loads are the forces that cause decks to shift horizontally, away from the supporting house framing. These forces include wind, differential settlement of soil below foundations, and changes in wood components due to seasonal conditions, such as swelling, shrinkage, and twisting. Eccentricity of ledger connections—that is, the downward force of the joists against the joist hangers that causes the bottom of the ledger to push into the wall and the top to pull away—is another horizontal force. Human activity on the deck—country line dancing, for example—also exerts lateral forces. In some areas, seismic events represent a significant lateral load; in fact, the IRC's lateral-load requirement is based on FEMA guidelines for improving homes' earthquake resistance. Even where seismic events are rare, the IRC requirements for lateral loads are a good idea and help to prevent deck failures from nonseismic-loading scenarios.

Frost Heave

BY DEBRA JUDGE SILBER

Frost heave occurs when freezing temperatures penetrate the ground, causing subsurface water to form ice structures that displace the soil along with anything that rests on or in that soil. While it was once thought that frost heave happens because water expands as it freezes, the process is actually more complicated, involving not only expansion due to freezing but also the accumulation of additional layers of ice as liquid water is drawn up from below the frost line.

Frost-susceptible soil—fine-grained, moist soil in certain climates—is the first prerequisite for frost heave. Engineers define this type of soil as either that in which more than 3% of the grains (by weight) are 0.02 mm in dia. or smaller, or that in which 10% of the grains are 0.075 mm or smaller.

Water is another requirement, as are subfreezing temperatures that penetrate beneath the surface. The depth to which freezing temperatures penetrate the ground is referred to as the freezing plane or frost front. The depth to which they can potentially extend in any given region is the frost line. Frost lines range from a few inches in Florida to more than 6 ft. in the northern United States.

If not controlled, frost heave can seriously damage buildings and other structures in cold climates.

Mitigation typically involves removal of one of the three elements (frost-susceptible soil, freezing temperatures, or water) required for frost heave to occur. Here's how it works.

Frost-Heave Formation

When freezing temperatures penetrate the ground, water trapped in voids in the soil forms ice crystals along the frost front. As it solidifies, this water expands by about 9%. In addition, the freezing process desiccates the surrounding soil, drawing unfrozen water from below the frost front through capillary action and vapor diffusion. This water freezes to the ice crystals that have formed above, thickening it to create an ice lens.

An Upward Force

As temperatures change, the depth of the frost front changes, leaving behind a series of ice lenses with layers of frozen soil between. As they grow, these ice lenses may attach themselves to vertical surfaces below ground, an action known as adhesion freezing, or adfreezing. The ice lenses continue to grow in the direction of the heat loss —that is, toward the surface—lifting soil and structures along the way.

When the air warms, thawing occurs from the ground's surface downward. As the ice lenses melt, water saturates the soil, weakening it. Structures raised by the frost heave slide back down, often resting askew from the combination of weakened soil and shifting load forces above. The cumulative effect of repeated heaving may aggravate the situation, causing a structure to collapse.

Controlling Frost Heave

FOOTINGS AND PIERS

Code mandates that support structures either extend below the local frost line or be protected by insulation so that the bearing soil is not subject to freezing and, thus, heaving. Frost heave also can be controlled by backfilling around piers with gravel to promote drainage, using a sleeve to prevent ice from gripping the concrete, or pouring footing bases that resist upward movement.

DRIVEWAYS, WALKWAYS, AND PATIOS

The occurrence of frost heave can be minimized by replacing fine-grain, frost-susceptible soil with coarse granular material that is not subject to heaving. Drainage measures can reduce the presence of moisture, which also prevents heaving. Providing a capillary break is another option; interrupting the capillary action that draws water toward the ice lenses can make frost heave less severe.

BASEMENTS

Frost heave can seriously damage a basement if the ground surrounding that basement freezes to the foundation walls. When this happens, heaving soil around the house can carry the walls with it. This situation does not occur with heated basements,

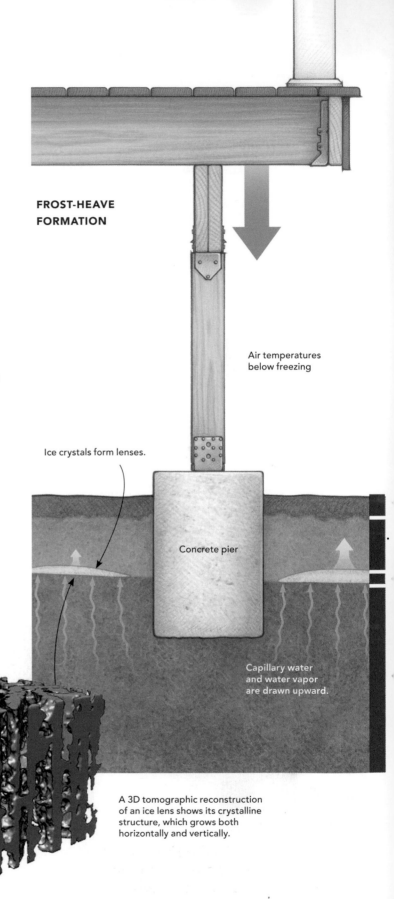

FROST-HEAVE FORMATION

Air temperatures below freezing

Ice crystals form lenses.

Concrete pier

Capillary water and water vapor are drawn upward.

A 3D tomographic reconstruction of an ice lens shows its crystalline structure, which grows both horizontally and vertically.

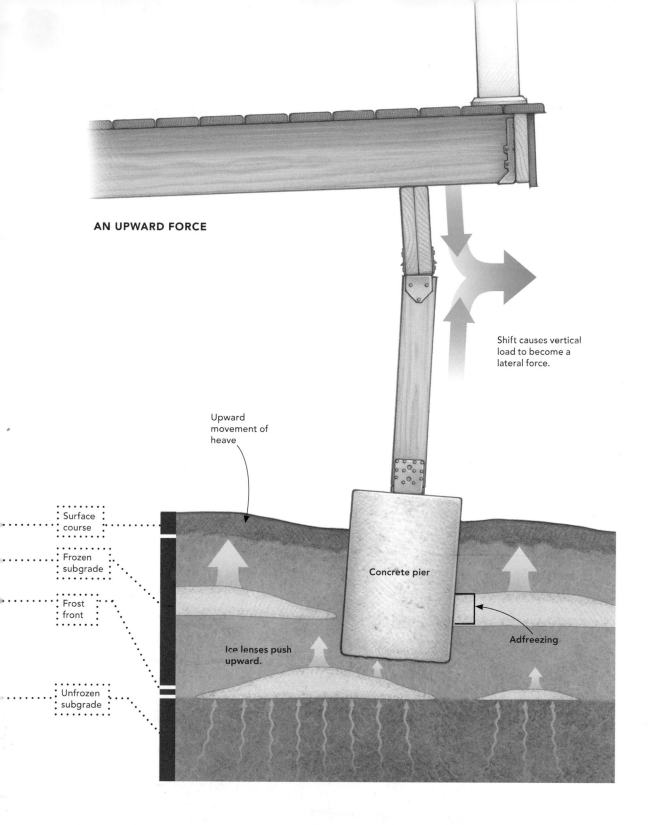

AN UPWARD FORCE

Shift causes vertical load to become a lateral force.

Upward movement of heave

Surface course

Frozen subgrade

Frost front

Unfrozen subgrade

Concrete pier

Ice lenses push upward.

Adfreezing

however. That's because a heated basement (insulated or not) loses heat to the soil surrounding it. This outward heat loss pulls moisture away from the foundation walls. Because moisture is required for adfreezing, less moisture means the frozen soil has a less tenacious grip on the foundation.

Sizing Deck Footings

BY MIKE GUERTIN

Footings transfer the weight of a deck and its occupants to the ground. How many footings you need and how big to make them is specific to each deck. Doing the calculations takes only a few minutes, ensures that I'm following best building practices, and keeps me from digging more than necessary.

The size and spacing of footings tie directly to the maximum spacing between posts of the beam they support. A larger beam can span a greater distance, requiring fewer but larger footings. The 2015 International Residential Code (IRC) contains a table for sizing deck beams (Table R507.6). The IRC assumes a 40-lb.-per-sq.-ft. (psf) live load and a 10-psf dead load. (Live load is the weight of occupants and furniture, while dead load is the weight of the structure.) Although the IRC table is valid in most jurisdictions, snow loads (found in the IRC) in northern New England or the Western mountains may exceed 40 psf, and you'll need to substitute that for the live load. Some local building codes may also require designing to a greater live load. In either case, you may then require an engineer's help.

Knowing the total load in psf, the size of the deck, and the number of footings, I can calculate what each footing has to support. The footing size is based on this load and the bearing capacity of the soil.

CHOOSE A BEAM

SEVERAL FACTORS DETERMINE WHICH BEAM SETUP to use. Should it overhang the end posts or end flush with them? Is there a backhoe at hand so that digging a few large footings makes sense? Or is this deck on a house with established landscaping that calls for a greater number of smaller-diameter footings that can be dug by hand around obstructions? What is the joist span?

After answering those questions, I choose a beam configuration, such as a double 2×8, from the IRC table and determine the number of footings needed based on the size of the deck. I prefer a double 2× beam because

it can rest on notched 6x6 posts. The 2½-in.-thick leg on the back of the notch bolts to the beam. Triple 2× beams sometimes make sense, but they require a structural connector to join to the post.

The IRC table allows joist overhangs (cantilevers) past the beam of up to one-quarter of the span between the beam and the ledger. The beams themselves can overhang the end posts by one-quarter of the post spacing. By cantilevering the end of the beam, you often can eliminate one footing.

THREE BEAM OPTIONS FOR A 14-FT. BY 20-FT. DECK

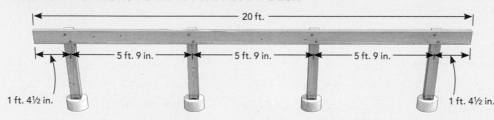

A double 2×8 beam offers a maximum span of 5 ft. 9 in. and a maximum overhang of 1 ft. 5¼ in., resulting in four posts spaced 5 ft. 9 in. apart and overhangs of 1 ft. 4½ in. at the ends.

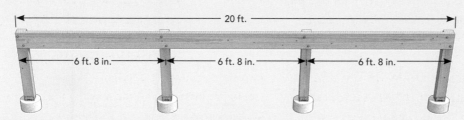

A double 2x10 beam with a maximum span of 6 ft. 9 in. results in four posts spaced 6 ft. 8 in. apart.

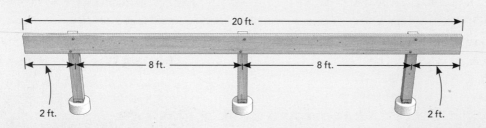

A double 2×12 beam with a maximum span of 8 ft. and a maximum overhang of 2 ft. results in three posts spaced 8 ft. apart and overhangs of 2 ft. at the ends.

POST SPACING FOR SOUTHERN-PINE BEAMS

		JOIST SPANS LESS THAN OR EQUAL TO:					
BEAM SIZE	**6 FT.**	**8 FT.**	**10 FT.**	**12 FT.**	**14 FT.**	**16 FT.**	**18 FT.**
2-2×8	8 ft. 9 in.	7 ft. 7 in.	6 ft. 9 in.	6 ft. 2 in.	5 ft. 9 in.	5 ft. 4 in.	5 ft. 0 in.
2-2×10	10 ft. 4 in.	9 ft. 0 in.	8 ft. 0 in.	7 ft. 4 in.	6 ft. 9 in.	6 ft. 4 in.	6 ft. 0 in.
2-2×12	12 ft. 2 in.	10 ft. 7 in.	9 ft. 5 in.	8 ft. 7 in.	8 ft. 0 in.	7 ft. 6 in.	7 ft. 0 in.
3-2×8	10 ft. 10 in.	9 ft. 6 in.	8 ft. 6 in.	7 ft. 9 in.	7 ft. 2 in.	6 ft. 8 in.	6 ft. 4 in.
3-2×10	13 ft. 0 in.	11 ft. 3 in.	10 ft. 0 in.	9 ft. 2 in.	8 ft. 6 in.	7 ft. 11 in.	7 ft. 6 in.
3-2×12	15 ft. 3 in.	13 ft. 3 in.	11 ft. 10 in.	10 ft. 9 in.	10 ft. 0 in.	9 ft. 4 in.	8 ft. 10 in.

*Area depicted above.
Note: Based on Table R507.6 of the 2015 IRC; only a portion of the table is reproduced here.

CALCULATE THE LOAD ON EACH FOOTING

THE IRC CALLS FOR DECKS to be designed for a minimum 40-psf live load and a 10-psf dead load; add the two together for a total load of 50 psf. Each footing carries the load imposed by a tributary area of the deck whose depth is half the distance from the beam to the ledger (7 ft. in the example here), plus any cantilever of the joists beyond the beam (2 ft. here, for a total of 9 ft.). The width of each tributary area is the sum of half the distance from that footing to the footings on each side. The two end footings are a little different, though. They carry the load halfway to the next footing, plus any overhang of the beam. So while the tributary area of the two middle footings has a width of 5 ft. 9 in., that of the two end footings is only 4 ft. 3 in.

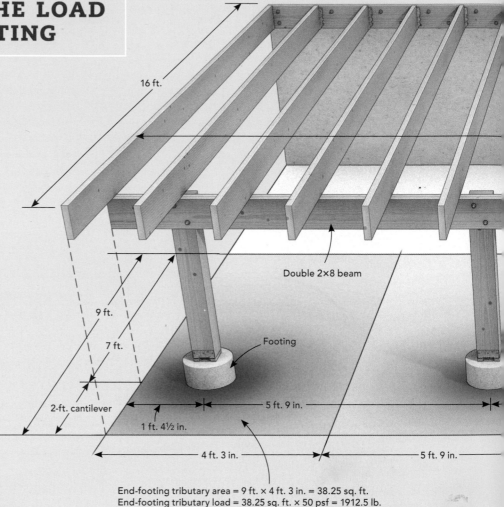

16 ft.

Double 2×8 beam

Footing

9 ft.

7 ft.

2-ft. cantilever

1 ft. 4½ in.

5 ft. 9 in.

4 ft. 3 in.

5 ft. 9 in.

End-footing tributary area = 9 ft. × 4 ft. 3 in. = 38.25 sq. ft.
End-footing tributary load = 38.25 sq. ft. × 50 psf = 1912.5 lb.

CARDBOARD TUBE FORMS CAN HANDLE SOME LOADS

CYLINDRICAL CARDBOARD TUBES ARE THE GO-TO FOOTING FORMS for a lot of deck builders. These forms create smooth sides that reduce the chance of frost attaching to the concrete and heaving the footing, and they isolate the concrete from the surrounding soil to prevent it from mixing in and weakening the concrete. Here's a quick guide to the area of typical footing-form tubes and footing bearing capacity based on common soil load-bearing values.

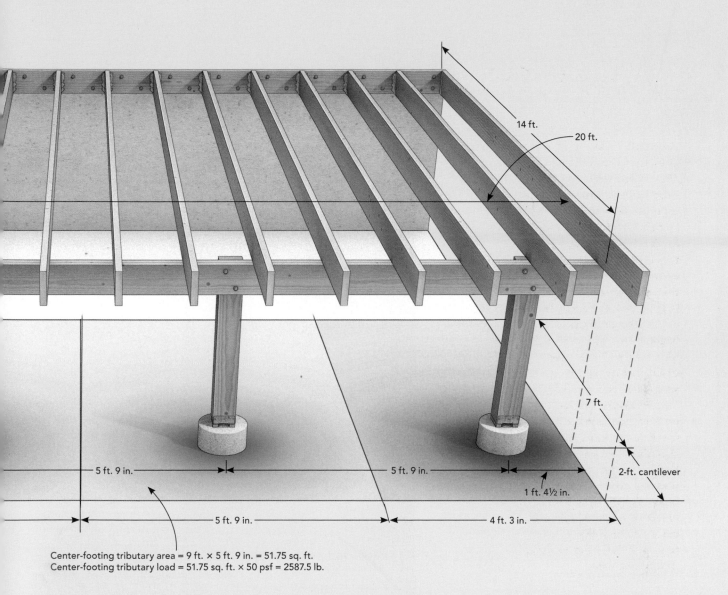

14 ft.

20 ft.

7 ft.

2-ft. cantilever

5 ft. 9 in.

5 ft. 9 in.

1 ft. 4½ in.

5 ft. 9 in.

4 ft. 3 in.

Center-footing tributary area = 9 ft. × 5 ft. 9 in. = 51.75 sq. ft.
Center-footing tributary load = 51.75 sq. ft. × 50 psf = 2587.5 lb.

FOOTING-FORM DIAMETER	AREA	1,500-PSF SOIL CAPACITY	3,000-PSF SOIL CAPACITY	4,000-PSF SOIL CAPACITY
8 in.	50.3 sq. in. (0.3493 sq. ft.)	524 lb. per footing	1,048 lb. per footing	1,397 lb. per footing
10 in.	78.5 sq. in. (0.54514 sq. ft.)	818 lb. per footing	1,635 lb. per footing	2,180 lb. per footing
12 in.	113.1 sq. in. (0.7854 sq. ft.)	1,178 lb. per footing	2,356 lb. per footing	3,142 lb. per footing

SIZE THE FOOTINGS

NOT ALL DIRT IS CREATED EQUAL

You need to know the bearing capacity of your soil before calculating footing size. The IRC lists the bearing capacity of five soil types, from "crystalline bedrock" at 20,000 psf down to 1,500 psf for "firm fine sand, silty sand, and silty gravel." Your building department may have soil maps that show local soil types and their bearing capacity. You also can have an evaluation done by a soils engineer, but it's probably cheaper simply to use the IRC's default 1,500-psf bearing capacity and to increase the size of the footings a little. Whether you're able to use cardboard tube forms or need to use one of the larger footing forms, odds are that there won't be forms for the exact footing size you calculate. In that case, always go to the next-larger form size.

CALCULATE THE FOOTING AREA NEEDED

Once you know the load a footing will support and the bearing capacity of the soil, you can determine the required footing size.

Total load ÷ bearing capacity = area

Convert the area into square inches.

End footings
1,912.5 lb. ÷ 1,500 psf = 1.275 sq. ft.
1.275 sq. ft. × 144 = 183.6 sq. in.

Center footings
2,587.5 lb. ÷ 1,500 psf = 1.725 sq. ft.
1.725 sq. ft. × 144 = 248.4 sq. in.

Convert the area into a round footing diameter or a square footing size.

$2 \sqrt{(\text{area} \div \text{pi})}$ = diameter of round footing (pi = 3.14)
or $\sqrt{(\text{area})}$ = length of sides of a square footing

End footings
Round: $2 \sqrt{(183.6 \div 3.14)}$ = 15.29 in. (15⁵⁄₁₆ in.) dia.
Square: $\sqrt{183.6}$ = 13.55 sq. in. (13⁹⁄₁₆ in.)

Center footings
Round: $2 \sqrt{(248.4 \div 3.14)}$ = 17.79 in. (17¾ in.) dia.
Square: $\sqrt{248.4}$ = 15.76 sq. in. (15¾ in.)

FROST LINES AND SOIL TYPE AFFECT FOOTING DEPTH

In areas not subject to freezing, footings must be at least 12 in. below the undisturbed ground surface. If there is any fill where the footings are placed, the footing holes must be dug at least 12 in. below the fill or disturbed soil into suitable ground. Compressive soil, expansive soil, and organic soil are a few common unsuitable types. Footing holes have to be dug through unsuitable soil to reach stable soil. When placed within 5 ft. of a house, footings must be at least the same depth as the house foundation to be sure they rest on undisturbed ground. Where the ground freezes, footings must be at least as deep as the local frost line. Your building department will know what this is, but it can be as deep as 60 in.

FOOTING-TO-POST CONNECTION

THE POST IS TIED TO THE FOOTING with a connector such as a Simpson ABA66Z or a USP PA66E-TZ, combined with a concrete anchor bolt.

CAST IN PLACE. Standard foundation bolts are a common way to attach post bases, but they must be placed accurately in the wet concrete.

GLUED IN PLACE. Chemical anchors that glue anchor bolts into drill holes offer great strength. Chemical anchors must be at least $3\frac{3}{16}$ in. from the footing edge.

WEDGED IN PLACE. Wedge bolts and sleeves fit into holes drilled after the concrete cures. Wedge anchors must be at least 5 in. from the concrete's edge.

BIGGER FOOTING FORMS

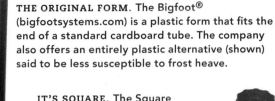

THE ORIGINAL FORM. The Bigfoot® (bigfootsystems.com) is a plastic form that fits the end of a standard cardboard tube. The company also offers an entirely plastic alternative (shown) said to be less susceptible to frost heave.

IT'S SQUARE. The Square Foot™ forms (soundfootings. com), which work with cardboard tubes, make it easy to calculate the area of the footing.

DESIGNED FOR REBAR. The WP Fail-Safe Form Footer™ (wpfailsafe .com) incorporates a proprietary rebar system, particularly useful in areas with seismic and wind-uplift concerns.

TAPERED TUBE. The Footing Tube (www .foottube.com) includes a concrete-saving tapered plastic tube in addition to the bell-shaped footing form. It offers little bite for ice to grab and lift, and it allows backfill to be compacted prior to placing the concrete.

SHIPS AND STORES FLAT. Flat-Forms (flat-forms.com) assemble quickly from cardboard packs to create a complete 48-in. bottom-to-grade form with a spread base.

DUCT-TAPE COMPATIBLE. The Redibase form (redibase-form.com) is used with standard cardboard tubes. It's designed to allow the joint to be sealed easily with duct tape to keep dirt out of the form.

WHAT ABOUT THE
WEIGHT OF THE FOOTING?

THE DEAD LOAD FIGURE (10 LB./SQ. FT.) in the IRC covers the weight of framing, decking, and railings but generally doesn't include the weight of the concrete footings. But should it?

Some people ignore the footing weight since the soil removed from the hole is close to the mass of the concrete filling the hole. Others add the full weight of each footing to the sizing calculations. And others just add the net difference between the mass of the concrete and the mass of the soil removed to the sizing calculations.

I actually weighed the silty gravel subsoil from a couple of footings and found that it weighed about 110 lb./cu. ft. Cured concrete weighs about 150 lb./cu. ft. Adding the full weight of a 12-in.-dia. footing tube that has an overall height of 4 ft.—which holds about 3 cu. ft. of concrete and has a total mass of 450 lb.—to a tributary deck load of 1,912.5 lb. yields a total load of 2,362.5 lb.

The net difference between the soil and the concrete is 40 lb./cu. ft., so the net difference between the concrete footing mass and mass of soil removed from the hole is 120 lb. Add the net difference to the tributary load for a total of 2,032.5 lb. (1,912.5 + 120). Note: the 12-in.-dia. footing is a guess at this point. The actual base of the footing may need to be greater or may be smaller. In practice, since the actual weight of the framing and decking materials often don't add up to 10 psf, there's probably enough prescriptive dead load capacity left to handle the difference in the weight of the concrete and the excavated soil for many decks.

ALTERNATIVE FOOTINGS

GARBAGE BAGS

I make adjustable footing forms from heavy-duty garbage bags. First, I dig a footing hole a little larger than the cardboard form and about 1 ft. shy of my final depth. Then I widen the bottom of the hole to the size required by the footing-size calculation.

Using duct tape, I attach a garbage bag to the bottom of the cardboard form and slip it into the hole. Before backfilling, I fill the bag with concrete so that it spreads out and fills the hole. At that point, I backfill the footing tube and fill the inside of the tube with concrete.

PIN FOOTINGS

Pin footings (pinfoundations.com) are engineered systems consisting of concrete anchor blocks cast with guide holes through which steel pins are driven diagonally into the earth. Each anchor block has an integral bolt on the top that is ready to accept post hardware. The pins are made of 1-in.-dia., schedule-40 galvanized steel. Residential models are sized for frost depths between 36 in. and 48 in., and commercial models can work with a 60-in. frost depth. The residential models have a load capacity of 2,700 lb. when installed in 1,500-psf soil and 3,600 lb. in 2,000-psf soil. The pins are driven into the earth in just minutes using a 1⅛-in. hex-shank demolition hammer.

HELICAL PILES

In areas served by a specialty contractor, helical piles can save a lot of digging. Galvanized-steel assemblies consisting of a helical plate (typically 12 in. dia. for decks) and a 2-in. pipe, residential helical piles are driven by a hydraulic motor on a small, dedicated machine. Once the pile reaches the minimum depth allowed by code, the operator monitors the hydraulic pressure required to drive the pile, which directly translates to the bearing capacity of the footing. Once the required bearing is reached, the pile is cut to length and a beam saddle is welded on. Depending on the contractor, you can end up with an engineer's report that verifies the load each footing can handle. One source for that service is www.technometalpost.com.

Deck Footings Done Right

BY MIKE GUERTIN

START WITH A GOOD HOLE

BUILDING CODES COVER MOST OF THE BASICS about footing size, frost depth, and the bearing capacity of soil and concrete. Codes don't, however, tell how to dig a proper footing hole. A good hole is smooth, straight, and flat-bottomed; includes a footing form; and avoids the pitfalls below.

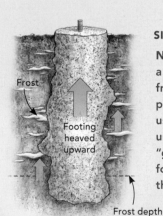

Frost

Footing heaved upward

Frost depth

SIDE ISSUES

No form: The smooth sides of a footing form minimize soil friction and act as a bond break, preventing heaving. If you don't use a form, concrete assumes the uneven shape of the soil. Frost can "grab" the rough sides and heave a footing even if the bottom is below the frost line.

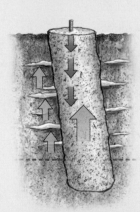

Slanted: The force on a slanted footing loads the side rather than the bottom of the footing, causing it to sink and rotate. Also, frost can heave up against the side.

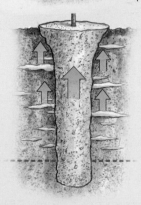

Inward taper/flared top: Footing forms prevent inverted-cone and mushroom shapes, the worst designs for footings. These shapes often have narrow bases that can sink under load, and frost pressing upward on the top can tilt the footing. Footing forms alleviate the problem even when the hole is dug overly wide at the top.

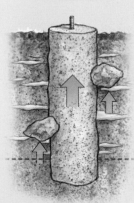

Debris: Rocks, roots, pipes, and other projections that impinge on the straight sides of footings can give purchase for frost to heave or tilt footings. They also leave defects in the footing that can lead to concrete fractures.

BOTTOM PROBLEMS

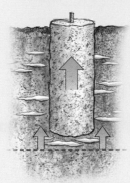

Too shallow: Decks connected to a house must be supported by footings that reach the frost line, the point below which the ground won't freeze. Otherwise, when moisture in the earth freezes and expands, it can push shallow footings upward. Frost depths vary, so check the local building department for your conditions.

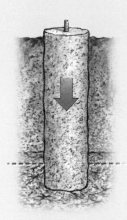

Unstable soil: Topsoil (loam) contains organic material (decayed plant matter and unconsolidated mineral matter) and a lot of air. Highly compressible and unstable, it can't reliably support a load. Footings must be dug through the topsoil, which can be several feet thick, even if that means going well past the frost line.

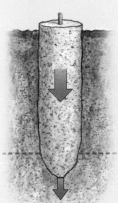

Rounded/pointed base: Footings are designed with flat bottoms for a good reason. If you dig them with round or pointed bottoms, then add a load, they can act like arrowheads piercing the soil. Make the bottom of the footing hole the same size as the footing form or larger. The bottom also must be flat and close to level.

Disturbed base: Footings can't rest on earth that has been disturbed by digging, even if that excavation took place many years ago. This is especially problematic for footings dug near a foundation wall. Even the couple of inches of loose soil at the bottom of a freshly dug hole must be removed or compacted by tamping.

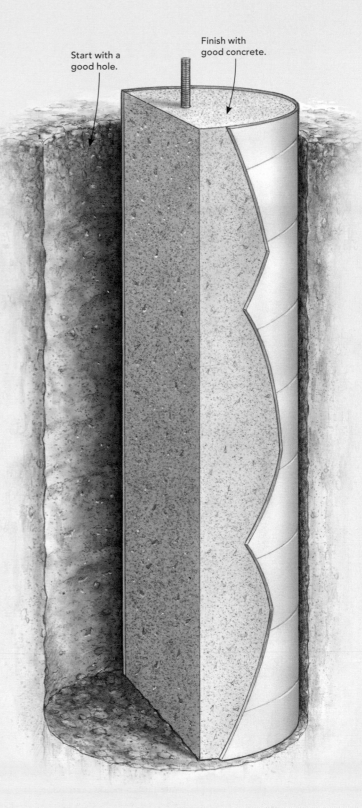

Start with a good hole.

Finish with good concrete.

FINISH WITH GOOD CONCRETE

THE MINIMUM COMPRESSIVE STRENGTH OF CONCRETE USED for footings should be 2,500 psi. Air pockets and other defects can reduce compressive strength, so the importance of properly mixing and placing concrete can't be overlooked.

GET THE MIX RIGHT

Too dry: A stiff, dry mix may not consolidate fully, so the footing could be left with air pockets and fracture lines that can lead the footing to crumble under load.

Too wet: Soupy concrete dilutes compressive strength. As the extra water dries away, tiny holes remain and weaken the concrete.

Just right: The concrete should be damp enough to hold together when squeezed into a ball and not crumble apart. It should keep a crown when shoveled and not spill off the edges.

Soil contamination: Soil can inadvertently fall into the concrete during placement, especially on footings poured directly into holes without forms. Soil contamination can weaken concrete and leave fracture lines. Use a footing form that's at least several inches above grade to avoid contamination.

AVOID THESE SETTING MISTAKES

Footing top below grade: Footings poured so that the concrete is below grade invite surrounding dirt to fill over the top. This puts the post-base connector at risk of corrosion and the post itself at greater risk of decay. Pour the footing at least 4 in. higher than grade.

Uneven tops: It's hard to plumb and secure a post base properly on top of a footing with a sloped top. Make sure to screed and level off the top of the concrete before it cures.

Rocks in the mix: Avoid the temptation to toss stones into the concrete pour. Soil on the stones will prevent the concrete from bonding, and there's also a risk of creating air pockets and weak spots.

Air pockets/cold joints: This problem often occurs when using a stiff concrete mix, when a pour is interrupted and fresh concrete is placed on top of curing concrete, or when large aggregate doesn't consolidate into the mix. Don't pause for more than 15 minutes during each pour, and vibrate or rod the concrete to ensure that layers are intermixed.

Water infiltration: If you hit water as you dig the footing holes or leave rainwater in a footing hole before pouring, the concrete will be contaminated and weak. Water must be removed from the hole, or the concrete must be isolated from the water by using a plastic bag or waterproof footing form.

Framing a Grade-Level Deck

BY CHRIS AHRENS

The traditional raised deck frame is a beautiful balance of structural function and adjustability. A ledger attaches through the wall sheathing and into the floor frame of the house, joists extend out from the ledger across the top of a built-up beam, and weight is transferred down support posts to footings below. The height of the deck is usually driven by the elevation of the house's floor framing, and then a set of stairs runs from the deck to the ground.

It's an easy template for any intermediate builder because it includes lots of flexibility when it comes to footing heights, post lengths, and beam leveling. It also offers plenty of underdeck access for grading and moisture management. Many builders assume that constructing a grade-level deck means shifting

THE LEDGER SETS THE ELEVATION. The ledger is not only the structural connection between the deck and the house; it's also what establishes the overall height and levelness of the entire deck frame. On this project, the 2×10 joists of the main deck frame sit just about even with the top of the foundation, and a landing framed with 2×8s sits atop the main frame, serving as a transition point between the lowered deck and the patio door. You don't have to bother adjusting the height of a laser to project a ledger guideline at just the right elevation. Instead, project a level line somewhere near where the ledger will attach, and then snap a line to be used as an offset benchmark for the rest of the elevations.

to a different technique—ditching the ledger and going to a freestanding structure, or swapping a carrying beam for a flush beam—but in fact, all of the traditional methods can still be used. You don't need to make drastic changes to the way the deck is assembled; you just need to modify how you tackle three of the structural components: the ledger, piers, and beam.

Working within a foot or so of ground level means that you have less room for adjustment. On the deck shown here, for instance, there wasn't enough space for posts, so the beam sits right on the footings. This single change meant that footings had to be poured level to each other and that their height couldn't be figured accurately until the ledger was set on the wall.

The Challenges Begin with the Ledger

A typical ledger-supported deck is fastened to the house at the rim joist. But to set the deck close to grade, the ledger might need to be attached to the foundation. This involves both challenges and advantages.

GAUGE BLOCKS GUIDE THE LEDGER. After determining where the ledger will attach in relation to the benchmark line, mark the offset on both ends of a pair of 2×8 cutoffs—the material that will be used to frame the landing. Align the marks on the blocks to the benchmark line, and screw them to the wall.

TWO NAILS LET YOU FOCUS ON THE DRILLING. Lift the ledger so that it's tight against the bottom edge of the gauge blocks, and then shoot a powder-actuated nail into each end of the ledger to tack it in place. Drill a hole and set a bolt on each end of the ledger before drilling all of the other bolt holes.

To start with, fastener options will change. On solid-concrete foundations like this one, you can attach the ledger with wedge bolts or with standard bolts set in epoxy or acrylic adhesive. Gone are the days of using lag shields for ledger attachments; they aren't up to snuff for structural deck connections. You can't use wedge bolts if you're attaching to a hollow-block foundation, but adhesive anchors will do the job as long as you set them in mesh screening or tubes, which gives the adhesive solid purchase inside the hollow block.

Attaching the ledger to the foundation may also mean spanning cast-in-place windows. On this job, we had two. Your building official has the final word on this subject, as there are no deck-specific requirements in the codes. From a structural standpoint, though, this is not a major departure from standard floor framing. Building codes for floor framing allow the use of a single structural header when spanning a space of 4 ft. or less, provided the header is the same size or larger than the joists attaching to it.

Another challenge that you might encounter is how to deal with a foundation that has dips and

humps on its face. Attaching a ledger to the rim joist generally goes easily because it would have been in the best interest of the framer to set that rim straight when building the first floor. By contrast, the dips and humps left in a foundation wall by its form boards aren't crucial to anybody but the deck builders trying to put a ledger onto that wall, so the concrete might be pretty out of whack.

Don't fuss with trying to get the ledger straight, though; just secure it tightly to the wall, and adjust things at the outer edge of the deck frame by letting joists run long, snapping a chalkline, and cutting the joists to an even length.

If all of this sounds like a hassle that you don't need, consider one major benefit: There's often no need to peel back siding or worry about ledger flashing—that is, unless you pulled off an old deck and had to patch in siding, as we did on this job. It's still a good idea to run flashing up under the bottom course of siding if the ledger will be set tight to the siding, but there's no need for that if the ledger is lower on the foundation wall. The only concern here is water getting behind the ledger and not being able to dry out easily. This problem is prevented by

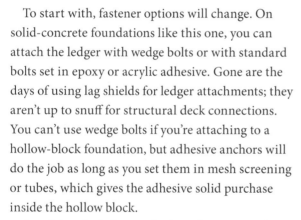

NUTS BEFORE HAMMERS. Use the predrilled ledger as a template for boring the holes in the concrete. But before whacking the wedge anchors into place, put a washer and a nut onto each bolt. A hammer can damage a bolt's leading threads and make it impossible to get the nut started if it's not already in place. Give the nut enough spins to ensure that it won't be hit by the hammer.

I use powder-actuated nails to tack temporary support blocks to the foundation to ease my back, free up my hands, and let me focus on positioning the ledger just right.

If you prefer, you can also tack the blocks to the wall framing above and then lift the ledger up tight to the blocks before pinning it to the foundation. This method is helpful if your deck will have a landing between the main part of the frame and the door to the house, which is the situation we had on part of this deck. In this case, we established our final height and then cut blocks from the framing lumber that would be used later for the landing, creating a sort of real-life story pole.

Whatever you do, take your time at the ledger. Installed carefully, it will make the footings, the beam, and the rest of your deck frame easier to build.

Piers Are Hard to Get Perfect

When digging 42-in.-deep holes 7 ft. apart in rocky soil, then placing footing tubes in a straight line and filling them with concrete to the same finished height, there are any number of ways for mistakes to creep in. It's important to aim for perfection, but it's crucial to understand how to deal with problems.

(Continued on p. 90)

LEDGER FASTENING BY THE CODE

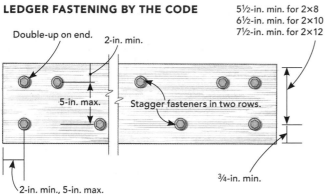

5½-in. min. for 2×8
6½-in. min. for 2×10
7½-in. min. for 2×12

Double-up on end.

2-in. min.

5-in. max.

Stagger fasteners in two rows.

¾-in. min.

2-in. min., 5-in. max.

applying a bead of sealant at the joint between ledger and foundation.

The last piece of advice I have on this topic is to think ahead about how to handle the logistics of holding, aligning, tacking, and permanently fastening the ledger. Wet pressure-treated lumber is heavy, but it seems to get even heavier when you're in a crouched position trying to hold a long ledger to a snapped chalkline while freeing up one hand to fasten the board to the wall. Whenever possible,

DEALING WITH A DROPPED DECK

ATTACHING A DECK LEDGER TO CONCRETE RATHER THAN THE HOUSE'S FRAMING can mean dealing with some new challenges. The most common ones I've found are jogs in the foundation that aren't square, concrete walls that aren't straight, and basement windows that are in the ledger's path.

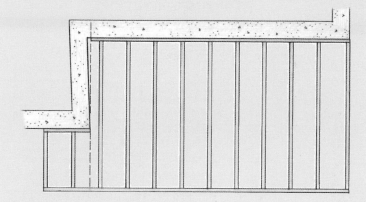

OUT-OF-SQUARE CORNERS

If the deck will wrap around corners or jogs in the foundation, check the foundation corners for square before setting the ledger. If you simply follow the jogs of the foundation, you could end up with an out-of-square frame.

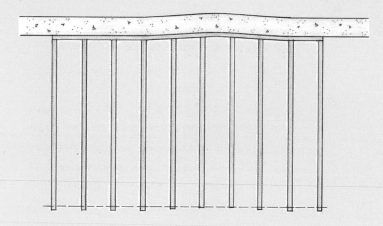

WAVY WALLS

Always knock off excess concrete left by the form ties to help ensure that the ledger lies flat against the wall. Even then, the ledger might not be perfectly flat. If you try to set joists cut to size, the opposite ends won't line up. Instead, let the joists run long over the beam. Before attaching the rim, snap a straight cutline, and trim the joists evenly.

BASEMENT WINDOWS

As long as the building official approves your plan, you can span the ledger right over small basement windows. In these cases, double-up the ledger fasteners on each side of the opening, holding them back from the window frames by about 3 in.

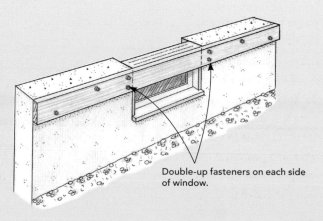

Double-up fasteners on each side of window.

2x10 ledger

2x10 beam

Post base

STRAIGHT TRUMPS PARALLEL

It's not crucial for the beam to be exactly parallel to the ledger and the deck rim; it just has to be straight and land fully on the piers. With the ideal beam centerline (red) marked on the two end piers, stretch a chalkline across the row of footings to visualize the centerline of the other post bases. Before snapping the chalkline, adjust the two ends of the line either in or out to be sure that each post base will bear fully on its pier.

Blue: Distance from ledger to pier center, according to plans

Red: Beam position adjusted to land on all piers

CALCULATE PIER HEIGHTS. The height of concrete piers isn't crucial on a raised deck because leveling the beam is a matter of adjusting the length of each post running between pier and beam. But for a grade-level deck, where the beam is set right on post bases anchored to the top of the concrete piers, there is far less room for error. To start, align a laser to the top edge of the fastened ledger, and then use a story pole to measure down the footing tubes to determine the finished height of each concrete pier.

NAILS MARK THE POUR. Rather than cutting the tubes at the finished height before pouring concrete, poke nails through the cardboard to serve as height indicators.

BUILD THE BEAM IN PLACE. It may be only inches from the ground, but the carrying beam in a grade-level deck does the same job as a structural beam 10 ft. overhead. It should be built strong, set level, and protected against rot. To start, one person holds the two halves of the beam so that the tops are in alignment before the second person nails them together. Building codes recommend the use of 10d threaded nails set in two staggered rows, with 16 in. between nails. The author nails more liberally.

DON'T FORGET THE SHIMS AND SPACERS

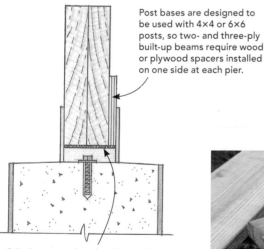

Post bases are designed to be used with 4×4 or 6×6 posts, so two- and three-ply built-up beams require wood or plywood spacers installed on one side at each pier.

If the beam needs to be shimmed to get it level, use shim stock that won't compress under load and won't deteriorate from rot or rust. Galvanized metal tie plates (sometimes called strap ties; photo at right) are a good option and can be bent in half for extra thickness.

PROTECT THE SEAM. The joint between pieces of lumber in a built-up beam is a notorious trap for water and debris and will eventually lead to damage, even with pressure-treated lumber. A strip of self-adhered flashing is a cheap weapon in the fight against the elements.

If piers aren't poured level to one another, the only option is to find the highest pier and then shim under the beam on the lower ones to meet the same finished height. In this situation, I still anchor the post bases to the concrete, but then I add shims between the post base and the underside of the beam after it's been nailed together and set in place.

If the piers aren't perfectly aligned to one another, then you have to find a new centerline for the beam. Forget about whether the beam runs perfectly parallel to the ledger—this really isn't important in a situation where deck joists run continuously over a beam anyway—and focus on setting the beam so that it bears fully on the piers. This desire for wiggle room in positioning the beam is why I use 12-in.-dia. footing tubes, even if I can get away with smaller ones, and why I opt for bolt-down post bases rather than the anchors that are cast in place.

The last thing to check before starting to set joists is that your site is graded and detailed to deal with moisture. A deck set low to the ground won't have much airflow below it. This will increase the risk of rot in the frame and of moisture-related issues above it, such as cupped deck boards.

The basics of moisture control are simple: Start by sloping the ground for drainage; you don't want water to settle under your deck. After that, put down several inches of gravel. Moisture wicks up to the surface through soil by capillary action, which only works when water can go from larger pores to smaller ones. Such a path is found easily in soil. Gravel creates a layer of larger pores that short-circuits capillary action, helping to keep the moisture in the soil and away from the deck. Landscape fabric below the gravel keeps dirt out and weeds from sprouting. Finally, never let any part of the deck frame touch the ground. Unless you're using lumber rated for ground contact—a rating that common pressure-treated lumber does not carry—the wood is not meant to be in direct contact with the ground.

Framing a Deck with Steel

BY ROBERT SHAW

My company focuses on building high-quality decks. Over the years, one of our biggest issues had been the quality of the pressure-treated lumber available for framing. The joists weren't uniform in depth, and they always twisted and warped as they dried.

When I heard about light-gauge steel deck framing in 2006, I was impressed by its apparent advantages: It's light, straight, and uniform in size. Still, the available information was limited, and I spent a few more years sorting through wet, heavy, pressure-treated framing lumber, culling out bad boards, crowning joists, sorting joists by variation in depth, planing the joists after installation, and trying my best to build a perfectly flat frame, only to come back the next day to more warped joists.

JOISTS + TRACKS = BEAMS

LIGHT-GAUGE STEEL IS IDENTIFIED IN DIMENSIONS like this: 800S200-54. That piece is an 8-in. stud (or joist) with a 2-in. flange made from 54-mil-thick (or 16-ga.) material. A piece identified as 800T200-54 is the same, except it's a track. The edges of a track's flange are straight, not curled like a stud's. Tracks are sized so that studs fit between their flanges.

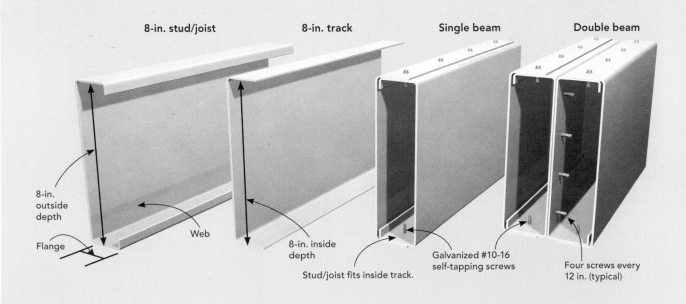

8-in. stud/joist

8-in. track

Single beam

Double beam

8-in. outside depth

Flange

Web

8-in. inside depth

Stud/joist fits inside track.

Galvanized #10-16 self-tapping screws

Four screws every 12 in. (typical)

In 2009, I decided to give steel framing a shot. I faced three main hurdles, however: dealing with building departments that were used to wood framing, finding a supplier, and learning how to work with steel. Once I overcame these hurdles, steel's advantages made it a no-brainer for me, even though it costs more per piece than lumber. Despite steel's higher cost, on a high-quality project with synthetic or hardwood decking and a manufactured rail system, the framing is a relatively small part of the whole cost.

Although it's lighter than wood, steel offers greater spans in smaller profiles than wood, allowing for more-flexible designs and fewer footings, which can compensate for some of steel's higher cost. Steel is rotproof (although it can corrode), noncombustible, termite-proof, and free of chemicals. It can be ordered in custom lengths to minimize field cuts, and any scrap is easily recycled.

First Hurdle: The Building Department

Even though the International Residential Code (IRC) devotes page after page to steel framing, it's much more common in commercial buildings than in houses. Most building departments aren't used to the idea of a steel-framed deck and so may be somewhat resistant. Despite the depth of coverage the IRC gives to light-gauge steel framing, most of it is specific to house walls, floors, and roofs, not to decks.

BEGIN WITH THE LEDGER. The ledger on a steel-framed deck is a piece of track that's bolted or screwed to the house. Just like a wood deck ledger, steel ledgers must be properly bolted to the house framing and installed level. Lay out the ledger so that the bolts don't interfere with joist connections. Unlike with a wood ledger, holes have to be drilled in steel even for structural screws. Drill ⅛-in. starter holes on layout, then switch to a step drill and enlarge the holes to fit the fasteners. After all the holes have been drilled, spray the exposed steel with Rust-Oleum® cold galvanizing compound.

DRILL HOLES IN THE LEDGER. Lay out the holes for the mounting screws so they don't interfere with the joist layout. Start the holes with a ⅛-in. twist bit, and finish with a step drill marked at the desired hole diameter.

DON'T CREATE OPPORTUNITIES FOR RUST. Coat all cuts and holes with cold galvanizing spray.

JUST LIKE CUTTING WOOD. Cut steel with a circular saw. The author likes Freud®'s Diablo® steel blades. The hot metal chips produced call for full-face protection.

GRINDER FOR THE NOTCHES. An inexpensive abrasive cutoff wheel in a die grinder makes short work of little cuts.

I've found that talking face to face with inspectors helps the process along best. Bring along some information (including this article) so that you can show them what you're talking about. Still, the line you'll probably hear is "I can approve this only with an engineer's design stamp."

If this happens, find an engineer who specializes in light commercial construction because he or she most likely will be familiar with the use of light-gauge steel. Once again, have some information to present. If you demonstrate a thorough understanding of steel framing and present high-quality, detailed drawings, an engineer might be willing simply to review and stamp your plans for a small fee. The big details on the plans won't be much different from those you'd see for a wood deck; there are still posts, beams, and joists. The main differences are in the details for fastening and blocking.

(Continued on p. 98)

BUILD THE BEAM. Single beams are built up by screwing together a track and a joist, typically with ¾-in. #10-16 self-tapping galvanized sheet-metal screws through the flanges every 12 in. Sight the length of a track to be sure it's supported flat and straight before joining it with a joist into a beam. A double beam consists of two single beams built together. Hot-dipped galvanized (HDG) screws are recommended in any moist environment. Commodity screws don't perform as well as some name-brand ones. Hilti and Starborn Industries both offer high-quality screws.

BUILDING BEAMS FROM TRACKS AND JOISTS

BEAMS ARE MADE BY COMBINING TRACKS AND JOISTS. A single beam consists of one joist nested inside one track and typically fastened with one screw through the flanges every 12 in. A double beam is made by screwing two joists together back to back, then adding a track on each side.

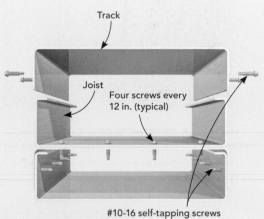

Track

Joist

Four screws every 12 in. (typical)

#10-16 self-tapping screws

A JOIST AND A TRACK MAKE A BEAM. Join the two nested members with self-tapping sheet-metal screws through their flanges.

WOOD POSTS ARE EASIER. In most cases, it's faster to notch and bolt a wood post to a steel beam than it is to assemble a steel post from tracks and joists.

INSTALL JOISTS AND BLOCKING. Without help, steel joists aren't as laterally stable as wood joists. So that they don't tip under load, steel joists require blocking (joist stock) where they bear on a beam. Depending on the span, additional blocking may be required at the center of the deck. You usually only need to block every other bay because each piece of blocking stabilizes the two adjacent joists. Alternating the joists so that flat faces flat simplifies blocking. Where the blocking is over a beam, add two screws through the flange of the block into the beam below.

STANDARD FRAMING ANGLES JOIN JOIST TO LEDGER. Joists attach to the ledger with standard Simpson Strong-Tie® or USP Structural Connectors framing-angle hardware. Fasten the framing angle to both members with self-tapping sheet-metal screws. Steel joists are dead straight, so there's no need to crown them before installation.

SCREW JOISTS TO BEAM. Fastening joists to a beam takes one screw through the flange and into the beam below.

BLOCK EVERY OTHER BAY. Each block stabilizes two joists.

BLOCK BETWEEN THE JOISTS. Self-tapping screws fasten framing angles to blocking and to the joists. Two additional screws secure the blocking to the beam.

SCREW RIM TO JOISTS. The rim is a piece of track that fits right over the ends of the joists and is then screwed through its top and bottom flanges. Sight along the rim as you screw it to the joists to keep the edge of the deck straight.

SCREW DOWN THE DECKING. You can install decking on steel frames in several ways. No matter which method you choose, you'll need to accommodate the protruding heads of the screws that secure the top flange of the rim to the joists. I mark the screw locations by holding the deck board in place and tapping it with a hammer and block. Then I flip the board over and drill shallow counterbores where the screw heads left dents.

FASTEN FROM BELOW. Short galvanized screws through joist flanges from below hold the edge boards.

Second Hurdle: Finding a Supplier

Your local lumberyard or home center probably won't have a clue about light-gauge steel. The place to buy light-gauge steel is usually a drywall-supply house that also deals in steel studs. Knowing this, I contacted drywall-supply houses and asked about material for decks. I got confused salespeople on the phone and funny looks at the store.

I changed my approach. Rather than explaining that I was building a deck and asking if they could supply the framing, I simply started using nomenclature from the engineer's plans. Once I learned how to speak the language, buying steel became a lot simpler.

Steel joists are technically referred to as studs. Studs fit inside tracks, which are supplied just slightly wider than the studs to ensure a proper fit. (Because of how I use these studs, I refer to them here as joists; when ordering, though, I call them studs to avoid confusing the supplier.) Like framing

lumber, steel framing is sold in certain depths, but it's also sold in a variety of flange widths, which is sort of like being able to buy 3x and 4x lumber as well as 2x lumber. Steel also comes in various gauges, or thicknesses. (For more information, go to the Steel Stud Manufacturer's Association website, www.ssma.com.)

Steel used outside must be galvanized. Many galvanization levels are available; G60, G90, and G135 are typical. The number indicates the ounces of zinc applied per square foot of material. For example, G60 has 0.6 oz. of zinc per sq. ft. (0.3 oz. on each side), while G135 has 1.35 oz. per sq. ft. This is the same system used for framing hardware intended for wood decks, which comes with a G185 coating. Before 2004, when the standard wood preservative was CCA, G60 and G90 coatings were commonly used on hardware. The G185 standard is a response to the greater corrosiveness of the chemicals that replaced CCA. Because it doesn't contact treated lumber, steel framing doesn't require the same

HIDDEN FASTENERS WORK WELL WITH STEEL FRAMING. You can install decking by drilling through the flange and screwing from below. I often mix this with biscuit-type hidden fasteners that engage in slots in the edge of the decking. The key is to use a biscuit-type fastener that relies on a vertically driven galvanized screw, not an angled screw, which won't engage in steel framing.

COVER THE STEEL. Fascia material—in this case, a pair of deck boards—hides the shiny rim joist from view.

galvanization level as hardware. Where I build, G90 is sufficient. If you live in a wetter environment or near a road that's treated with deicing salt, consider thicker galvanization. If you live on the seacoast, steel framing may not be acceptable at all.

Steel studs typically come with holes already punched for wiring and plumbing. Order yours without them. They're unsightly, unnecessary on a deck, and could line up with a spot where a screw is required.

Third Hurdle: Putting It Together

There's a lot about framing a steel deck that's no different from framing a wood deck. The footings are the same, although there may be fewer of them. Ledger flashing is the same, with one caveat: If your flashing will contact the framing, use either vinyl or galvanized-steel flashing; other metals will corrode. Most important, do not combine stainless steel with galvanized framing. Stainless steel and zinc are on

opposite ends of the galvanic scale. This means that in the presence of moisture, the zinc galvanization will rapidly oxidize and will expose the underlying steel, which then will rust.

BUILD STAIRS AND ATTACH RAILING POSTS

For railings, I use a lot of top-mount posts and a locally sourced welded railing or a system from Fortress Iron or RDI. These systems require solid-wood blocking. Conventional wood posts can be installed with blocking and ½-in. through bolts. Where stairs attach, I add a track to the joist to support the extra weight. Stairs can be steel, with the stringers consisting of single beams, painted to match the decking that covers the steel subtreads and risers. Sometimes I use 2×12 treated-wood stringers, which fasten to the deck with Simpson's LSSU210Z or LSCZ brackets.

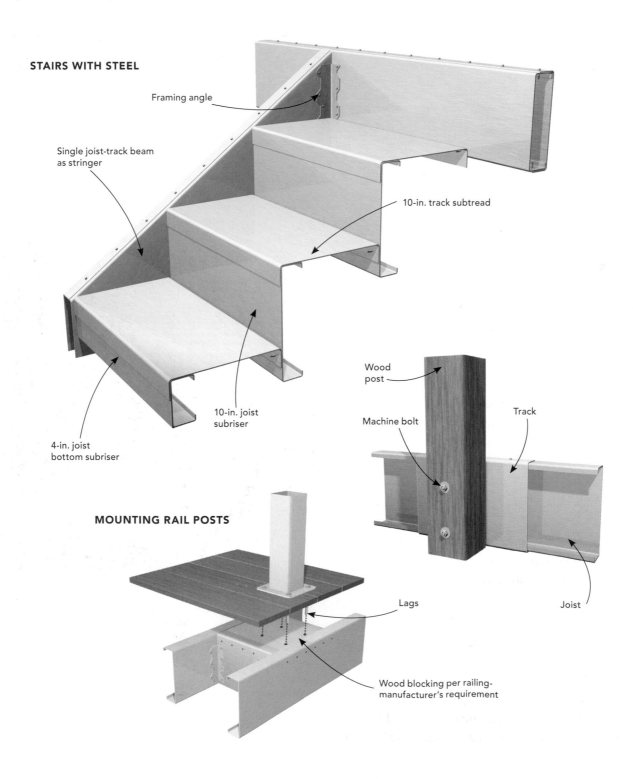

STAIRS WITH STEEL

Framing angle

Single joist-track beam as stringer

10-in. track subtread

10-in. joist subriser

4-in. joist bottom subriser

MOUNTING RAIL POSTS

Wood post

Machine bolt

Track

Joist

Lags

Wood blocking per railing-manufacturer's requirement

Top 10 Deck-Building Mistakes

BY GLENN MATHEWSON

The process of building decks is not nearly the same today as it was a decade or more ago. While the outdoor environment and the endless design possibilities have remained constant, emerging technologies and new products and materials require a stronger sense of industry codes and best practices for you to be able to build a deck properly.

As a deck builder, inspector, and plans analyst, I have seen a lot of inferior deck-building practices from professionals and do-it-yourselfers. I've also seen an abundance of bad information that perpetuates problematic designs and poor construction practices. A badly built deck is more prone to failure than a correctly built one, and it's dangerous for those who use it.

Here, I highlight the most common errors I see in deck building and offer solutions to help ensure that your next deck is safe and that it lasts.

1. Failing to Install a Continuous Handrail on Stairs

THE ERROR:

For construction or aesthetic purposes, builders regularly install handrails interrupted with newel posts. It's also common to see a guardrail used as a handrail.

INCORRECT. The post in the middle of this flight of stairs interrupts the top of the railing, which was designed to serve as the handrail. A new continuous handrail, albeit an unsightly one, had to be added.

THE SOLUTION:

Code provision R311.7.8.2 requires that a continuous handrail be installed on any set of stairs that has four or more steps. A continuous guardrail free of midspan posts extending through the top can be used as a handrail but only if it meets specific geometric requirements. To be considered a handrail, the guardrail must be graspable by those walking up and down the stairs.

If a post interrupts a guardrail, a true handrail must be added to the guardrail running along the stairs.

2. Installing Hardware Incorrectly and Using the Wrong Fasteners

THE ERROR:

Incorrect fasteners in hangers are a notorious mistake. For example, deck screws are not a proper way to attach joist hangers, and using 1¼-in.-long 10d nails where 3½-in. 16d nails are required is a sure sign that manufacturer instructions were not followed.

Fasteners that don't have the correct corrosion-resistance rating will fail quickly when installed in treated lumber. Also, using only one-half of a two-part post-to-beam connector and installing undersize bolts in 6x6 post bases are common installation errors.

THE SOLUTION:

For hardware to work as the manufacturer claims it will and the way the inspector expects it to, follow the manufacturer's installation instructions. Proprietary hardware is not specified in the code; therefore, it is considered an alternative. Alternatives are approved via testing or engineering, and that information must be provided to the building official. The only way to be sure hardware will perform as expected is if it is installed as it was tested or designed. Beyond code compliance, valid product warranties depend on proper installation.

INCORRECT. Always follow manufacturer guidelines for appropriate fastener types and sizes, and use stainless-steel or galvanized fasteners if you are using pressured-treated lumber.

3. Bolting Beams to the Sides of Posts

THE ERROR:

A tragedy brought to us from the aisles of big-box stores: directions to deck builders to bolt deck beams to the sides of support posts. The average backyard deck has relatively few posts. Fewer posts result in

INCORRECT. Bolting beams to posts as shown here can result in failure. The bolt may not shear, but the wood can shred. Use a galvanized-steel post cap, and keep the beam firmly seated atop its support post.

BEAM-TO-POST CONNECTION

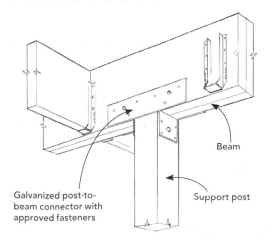

Beam

Support post

Galvanized post-to-beam connector with approved fasteners

greater loads at beam connections. It would take a huge load to shear a ½-in.-dia. machine bolt, but long before that occurs, the wood around the bolt would be crushed and distorted, resulting in a failed connection.

THE SOLUTION:

A beam should be bolted to the side of a post only for low-level decks that have short-spanning joists and beams and many support posts. Of course, that means lots and lots of foundation piers, which are not the best choice in a region with a significant frost depth. With all the hardware available to handle various direct-bearing applications of different-size beams and posts, there is little reason not to place deck posts directly beneath beams.

4. Overspanning Composite Decking

THE ERROR:

The maximum span of wood-and-plastic composite decking generally depends on the type of plastic used in the product. It's important to follow the span limits of a specific product as outlined in the manufacturer's installation instructions, which some builders fail to review. Overspanning composite decking is most commonly a problem when deck boards are run diagonally over joists or when they're used as stair treads.

THE SOLUTION:

Floor joists for a deck are typically installed at 16 in. on center, which won't properly support some composite-decking products when installed on an angle. In new construction, be sure floor joists are installed at the correct spacing. In existing decks, adding more floor joists is the only remedy. Similarly, additional stair stringers might have to be added to stairs where composite decking is used for the treads. Stair treads must be able to resist a concentrated load of 300 lb. over an area of 4 sq. in. This requirement puts a lot of pressure on the actual tread

CORRECT. To meet the span tolerance of this diagonally installed composite decking properly, additional joists and hangers had to be added to the existing deck framing.

material to support concentrated loads. Some composite products are limited to an 8-in. maximum span when used as stair treads, which require the support of four stringers in a 36-in.-wide stairway.

5. Building Stairs with Incorrect Riser Heights

THE ERROR:

Often, the bottom step on a set of deck stairs is roughly 1 in. taller than the rest. Code allows a maximum variation of only ⅜ in. between riser heights. This guideline often confuses inexperienced carpenters, who insist that they cut every notch in the stringer the same.

THE SOLUTION:

Every notch cut into a stringer has an identical riser height except for the bottom one. The steps notched out of the stringer in the middle of the flight have treads placed above and below each step, effectively adding the same tread thickness to each riser height

SIZE RISERS CORRECTLY

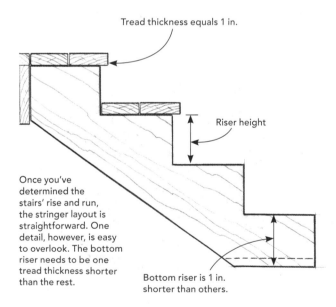

Tread thickness equals 1 in.

Riser height

Once you've determined the stairs' rise and run, the stringer layout is straightforward. One detail, however, is easy to overlook. The bottom riser needs to be one tread thickness shorter than the rest.

Bottom riser is 1 in. shorter than others.

so that they remain constant. The bottom step doesn't have a tread below it, though, so you must subtract the thickness of the tread from the height of the bottom riser, which is the bottom of the stringer.

6. Ignoring Clearances and Inhibiting Access

THE ERROR:

Although well constructed, some decks create code violations and safety hazards just by how they interact with the house. For example, some stairs on multilevel decks end up near windows that the builder has not replaced with tempered-glass units. Other decks are built too close to the house's main electrical service panel or the service conductors overhead—which need to be at least 10 ft. above a deck or 3 ft. to the side of a deck, according to code (E3604.2.2).

THE SOLUTION:

No matter what features exist on the exterior of a home—windows, air-conditioning compressors, low-hanging soffits, exterior lights, outdoor receptacle outlets, dryer vents—identify the required clearances before starting a deck design. While some features will influence the shape and location of the deck, other features may require only that appropriate access be integrated into the design of the deck.

CONSIDER THE CLEARANCES

Some clearances around a deck are code-required, like providing a minimum 36-in.-tall escape path from a basement egress window, while others are simply practical, like ensuring access to hose bibs. Each clearance should be considered with equal diligence.

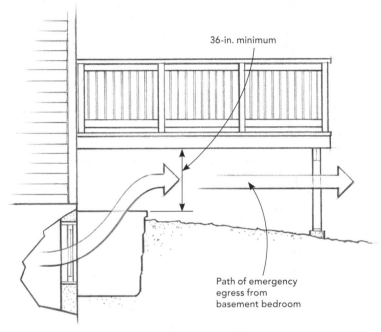

36-in. minimum

Path of emergency egress from basement bedroom

CORRECT. If sistering deck joists to floor joists isn't an option, adding a beam, posts, and footings can help to relieve some of the stress placed on the fasteners connecting the ledger to the end grain of the cantilevered floor joists.

7. Attaching Deck Ledgers Poorly

THE ERROR:

The majority of deck plans end with a straight, continuous line at the ledger, rather than details as to what the ledger is connecting to. Unfortunately, the way a ledger attaches to a house is one of the most critical elements in deck construction, and many builders get it wrong. For example, they bolt ledgers straight to brick, stucco, or EIFS cladding. These practices violate the code.

One of the more egregious ledger mistakes is connecting the ledger to a rim joist nailed to the end grain of cantilevered floor joists—those that support a kitchen bump-out, for example.

THE SOLUTION:

Detailing a ledger properly depends on the building type, the cladding material, and the site conditions. Of all the parts of a deck, the ledger can rarely be treated the same from job to job. Long before construction begins, considerations must be made as to, for example, whether stucco needs to be cut back with new weep screed installed or whether a few courses of lap siding need to be removed to bolt and flash the new ledger properly.

A ledger connection to a cantilevered floor requires specific considerations. Instead of attaching a ledger to the ends of the cantilevered floor joists, it's often stronger to sister the deck joists to the existing floor joists.

8. Setting Piers in Disturbed Soil

THE ERROR:

When it comes to digging footings for their deck piers, some builders are lazy. Usually, a deck's foundation piers are not set below the region's frost line. To avoid deck-ledger failures, freestanding decks are becoming popular, but the piers nearest the home's foundation are often set atop backfill.

In areas where the frost depth is not an issue and precast foundation blocks are commonplace, they're often set on top of the exposed grade.

THE SOLUTION:

Just about every deck is built on an isolated-pier foundation system. Foundation systems are required to extend a minimum of 12 in. into undisturbed soil (R403.1.4). In cold climates, where the earth is subject to freezing, a pier foundation must extend to a depth below that which is likely to freeze—anywhere from 36 in. to 48 in. This prevents the soil below the pier from freezing and heaving the pier upward.

To install deck piers properly, the piers must bear on undisturbed soil and be set below the frost line in cold-climate regions. However, if the piers are in a backfill region, as is the case with piers nearest the house on a freestanding deck, the footing depth may have to be as deep as 10 ft. to reach undisturbed soil and to comply with code.

Precast foundation blocks must be set at least 12 in. into the ground. However, even in the middle of a lot, the topsoil is tilled roughly 6 in. prior to seeding, so it's likely that the footing needs to be at least 18 in. deep to comply with code.

INCORRECT. When set above an area's frost line, footings can heave (left). Even where the ground doesn't freeze, footings must be set 12 in. into undisturbed soil and not directly on grade (right).

CORRECT. Piers set below the frost line with bell-shaped bases stay in place and distribute the deck's weight.

Assume that all deck piers and foundation blocks require some digging.

9. Incorrectly Attaching Guardrail Posts

THE ERROR:
Insufficiently connecting a guardrail post to a deck is among the most dangerous deck-building errors. Fastening guardrails to deck rim joists or floor joists with wood screws is not acceptable. While some builders get the guardrail-to-rim-joist connection correct, they don't always ensure that the rim joist is attached to the deck framing properly.

THE SOLUTION:
The code (table R301.5) requires a guardrail to be capable of resisting a concentrated load of 200 lb. in any direction along its top. Depending on the design of the guard assembly, a stout guardrail-post-to-deck connection can be accomplished with blocking and through-bolts or with horizontally oriented hold-down hardware. In some rail designs, most of

INCORRECT. Don't use nails or screws to fasten railing posts to deck framing. Use bolts.

CORRECT. More specifically, use blocking and bolts to create a stronger railing than one with posts connected to rim joists that are nailed only to the end grain of the joists.

the load resistance is handled by the post connection to the deck. In those instances, the post should be attached to the joists, not the rim, because the rim is not usually fastened to the joists in a manner capable of transferring the load. Rims are typically nailed into the end grain of the joist, the weakest possible connection for withdrawal resistance.

The design methods for guardrail assemblies are as vast as the imagination, and homeowners admire that creative expression. However, serious consideration must be made as to how the guardrail is ultimately assembled.

The strength of a guardrail assembly is provided by a lot more than just the post-to-deck connection. The concentrated load must be resisted at any point along the top of the rail. With a common 5-ft. to 6-ft. distance between the posts, the load must transfer through the connection of the horizontal rails to the post. When a continuous top cap runs across the posts, it acts like a horizontal beam to help distribute the load over a larger area. When a post is run long, through the top of the guardrail, there is a considerable reduction in strength.

10. Making Beam Splices in the Wrong Places

THE ERROR:

When a long built-up beam spans multiple posts, many builders run one ply long and extend it beyond the support posts. Many builders believe this practice is good because splices of opposing beam plies are greatly separated as opposed to being only inches apart on top of a post. Unfortunately in these cases, an engineer's evaluation or a rebuild of the beam is required.

THE SOLUTION:

Beams are under two stresses: bending and shear. Shear forces act perpendicular to the length of the beam and are greatest near the bearing ends.

Bending changes the beam's shape, a force called deflection, and is greatest in the center of the beam span. The code lists maximum allowable limits for deflection. In deck beams, the deflection limit is typically reached long before shear limits are a consideration. Any reduction in bending resistance also increases deflection potential and ultimately ends in code noncompliance.

Beam splices that miss the bearing point by a small amount don't greatly affect bending or deflection, and the shear strength of one fewer ply

is likely still sufficient. In these cases, the cost of an engineer's review might just get you the OK to build. If a design calls for a splice in the center of a span, it will be smarter and cheaper to build the beam so that splices land atop posts.

INCORRECT. Beams suffer the greatest amount of deflection at the center of their post-to-post span. Therefore, strong beams are spliced atop posts. If you can't stagger splices over different posts, then placing them over a single post is permissible.

BEAM SPLICES

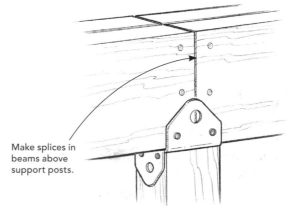

Make splices in beams above support posts.

Make an Old Deck Safe

BY MIKE GUERTIN

Broken balusters

Leaky flashing

Unsafe handrail

Unsecure ledger

Weak stairs

Posts don't support the beam

No lateral load connectors

Shallow footings

I was at a client's house only to estimate a front-door replacement, but my eyes were drawn to the second-story deck. From a distance, I could see that the joists weren't supported by a regular beam but were attached to a single rim joist that in turn was nailed only to the side of the 4x4 posts. A closer inspection revealed many other problems: corroding hardware; missing hardware nails; inadequate ledger attachment and flashing; stair stringers pulling away from the frame; and loose, warped guard balusters.

I wasn't surprised. The houses in the neighborhood were built in the 1970s, and the decks were

THE PROBLEM: SHALLOW FOOTINGS. The footings are tilted and the posts are sliding off the tops. They also don't extend below the frost line.

ADD TEMPORARY SUPPORT. Before excavating the footings, brace the deck with temporary support columns. Set the columns plumb, and tack them in at the top with staging nails or structural screws.

A BETTER FOOTING. After removing the old footings, dig the holes deeper and wider. Based on the footing-size table in DCA-6, footings need to be 16 in. dia. Local code specifies a 40-in. depth. On this job, the author used 12-in.-dia. form tubes with garbage bags taped to the bottom. The bags contain the concrete while permitting it to fill the 16-in.-dia. base entirely at the bottom of the hole. The bags also isolate the concrete from groundwater and soil contamination.

ATTACH THE HARDWARE, THEN POUR. After locating and backfilling the tube, fasten the galvanized post base to the existing post.

OFFSET FOR A REASON. With the concrete in place, it's apparent that the post is not centered. The author offset the footing to make room for an additional post to support a new rim beam.

slapped on without attention to good building practices. There had been local cases of deck collapses. Without preemptive repairs, this deck was a catastrophe waiting to happen.

According to the North American Deck and Railing Association, more than 40 million decks are over 20 years old. You have to wonder how well those decks were constructed before model building codes ramped up minimum standards, not to mention the wear and tear nature inflicts on a deck year after year.

As it turned out, this deck was worth saving. The framing was solid, and repairs were straightforward because I had easy access to the deck's underside. I figured it would take only three days of labor and $600 in materials, much cheaper than dismantling and disposing of an old deck and building a new one. I used the American Wood Council's Prescriptive Residential Wood Deck Construction Guide (also known as the DCA-6), based on the 2009 IRC, as a reference.

Shallow Footings

Starting at ground level, the first thing I noticed was that the footings appeared tilted and that the posts were sliding off the tops. I dug around a couple of footings and found that they didn't extend below the frost line. Combined with their mushroom-shaped tops and unstable surrounding soil, their shallow depth had led to frost heave.

Posts Don't Support the Beam

The single rim joist carrying the deck joists was face-nailed to the 4x4 posts, which extend up to become railing posts. Without additional support, nails have the potential to pull out. Ideally, the rim beam should be doubled and should rest directly on top of the support posts.

THE PROBLEM: THE POSTS DON'T SUPPORT THE BEAM. The rim beam should rest directly on top of the support posts, but that isn't the case here.

DOUBLE THE POSTS. Attach new 4×4 posts to the existing posts with structural screws. The new posts are cut to the height of the rim and rest on galvanized post bases anchored to the new footings.

REINFORCE THE SPAN. The single rim joist spans nearly 6 ft. between posts, far greater than allowed for the deck load. The DCA-6 beam-span table allows a maximum 6-ft. 2-in. span for a double 2×8 south-ern-yellow-pine beam that carries a joist span of 12 ft. After removing the outside decking board, nail a new rim to the existing rim with 16d galvanized nails, then secure each post-rim connection with a galvanized post cap (here, Simpson AC4Z).

THE PROBLEM: AN UNSECURED LEDGER. Not only is the ledger inadequately attached, but also the joist hangers are beginning to rust.

WILL HANG. The new joist hangers have two times the galvanized coating of the old hangers. The hangers mounted to the rim beam are nailed with 3-in. HDG common nails. The hangers on the ledger are face-nailed with 1½-in. 10d hanger nails or 1½-in. structural screws.

SPACE NEW STRUCTURAL SCREWS ACCORDING TO THE MANUFACTURER'S INSTALLATION TABLE FOR THE DECK LOAD AND JOIST SPAN. These 3⅝-in. screws are long enough to penetrate through the ledger, the wall sheathing, and the house rim joist. They're staggered 1¾ in. from the top and bottom edges of the ledger and are doubled at the ledger ends and joints.

Unsecure Ledger

The ledger is inadequately attached to the house with washerless 5/16-in. lag screws and a few randomly driven structural screws. In addition, all the joist hangers are beginning to rust and are missing nails. Where there are nails, they're the wrong type (6d common nails and 2-in. roofing nails).

No Lateral Load Connectors

Lateral load connections have been prescriptively addressed in the code only since 2007. While not required on existing decks, they're a well-advised upgrade to elevated decks. The lateral connection joins a deck joist to a joist inside the house. Two connections per deck are all that's needed. After running the bolt or rod from the inside out through the ledger, position the deck-joist hardware and screw it in place. Add a bead of sealant to waterproof any gap between the rod and ledger.

LATERAL LOAD CONNECTORS

The lateral connector joins a deck joist to a joist inside the house. All that's needed are two connections per deck.

Leaky Flashing

The thin aluminum ledger flashing is inadequate and is corroded in several spots. Left as is, the flashing will allow water behind the ledger, which in turn will cause rot and a potential deck failure. A more robust flashing system should include self-adhering membrane and flashing with a taller wall leg.

THE PROBLEM: LEAKY FLASHING. The ledger flashing is corroded and inadequate.

PREPARE FOR FRAMING. Remove the door riser board, the siding, and the first deck board to inspect for rot. After folding up the housewrap, cut a shallow kerf in the joist tops for the flashing edge.

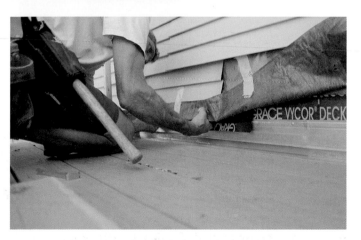

LAYERS OF PROTECTION. After applying a strip of self-adhering membrane to the top of the ledger and onto the wall, install new flashing (everflashing.org) over the ledger. Counterflash the metal flashing with another piece of self-adhering membrane, and fold the housewrap back down over the wall leg.

Broken Balusters

The spaces between most of the guard balusters are greater than the code limit of less than 4 in. Several balusters are warped or broken, and most are loose, attached only by a single nail at each end.

THE PROBLEM: BROKEN BALUSTERS. The balusters are warped, broken, and loose. They also are spaced farther apart than the code limit of less than 4 in.

A BETTER WAY TO SPACE BALUSTERS. Stretch a length of ¾-in.-wide waistband elastic, and mark lines at 5¼-in. increments (4-in. space plus the width of a baluster). Pin a line at one end of the deck rail, and stretch the elastic to the opposite end. Adjust the stretch until the spacing between lines is less than 5¼ in. (the code baluster-space limit of less than 4 in. plus the baluster width). Pin a line 1¼ in. past the end of the rail. Transfer the lines onto the railing, and align the baluster edges with the lines.

SECURE THE RAILING. Remove the balusters from each rail section, and replace the bad ones. For a better connection, drill pilot holes into each end of the balusters, and fasten them to the 2×4 rails with four screws, two at each end.

Unsafe Handrail

According to code, stairs need at least one handrail continuous from top to bottom and whose ends either terminate onto newels or return safely. Here, the handrail ends run long and don't have safety returns onto the guardrail.

THE PROBLEM: AN UNSAFE HANDRAIL. To meet code, the handrail must either terminate onto newels or return safely. This rail does neither.

RETURN FOR SAFETY. The author trimmed the extralong handrail and guardrail, then mitered the handrail to make a safety return. He glued and screwed the top and bottom returns to the rail to wrap around the end of the guardrail.

Weak Stairs

After a quick inspection, I found a handful of problems with the stairs. The tops of the stringers had pulled away from the header. The stringer cuts extended past the notches into the structural area. (The DCA-6 requires an uncut structural area of at least 5 in.) The stringer's span was too long and spaced too wide without intermediate support. Finally, the stringer header itself had no supporting jacks and was nailed only to the posts.

Stringers pulling away

Weakened stringers

Too long, too wide

DOUBLE UP. Issues of span, spacing, and overcut stringer notches can be resolved by sistering 2×6s along each stringer. To make it easier to fit them into place, cut the 2×6s short so that they can rest on ground-contact pressure-treated 4×4 blocks. Nail the 2×6s to the stringers with two rows of 12d galvanized nails, 12 in. on center.

HARDWARE REINFORCES THE CONNECTION. Screw galvanized stringer connectors (Simpson LSCZ or similar) to the header and to the new 2×6s to prevent the stringers from pulling away.

THE HEADER NEEDS SUPPORT. Position 2×4 pressure-treated jacks from the footings to beneath each end of the stringer header, and attach them to the 4×4 posts with structural screws.

PART 4

Decking

DECKS THAT STAND UP TO WILDFIRE 118

SITE-BUILT DECK DRAINAGE 126

DECKING OVER A ROOF 130

DECK REFINISHING 138

Decks That Stand Up to Wildfire

BY PAUL DEGROOT

Think about it. In the event of a wildfire, a deck is a giant surface that's likely to get peppered with wind-borne embers. If the deck catches on fire, the house is probably next. Not even brick or stucco siding can prevent a deck fire from shattering the glass in patio doors or windows and igniting a home from within.

With the spate of disastrous wildfires across the country in recent years, local building and fire codes may demand fire-resistant decks on lots that border undeveloped land at risk for wildfires. Fire marshals and code officials know these locations collectively as the wildland-urban interface (WUI). According to a 2013 report by the International Association of Wildland Fire, 46 million homes are situated in WUI zones. Particularly in the Rocky Mountains and the Southwest, the spread of housing into low-elevation forested land has resulted in nearly every urban area having a large ring of WUI. Multitudes of decks are already in harm's way, and more are being built all the time.

Code Requirements Vary with Jurisdiction

The most comprehensive code written to reduce the hazard to life and property from fire in wildland settings, including preventive measures pertaining to decks, is the International Code Council's International Wildland-Urban Interface Code (IWUIC). Based on an area's terrain, fuel type (trees, grasses, etc.), fuel abundance, and the number of days that critical fire weather occurs annually, the IWUIC defines fire-hazard severity classifications of moderate, high, and extreme. Local jurisdictions (building or fire departments, for example) use this information to map their particular zones of wildfire risk.

Where in force, the IWUIC requires ignition-resistant construction for a home's exterior components, including decks and other projections. The details depend on the fire-hazard severity, the water supply, and the distance between the home and vegetative fuel (known as defensible space). Although the ignition-resistant construction specs are divided into three categories—class 1 (most resistant), class 2, and class 3 (least resistant)—the requirements for decks are identical in classes 1 and 2. Class 3 permits all deck types.

California's Office of the State Fire Marshal developed its own requirements for wildfire zones, which are in section R327.9 of the California Residential Code. Individual jurisdictions in the state have adopted these specifications verbatim

or with modifications that are more restrictive. California divides land into three levels of fire-hazard severity: moderate, high, and very high. The code applies to all unincorporated land designated as State Responsibility Areas by the state's Board of Forestry and Fire Protection. It also applies to any areas deemed by cities and local agencies as Very High Fire Hazard Severity zones or Wildland Interface Fire Areas. Unlike the IWUIC, the California code only regulates the top decking surface.

Using the IWUIC code as the model, I show here three ways to build a deck that can help keep flames at bay. It is possible to mix and match parts

and come up with other code-compliant designs. Because the lumber framing is combustible, the first approach only fits the IWUIC's class-3 ignition resistance and cannot be built in high- or extreme-hazard locations. Nonetheless, it's an upgrade. The last two methods meet the class-1/class-2 ignition-resistance requirements of the IWUIC and can be used in moderate- and high-hazard areas, as well as in some extreme-hazard zones. Even if you build in a lower-hazard area—or in parts of California where only the decking is considered for purposes of wildfire codes, or in a location where the IWUIC hasn't been adopted—it still might be a good idea to upgrade your deck beyond what code requires.

DECK-BOARD FLAME-SPREAD RATINGS

DECK BOARDS ARE TESTED FOR THEIR ABILITY TO SUPPORT COMBUSTION. The test measures flame growth on the underside of a horizontal test specimen. The result is the Flame Spread Index, a relative scale in which asbestos-cement board has a value of 0, and red oak has a value of 100. For a board to earn the top class-A flame-spread rating, it needs to test in the 0 to 25 range, which also includes ordinary gypsum drywall (15) and fiber-cement siding (0). Deck boards scoring in the 26 to 75 range are class B, and those in the 76 to 200 range yield a class-C flame-spread rating. For comparison, according to the American Wood Council, redwood (70) and western red cedar (70 to 73) are class-B decking, while untreated southern yellow pine (130 to 195) is class C. The domestic wood with the lowest flame spread is western larch, at 45.

California's Office of the State Fire Marshal keeps a listing on its website of materials approved for use in WUI areas. Of the many manufacturers who have paid to have their decking tested (it is not mandatory), most wood and wood-composite deck boards have either class-B or class-C flame-spread ratings. There currently are a handful of class-A earners, including cellular-PVC deck products (Interplast TUFboard and Enduris Endeck) and a few dense, imported hardwoods such as cumaru, red balau, machiche, and merbau.

Method 1:
Upgraded Class-3 Deck

This option is a way to make a conventional wood deck more ignition resistant without resorting to exotic means. Support posts are 6x6s, which have a longer burn-through time than 4x4s. Built-up or solid heavy-timber beams, although standard details, also offer better performance in a fire than thinner members. The deck boards are a key part of the upgrade, carrying the top class-A rating in their ability to limit the spread of flames (see "Deck-board flame-spread ratings," at left). Class-A deck boards include some dense imported hardwoods, several PVC options, fire-retardant-treated (FRT) wood, and aluminum decking.

Embers alighting in the narrow gap between the house and the first deck board can easily kindle the dry pine straw, leaves, and twigs that collect in this crevice and can ignite flammable siding and the combustible materials behind it. Metal flashing will help to keep out debris.

Finally, you can diminish the chances of embers starting a fire below by covering the ground with gravel and keeping it clean of debris and combustibles, a fire-safety upgrade that costs very little.

CALIFORNIA BURNING. In this test to determine flame spread for product listing in California, a specifically sized ignition source, or "brand," is placed on different deckings. While the brand ignited the class-C decking on the left, it burned out on the class-B decking on the right.

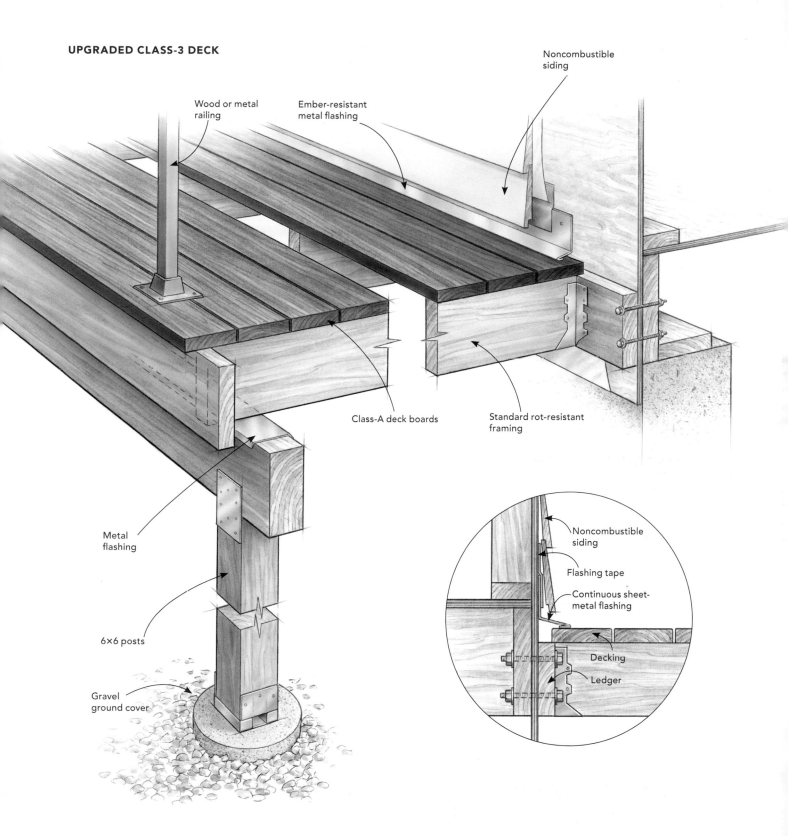

UPGRADED CLASS-3 DECK

Wood or metal railing

Ember-resistant metal flashing

Noncombustible siding

Class-A deck boards

Standard rot-resistant framing

Metal flashing

6×6 posts

Gravel ground cover

Noncombustible siding

Flashing tape

Continuous sheet-metal flashing

Decking

Ledger

MAKE THE SPACE NEAR THE DECK FIRE RESISTANT

VEGETATION CONTROL, ALSO TERMED FUEL MODIFICATION, IS CRITICAL to establishing and maintaining a clear zone, known as defensible space, around your home. According to the International Wildland-Urban Interface Code (IWUIC), 30 ft. is the minimum fuel-modification distance for moderate fire-hazard areas, while 50 ft. and 100 ft. are required in high and extreme fire-hazard zones, respectively. (Grasses, ground covers, shrubs, and trees can be incorporated into defensible spaces; see readyforwildfire.org/docs/files/calfire_ready_brochure.pdf for more information.)

Don't store firewood and other combustible items near or under the deck. Cover the ground below and around the deck with a layer of stones. Remove dried leaves, pine straw, and limbs from the hard-to-reach spaces common with decks that are near the ground. Use gravel paths, flagstone patios, and masonry retaining walls to isolate your home and deck from nearby plantings. Remove any dead wood, plants, or grasses, as well as flammable plantings near decks. Separate trees by at least 10 ft., and trim overhanging branches to at least 6 ft. above any part of the deck.

Method 2: Traditionally Framed Class-1 and Class-2 Deck

This method combines ignition-resistant wood framing with nonflammable aluminum decking. FRT wood is pressure-impregnated with chemicals that greatly reduce the wood's ability to propagate flame. Although it remains a combustible material, FRT lumber has a class-A flame-spread rating, so it will not burn readily. Hoover Treated Wood Products (Exterior Fire-X®) and Lonza Wood Protection (FRX®) both produce FRT lumber. For exterior applications, manufacturers use a treatment engineered to keep the protective chemicals from leeching out. However, the treatment does not make the wood rot resistant, so naturally rot-resistant western red cedar is usually the species chosen for FRT lumber intended for exterior use. Lumberyards that don't stock FRT wood can order it, but expect to pay 40% to 60% more than for untreated lumber. Light-gauge steel framing could substitute for the FRT lumber.

Aluminum isn't a go-to decking choice for many builders, and you can substitute another class-A decking and get similar results. But aluminum is a fireproof surface on which embers self-extinguish, which is reason alone to choose it. Just make sure to isolate the aluminum from the framing, as contact with most treated lumber (or steel framing) can corrode aluminum when moisture persists. Strips of heavy-duty roof underlayment, such as Grace Ice & Water Shield®, make excellent isolators.

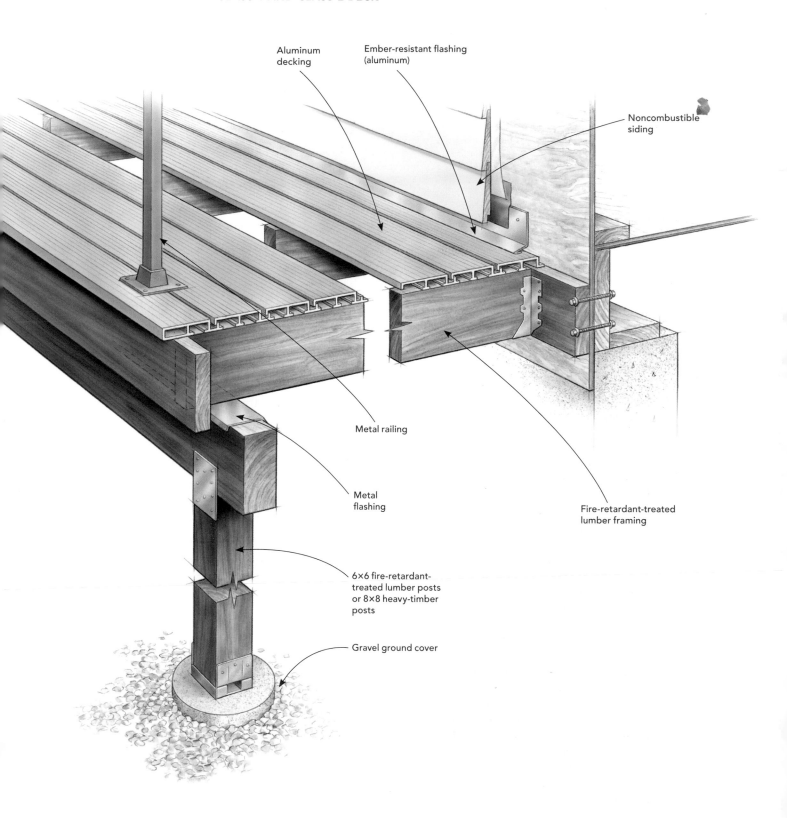

Aluminum decking

Ember-resistant flashing (aluminum)

Noncombustible siding

Metal railing

Metal flashing

Fire-retardant-treated lumber framing

6×6 fire-retardant-treated lumber posts or 8×8 heavy-timber posts

Gravel ground cover

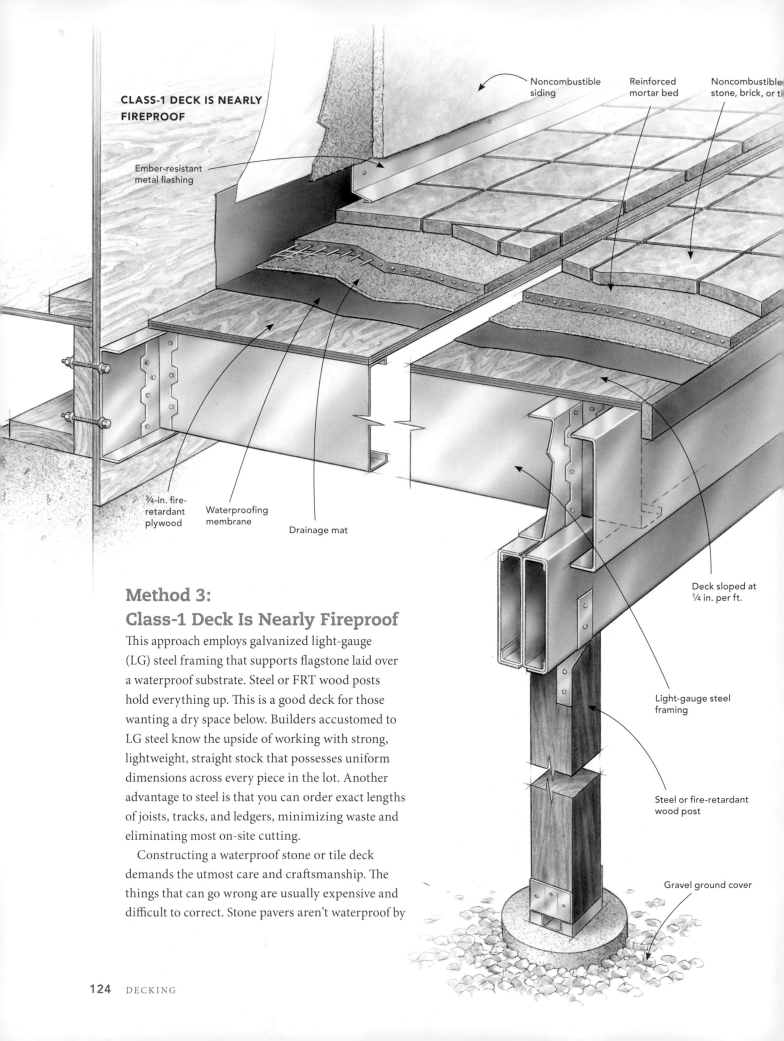

Ember-resistant
metal flashing

Noncombustible
siding

Reinforced
mortar bed

Noncombustible
stone, brick, or ti

¾-in. fire-
retardant
plywood

Waterproofing
membrane

Drainage mat

Deck sloped at
¼ in. per ft.

Light-gauge steel
framing

Steel or fire-retardant
wood post

Gravel ground cover

Method 3:
Class-1 Deck Is Nearly Fireproof

This approach employs galvanized light-gauge
(LG) steel framing that supports flagstone laid over
a waterproof substrate. Steel or FRT wood posts
hold everything up. This is a good deck for those
wanting a dry space below. Builders accustomed to
LG steel know the upside of working with strong,
lightweight, straight stock that possesses uniform
dimensions across every piece in the lot. Another
advantage to steel is that you can order exact lengths
of joists, tracks, and ledgers, minimizing waste and
eliminating most on-site cutting.

Constructing a waterproof stone or tile deck
demands the utmost care and craftsmanship. The
things that can go wrong are usually expensive and
difficult to correct. Stone pavers aren't waterproof by

themselves, nor are the grout joints between them. Pavers, as well as exterior tiles, must be installed over a waterproof substrate built and sloped ¼ in. per ft., like a flat roof. Atop a waterproof membrane goes a drainage mat that directs water that gets through the pavers downward to the deck edge. On top of the drainage plane goes the reinforced mortar bed necessary for embedding the flagstone. At up to 30 lb. per sq. ft., the stone and the mortar bed are heavy. An engineer can design the LG framing accordingly.

Because of the volume of water that collects in the masonry, flagstone set in a mortar bed would not be a wise choice for a deck subject to wet and freezing weather. Freeze-thaw cycles would likely cause cracking, spalling, and delaminating. Impervious porcelain tile is the answer in freeze-thaw climates. The tiles are placed onto an additional waterproof membrane that covers the plywood and is bonded to the mortar bed, sealing it against water penetration. Any water that happens to get past the main line of defense will be stopped by this barrier.

BELOW-DECK PROTECTION

DECKS BUILT ABOVE TERRAIN THAT FALLS DOWNWARD AND AWAY ARE MORE SUSCEPTIBLE TO WILDFIRE ENCROACHMENT, and extra fire protection is mandated by the IWUIC in these cases. The California Building Code does not require below-deck enclosure, but local jurisdictions may require it. Specifically, the space below an attached deck must be enclosed with fire-resistant exterior walls if any portion of the deck projects over a descending slope with a grade greater than 10%. The walls must extend to within 6 in. of the ground and can be built in a variety of ways. Noncombustible walls of brick, stone, or concrete block work great, but they require footings. Stud walls that hang from the deck and are built with one-hour fire-resistance-rated assemblies on the exterior are permitted—for example, metal studs with Type-X gypsum sheathing covered with fiber-cement siding or cement stucco. Also suitable are walls faced on the exterior with ignition-resistant materials such as fire-retardant-treated (FRT) wood siding. Other walls that comply but may be less common are heavy-timber or log walls.

Obviously, you must allow for drainage and ventilation of the enclosed area if your deck boards have gaps between them. This is why the walls can be open at the bottom to within 6 in. of the ground. Don't like the idea of that big space at the bottom? Build a waterproof deck, pour a concrete slab under it, and put fire-resistant enclosure walls on the slab. Now your drainage issue is gone, and you're fully protected from below. If you want to ventilate the space, use wall vents designed to keep embers and flames out. Vulcan Vents™, Brandguard Vents, and Vivico FireGuard Vents are examples approved for use in California.

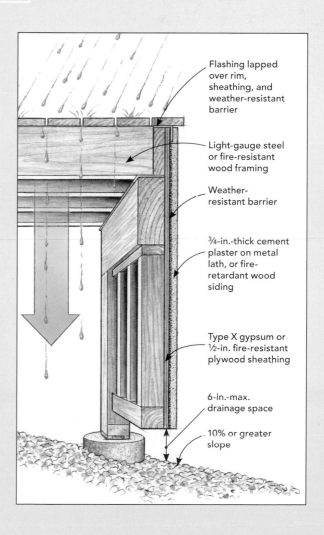

Flashing lapped over rim, sheathing, and weather-resistant barrier

Light-gauge steel or fire-resistant wood framing

Weather-resistant barrier

¾-in.-thick cement plaster on metal lath, or fire-retardant wood siding

Type X gypsum or ½-in. fire-resistant plywood sheathing

6-in.-max. drainage space

10% or greater slope

Site-Built Deck Drainage

BY MIKE GUERTIN

When I build a deck with more than 4 ft. of space between the framing and the grade, I install an underdeck-drainage system. Consisting of a membrane installed under the decking, the system collects and channels water into a perimeter gutter system and away from the building. The area beneath the deck is kept dry and can be used for storage or, with enough headroom, a covered patio.

Several commercial underdeck-drainage systems are available for installation during deck construction or as a retrofit (Sources, p. 129). I prefer to fabricate my own system from ethylene propylene diene monomer (EPDM) rubber-roof material and

BEFORE THE LAYOUT, GAUGE THE DROOP. The easiest way to estimate the amount of membrane needed is to make a gauge from a piece of rope or a strip of EPDM. Hold the piece across a joist bay, and slide one end inward until you reach the target droop in the middle. Mark the gauge at the center of the joists and measure. To estimate the material at the shallow end, repeat the process at the opposite end of the joist bay.

an aluminum gutter. It's relatively fast and easy to install before the decking is laid, and this method costs less than commercial systems.

EPDM rubber is a roofing material used on flat and low-slope roofs. It's available from roofing-supply houses in two standard thicknesses, 0.45 in. and 0.60 in., and in 10-ft.- or 20-ft.-wide rolls 50 ft. to 100 ft. in length. I usually use the thicker material, but the thinner grade works fine for this application. When working alone, I find 10-ft.-wide rolls easier to handle.

Start with a Plan to Drain the Water

Working backward, it's best to figure out where the water will go before engineering the membrane. A standard aluminum gutter is a cost-effective, simple solution. On this project, I located the gutter along the outer perimeter, beneath the joists. I design decks with an integral rim beam made of double 2x12s with the floor joists (typically 2x8) flush with the beam top. This leaves enough of the beam hanging below the joists to hide all or part of the gutter. Alternatively, an extrawide trim board that conceals the bottom edge of the rim board will also hide the gutter on decks that have a flush rim beam or cantilever over a beam.

CHALKLINES MAKE LAYOUT EASY. Because of the graduated swale of the membrane between the joists, each piece of membrane must be fan-shaped. Start by finding the center of the sheet at each end; this locates the center joist in the series. Step off the head measurement along one end of the sheet on each side of the center mark and again along the gutter end. (If you're marking out more than two or three pieces of membrane with the same joist spacing and membrane droop, make story poles for each end of the sheets.) Snap chalklines between the marks at the head and foot of the sheet. Trim off the excess membrane along the edges, leaving about 3 in. beyond the last joist line. The EPDM strips can be saved and used as sleeper cushions for decks over flat roofs.

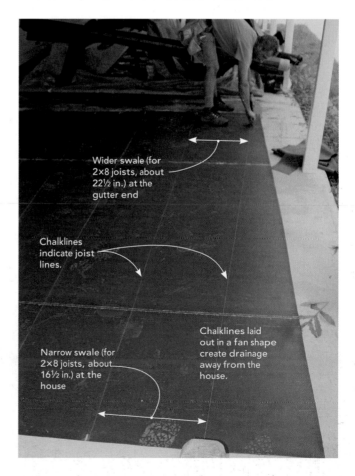

Wider swale (for 2×8 joists, about 22½ in.) at the gutter end

Chalklines indicate joist lines.

Chalklines laid out in a fan shape create drainage away from the house.

Narrow swale (for 2×8 joists, about 16½ in.) at the house

ROLL OUT AND STAPLE. Align the centerline of the sheet with the center joist of the area it covers. Let about an inch of the sheet run up the wall. Staple the sheet every 12 in. along the joist with hammer-tacker staples. The staples need to hold the sheet only temporarily until the decking goes down. Leave the last foot of the sheet at the gutter end loose for trimming later. Shift the sheet sideways to align the next chalkline with the center of the adjacent joist, and staple it down. Continue until you reach the last joist on both sides.

Before launching into a project, it's a good idea to identify the type of decking that will be used. Some plastic and composite decking brands require a minimum ventilation area beneath the boards. Check with the manufacturer's requirements when selecting decking to see if underdeck-drainage systems are permitted.

Determine the Slope of the Membrane

To drain the water toward the gutter, I create a graduated swale in the membrane between the joists that drains the water into the gutter. The swale is tighter at the house, about 1 in. to $1\frac{1}{2}$ in. of droop at the head of the joist bays and a droop $\frac{1}{2}$ in. shy of the full joist depth at the gutter end.

The trick here is an accurate layout of the membrane. Because of the graduated swale between joists, each piece of membrane must be cut into a fan shape. To account for the distortion created by the swale, I add an extra 8 in. to the length of the membrane for decks built of 2x6 and 2x8 joists and

CLEAN IT UP. Trim off the excess membrane along the last joist, the gutter, and the house, leaving about 1 in. of overlap into the gutter and over the siding, respectively.

FLASH AT THE HOUSE. Lap siding makes flashing the underdeck-drainage system easy. Bend a piece of metal or vinyl flashing to slip under a butt joint and over the membrane by several inches. When it's time to install the decking, first lay strips of cedar shingles on top of each joist to create a drainage space over the flashing. Any water collected by the flashing can then drain onto the membrane instead of being trapped between the decking and the flashing.

A CEILING IS BETTER THAN BARE JOISTS. Finish the underside of the deck when the area will be used as outdoor-living space. The beam and gutter get wrapped first with aluminum or vinyl coil stock for a clean look. The joists are covered with vinyl soffit stapled into place. Tongue-and-groove boards or plywood also can be used.

12 in. for decks framed with 2x10 and 2x12 joists. Each 10-ft.-wide sheet will span four 16-in.-on-center bays and cross five joists.

A Long Life Span Still Requires Maintenance

EPDM roofing has a 20- to 30-year or longer life span when exposed on a flat roof. Given that the decking shades the EPDM, I'm hoping for a 75-year-plus life. Don't expect to get away without any maintenance, though. Leaves and debris will inevitably get between the deck boards. Chances are that regular rain will flush everything clean. However, plan access points for periodic washing. If you nail down deck boards or use a hidden-fastener system, consider screwing one course of decking near the house side and another course close to the outside edge of the deck. The screwed boards can be removed so that the drainage system can be hosed out and the gutter cleaned.

SOURCES

THIS IS JUST A PARTIAL LISTING of commercially available deck-drainage systems manufacturers. Please consult your local building-supply store or the web for more options.

AMERICAN DRY DECK™
www.americandrydeck.com

DRYSNAP®
www.drysnap.com

ARIDDEK
www.wahoodecks.com

DRYSPACE™
www.timbertech.com

DEK DRAIN®
www.dekdrain.com

RAINESCAPE®
www.trexrainescape.com

DRYJOIST™
www.wahoodecks.com

UNDERDECK™
www.underdeck.com

EPDM membrane

Tapered sleeper

½-in. fiber roof underlayment

¾-in. plywood sheathing

EPDM membrane

Peel-and-stick EPDM tape

Drip edge

Decking over a Roof

BY EMANUEL A. SILVA

There are tons of reasons to build a deck over a roof, from creating a romantic outdoor breakfast nook off a second-floor master bedroom to providing a second-floor porch on a city house. No matter the reason, the keys to a long-lasting deck above a living space are the same: a reliable roof membrane and details that minimize any damage to the roof from the deck loads. I like rubber roofing for this, combined with a floating deck floor. The rubber roofing I've been using for 15 years—a glue-down, 60-mil EPDM membrane from International Diamond Systems—offers several advantages. It's reliable, it's fairly easy to work with, and

it requires no special tools. That said, a lot of people subcontract the roofing work and build the deck themselves. Either way, the roofing has to be right.

Framing the Roof

Whenever I install decking over a roof, I make sure the framing is structurally sound and properly pitched to drain water. The project illustrated here was a complete teardown and rebuild, so I framed the roof with 2x8s spaced on 16-in. centers, supported by a beam and a ledger as on most decks. Because these 2x8s were also the framing for the

FIBER UNDERLAYMENT PROTECTS ROOFING (LEFT). Nails can back out of plywood or OSB over time. A layer of fiberboard prevents them from penetrating the roofing. Don't overlap the seams. Offsetting the joints in the fiberboard from those in the sheathing makes a smooth surface.

USE THE BIG WASHERS (RIGHT). Screws and 3-in.-dia. sheet-metal washers mean that only 16 1⁵⁄₈-in. fasteners are needed per sheet. The washers are sold by roofing-supply houses.

RUNNING THE RUBBER. Installing large sheets of rubber is easier than it looks, although it's a big help to have a second pair of hands on the job. Dry-fit the rubber first. Roll out the rubber sheet so that it's square to the roof, then use scissors to make the cuts needed around penetrations such as posts. Before gluing the rubber, be sure to clean it with a manufacturer-recommended solvent.

ROLL THE RUBBER MEMBRANE HALF-WAY BACK. Working in approximately 2-ft. swaths, spread the adhesive on both the rubber and the substrate.

MAKE IT PERMANENT. Once the glue is barely tacky, unroll the rubber over the glued area, and smooth it out with a J-roller.

UP THE WALL. Adhering the rubber about 2 ft. up the adjacent wall is part of creating a watertight system.

ceiling below, and because I wanted to keep all the cuts square, I framed the roof level. To pitch the upper surface ¼ in. per ft. for drainage, I ripped 2x4s on a taper and screwed them to the tops of the joists.

It might seem as though it would have been easier to start with 2x12s and rip them to a taper. The trouble with that approach is that the allowable span of a joist or rafter depends on both its species and its grade. The grade depends largely on how close knots and other defects are to the edge of the board. In ripping a board, a knot that had existed harmlessly in the center is now close to the ripped edge, compromising the board's strength. For that reason, code does not allow the use of ripped lumber for structural purposes.

Continuous notched 4x6 posts support the framing and also serve as rail posts. The roof sheathing is ¾-in. CDX plywood, glued and screwed to the framing.

To create a smooth surface and to protect the bottom of the rubber roofing from any fasteners or rough edges on the plywood, I installed ½-in. fiber roof underlayment as a final substrate. Each board is secured with 16 1⅝-in. screws and 3-in.-dia. sheet-metal washers.

Where the roof ties into the house, I removed the siding about 2 ft. up the wall and about 1 ft. out on each side. This enabled me to fully adhere the roofing membrane about 2 ft. up the sheathing and then counterflash with a self-adhering butyl membrane. I pulled back the existing building paper after stripping the siding, installed the butyl membrane, and lapped the building paper back over it. This procedure makes for a watertight connection on ordinary rainy days, but it also protects against wind-driven rain or deep snow sitting on the deck up against the house.

Glue Down the EPDM Roofing

EPDM roofing is available in a variety of widths and in lengths up to 100 ft. Here, I needed enough

DETAILING THE ROOF EDGE. Use permanent trim around a permanent roof. PVC won't rot, it takes paint well, and you can glue rubber roofing to it. To start, glue the roofing to the fascia. Spread the adhesive on the rubber roofing and about 2 in. onto the board below.

DRIP EDGE PROTECTS THE CORNER. Nail a 3-in. aluminum drip edge over the corner of the roof. Guide a knife along it to trim the excess rubber.

SEAL THE DRIP EDGE. Use uncured EPDM tape to cover the nails and seal the drip edge to the roof. Uncured EPDM must be protected from UV rays, which the decking will do once installed.

rubber to overhang about 1 ft. on each end, and it had to be wide enough to run about 2 ft. up the house wall and to overhang the edge of the deck by at least 2 in. Because I was using up leftovers from another job, I did this roof with two pieces of rubber, which I joined in the middle with Rubberall® Splicing Adhesive. In most cases, though, I'd simply buy membrane big enough to cover the roof in one piece. After sweeping the underlayment clean and making sure there were no protruding fasteners, my helper and I laid the rubber down on the underlayment and fitted it to the house and against the posts. I made cutouts for the posts, then split the rubber beyond the cutouts so it could be placed around each post.

Next, we rolled back the rubber about halfway toward the posts. Working about 2 ft. at a time, we wiped the membrane with Rubberall's membrane cleaner and then spread its bonding adhesive on both the underlayment and the membrane using a paint roller. It's a contact adhesive, so once the glue was set enough that my finger barely stuck to it, we slowly rolled the membrane over the glued area, making sure not to make any air bubbles, and smoothed it with a J-roller.

We continued toward the house in 2-ft. sections and finished by gluing the rubber about 2 ft. up the wall. We then turned around and glued the rubber around the posts and over the PVC fascia. The glue extends about 2 in. down the fascia. We let the excess rubber hang for the time being.

To protect the outer edge from damage, we installed a 3-in. aluminum drip cap all around the perimeter, fastening it every foot with 2-in. hot-dipped galvanized roofing nails. I trimmed the rubber with a knife so that it would be even with

FLASH THE POSTS. Any penetration in the EPDM membrane is a potential leak, so the posts on this roof required special attention. They were wrapped with rubber and then flashed to the roof with scraps of rubber and splicing adhesive. The challenging areas to flash are the post corners. The first step was to wrap the post. Wrapping the post with membrane provides a reliable base for gluing additional rubber for flashing.

PAINT ON THE GLUE. Spread splice adhesive on the roof and on the post wrap.

the bottom of the drip edge. To waterproof the inside edge of the drip cap and to protect the nail penetrations, I covered the joint with uncured-EPDM peel-and-stick tape. Starting with the bottom edge of the roof and finishing up with the sides yields a shingle effect that will prevent water from entering.

Integrating the posts into the roofing is the hardest part of this job; getting roofing to seal around the corners of the posts is both vital and challenging. I could have bought premade corners for the posts, but they're expensive. Instead, I made corners from membrane scraps, overlapping them and gluing them in place with splice adhesive. I counterflashed with a butyl membrane to about 3 ft. up the post, and eventually wrapped the posts with PVC trim.

Let the Sleepers Lie

The next step was to lay out the sleepers 16 in. on center, on top of the joists below. To prevent the sleepers from wearing through the EPDM roof, I laid additional 4-in.-wide strips of rubber membrane below the sleepers' locations.

I wanted the tops of the sleepers to be level, so I ripped pressure-treated 2x6s in half so that their bottoms tapered to match the roof pitch. At their thinnest part, the sleepers are 1½ in. deep, so the 2-in. decking fasteners won't stick through. Cutting pressure-treated lumber exposes the untreated core, so I applied Wolman™ CopperCoat™ wood preservative to all the cut sides and ends to help prevent rot.

Any penetrations in the roof membrane made by fasteners are potential leaks, so the sleepers just rest in place. The post wraps help prevent the decking from uplifting.

START AT THE BOTTOM. Split a scrap of rubber so it can go around the corner while lying flat on the roof. Stretch the rubber a little so the apex of the split is placed above the roof plane.

OVERLAP THE FIRST LAYER. Split a second scrap of rubber like the first. Install it to wrap the corner and splay onto the roof. The apex of its split must be on the roof so that the two apexes don't align and create a potential leak.

COUNTERFLASH. Once the post is fully flashed to the roof, counterflash with layers of bituminous membrane going up the post about 3 ft.

FINALLY, IT'S TIME TO DECK.
Installing the decking is straight-forward. Tapered sleepers ripped from 2x material ensure a level walking surface. Strips of 4-in.-wide EPDM provide a layer of protection between the sleepers and the roof. The sleepers aren't fastened in place, and the floor floats.

GLUE DOES THE WORK. The decking nails are mainly there to clamp the boards until the urethane sealant sets up.

NAIL DOWN THE DECKING. Short, 2-in. stainless-steel finish nails fasten the mahogany decking to the sleepers. PVC trim will hide the gap between the decking and the post and help to hold the decking down.

JUST DETAILS LEFT TO GO. A second coat of Penofin (the boards were all coated and dried before installation), rails, trim, siding, and paint are all that's left.

So that the finish would have time to dry, I had coated all six sides of the mahogany deck boards with Penofin® a week earlier and had stacked them with sticks between the layers. As I worked, I recoated all the cut edges. To secure the decking, I used 3M™ 5200 Marine Adhesive Sealant, a tough, waterproof urethane normally used as boat glue. I followed the adhesive with stainless-steel finish nails. The nails' main function is to clamp the boards while the glue cures, which is what provides the real strength. I finished up by applying another coat of Penofin to the boards. This helps to hide and seal all the small nail holes and gives the boards one more layer of protection.

With the decking down, the rest of the job was the same as any other porch. I wrapped the posts with a ¾-in. PVC trim board and added railings, then replaced the siding and called in the painter.

Deck Refinishing

BY JIM GRANT

Keeping decks looking good in a sunbaked climate can be a challenge, but it provides me plenty of work as a professional deck refinisher. In San Diego, where I live and work, outdoor living space is important, and my clients expect a deck to look as good as the interior of a house. Maintaining a deck can be a huge challenge. Poorly handled cleaning or refinishing usually results in a deck that has to be redone.

I was recently called to look at a hardwood deck in Solana Beach, Calif. This deck, which was about three years old, needed a good cleaning and refinishing. In addition, black streaks emerged from every fastener on the stairs, the privacy fence, and the glass-paneled walls that protect deck occupants from coastal winds (sidebar, p. 144).

The stains resulted from the nails' rusting. Apparently, the builder had used galvanized nails to fasten everything but the decking. I see this black staining regularly despite the sound advice of distributors who suggest stainless-steel fasteners for tropical hardwoods. Fortunately, the deck surface was unaffected because the decking was attached with blind fasteners (www.ebty.com).

1. START WITH A GOOD CLEANING. Starting with vertical surfaces and working from the top down, apply deck cleaner. Allow it to work for 10 to 15 minutes.

Begin with a Thorough Cleaning

This project was typical of the deck-refinishing work my crew undertakes. First, we clean the wood with a concentrated detergent. Then we follow up with a wood brightener. After each step, we power wash using a wide-angle (40°) nozzle.

3. POWER RINSE. Starting with the vertical surfaces and working from the top down, rinse the deck clean with a pressure washer equipped with a wide-angle (40°) nozzle. Nozzles with a tighter spray pattern can strip out soft areas, leaving gouges.

2. SCRUB THE SURFACE. Moving in the direction of the wood grain, use a stiff-bristle brush on a telescopic pole to clean the wooden surfaces. Horizontal boards are usually the dirtiest. Use smaller handheld brushes for hard-to-reach areas.

A BETTER SPRAYER

FRUSTRATED WITH CONSTANT PUMP-ING and all-too-frequent refills when using a garden sprayer, the tool commonly used to apply cleaner and wood brightener, the author devised his own spray rig. At its heart is a small AC-powered transfer pump. The inlet has a short hose that's dunked into a bucket of cleaning solution. The outlet side has a TeeJet® spray wand (www.teejet.com). To make transport easier, the rig is contained in a plastic tool-box that holds the pump, cord, and inlet hose.

A pressure washer in the hands of a novice can destroy landscaping, force water into a house, and ruin a wood deck. We've handled many projects where homeowners or contractors have damaged the deck surface with a power washer. Fixing the resultant gouges requires extensive sanding and sometimes new decking. Before I let new employees touch someone's deck with a pressure washer, I teach them how to feather the stream of water onto the surface when starting out and how to let the cleaning chemicals do the majority of the work. We always use a wide-angle nozzle on decking, even if it takes a little longer to get the surface clean.

1. USE BRIGHTENER TO MAKE OLD WOOD LOOK NEW. After allowing the wood to dry, apply an oxalic-acid-based wood brightener to all surfaces. Mix 1 gal. of the brightener with about 3 gal. of water. The author uses a homemade spray rig to apply it (sidebar, at left). Allow the brightener to work for about 15 minutes, then scrub the wood with a stiff brush and rinse it with a pressure washer.

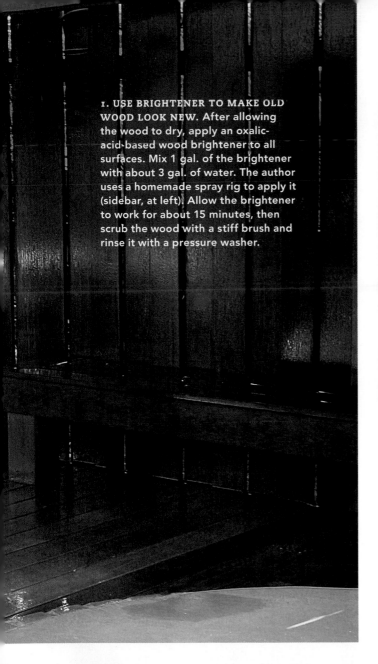

2. SCRUB AGAIN. Once the wood brightener has worked for about 15 minutes, scrub the surfaces with stiff-bristle brushes. A long handle provides additional leverage.

3. RINSE CLEAN. A gas-powered pressure washer equipped with a wide-angle (40°) nozzle rinses and cleans the surface without damage. The pressure washer doesn't apply the two cleaning chemicals; it sprays only water.

1. ONE BOARD AT A TIME. To prevent lap marks, coat the deck boards with finish individually. After covering each board, stop spraying, and wipe away excess coating as necessary.

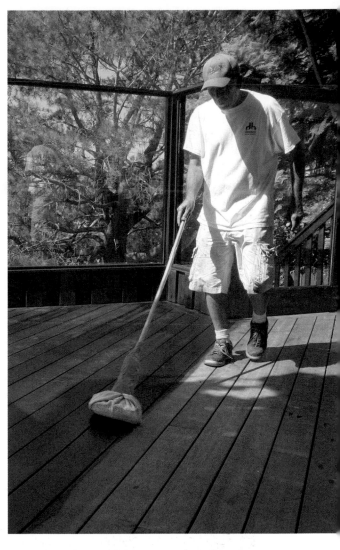

3. WIPE OFF THE EXCESS. Once the finish has had a chance to be absorbed fully by the decking (10 minutes), remove the excess with a rag (small areas) or a rag-covered scrub brush (large areas).

2. SPRAY, THEN SMOOTH. A painter's pad on a long pole helps to smooth the layer of finish applied with the sprayer. The pad works the finish into the grain and evens the application so that it's absorbed uniformly.

On this deck, once the wood was cleaned and brightened, we turned to the rusting fasteners. To prevent water from getting into the nail holes and causing a recurrence of staining, we filled the holes with a wax-based exterior filler. We heated the filler slightly with a tea-light candle and carefully pushed it into the 400-plus holes. Minor sanding with a medium-grit sanding sponge removed the excess filler. We used a light touch, because excessive sanding can result in a noticeable change in the wood texture that shows up later when the deck is finished.

Apply the Finish

With the surface clean and free of rust stains, it was time to apply the coating. Choosing a coating can be confusing to homeowners and contractors alike, and mistakes in application can result in serious problems, including peeling from improper adhesion, blotchiness from improper surface prep, or the use of too much finish. Usually, the coating has to be chemically removed and the deck recoated.

I've done my own testing on 50 products over the past 23 years and continue to test finishes. For this deck, I used an oil-based stain for hardwood decking from Superdeck® (www.superdeck.com). This coating enhances the natural look of the wood with penetrating oils that protect the surface and prevent mildew and water damage. The high density of hardwood decking makes using the proper application method important. We use several different types of applicator pads and make long strokes to avoid leaving lap marks and applying too much coating. After the coating has fully penetrated (usually in 10 to 15 minutes), we use a lint-free cloth to remove the excess material.

For tight corners and other hard-to-reach areas, we use a natural-bristle brush and then wipe away the excess coating with a lint-free cloth. We also watch the amount of absorption, because the density of individual boards can vary. As a result, some boards need more finish than others.

A FIX FOR RUSTY FASTENERS

DESPITE RECOMMENDATIONS TO USE STAINLESS-STEEL FASTENERS for hardwood decks, we often see decks built with galvanized fasteners. Unfortunately, it doesn't take long for the nails to rust, leaving black streaks that can make an otherwise beautiful deck look really bad.

In most cases, the cleaner and brightener remove the marks, but in some badly stained areas, only a sander can remove them. This is a last resort, however, because it means sanding the whole board or having a board with an inconsistent appearance between sanded and unsanded areas.

Once the black marks are gone, we fill the holes with a color-matched, wax-based wood filler. It's important to pick the right color, or the filled holes will be as obvious as the black stains.

SAND AWAY MARKS. In spots with the worst black staining, the cleaner and wood brightener are not fully effective at removing discoloration. In these spots, the only solution is to use a random-orbit sander equipped with 120-grit paper over the board.

FILL AND SMOOTH. Once a matching color has been found, the wax filler (www.fastcap.com) is applied with a plastic spatula included with the kit. The same tool scrapes away the excess.

TIPS FOR A BETTER FINISH

MIX THOROUGHLY. Stir the individual cans of finish so that any settled pigments are mixed with the solvent. Mix together all the cans for a uniform color.

BRUSH TIGHT SPOTS. Use a brush to cover stairs and other areas too awkward to spray. Allow the coating to penetrate for a few minutes, then wipe away the excess with a clean lint-free cloth.

START AT THE TOP. The author applies the finish with a Wagner® 1075 airless sprayer, but you also can use a 7-in. painting pad. Cover any surfaces and vegetation that could be damaged from overspray with canvas drop cloths.

USE A SMALL PAD FOR SMALL SPACES. A disposable, handheld painting pad is good for applying finish to areas too small to spray and too big to brush.

PART 5

Railings and Stairs

147 MANUFACTURED RAILING SYSTEMS

156 RAILING RETROFIT

164 2 IDEAS FOR CUSTOM RAILINGS

169 MOUNTING DECK STAIRS

Manufactured Railing Systems

BY JEFFERSON KOLLE

It used to be that most pressure-treated decks were surrounded by pressured-treated railings nailed together almost as an afterthought. Serviceable and cost-effective, these railings looked OK until they went through a few seasons in the weather, after which they'd look more like a hog fence than the crown on your beautiful outdoor space.

Pressure-treated decking and railings are still the most popular, but the incredible array of engineered deck boards that have hit the market in the last few decades has brought with it elaborate railing systems made from the same materials by the same manufacturers. These engineered railing systems include rails, balusters, posts or post sleeves, and assorted accessories.

The initial beauty of these systems is that they match the decking product you've chosen. They also share the same low-maintenance characteristics, which you'll appreciate if you've ever spent a Saturday scrubbing and sealing a 100-ft. run of pressure-treated balusters and rails. Yet another plus is that the manufacturers of these railing systems have already contracted third-party testing facilities to get their products code-approved. (Avoid any railing-system company that hasn't done this.)

Components for railing systems are packaged by type—you order just what you need in the way of rails, post components, and balusters. Most systems include the requisite fasteners, and all include installation instructions ranging in quality from a single sheet to printed pamphlets and online videos. None of the railing systems discussed here are that complicated to install, but there is a learning curve. After a little practice, though, you should be able to install a complete 6-ft.-long system in under 30 minutes. Sure, armed with a chopbox and pneumatic gun, you could possibly smack together a similar length of pressure-treated railing in a little less time, but consider the aesthetics of the final result.

A Wealth of Options

Engineered railing systems are available in the same materials as engineered decking—metal (generally aluminum), vinyl, composites, and capped composites—and all have their advantages in terms of cost, appearance, and maintenance. Vinyl railing systems are lightweight, but colors are usually limited to lighter hues. While vinyl is generally the least expensive of the engineered materials, vinyl railings still cost more than simple, site-built wood railings. Aluminum railings are available in a wide variety of colors, but they cost more than vinyl. Also, while their powder-coated surfaces are tough, site-cut edges can corrode in salty environments.

(Unlike paints that adhere to a surface, powder coats are applied electrostatically, then heat cured.) Heavy composite railings—made from a fusion of wood fiber and plastic—come in deep, rich colors, but they've been outshined lately by the current darlings of the deck-board business: capped composites. The most expensive railings out there, these have an outer layer of a vinyl-like material that can be embossed and striated with wood-grain patterns.

How to Choose

Any contractor you hire will probably have a preferred railing system, either because of previous experience with a product or its local availability. If you're installing the railings yourself, you might be inclined simply to choose the company that made the decking you used. But if that manufacturer's railing system doesn't appeal to you, look elsewhere. Here are a few tips to help you make the right choice.

APPEARANCE

You'll spend a lot of time looking at the railing, even in the winter when you're inside your house. Saving a few bucks won't make an ugly railing beautiful.

AVAILABILITY

Most lumberyards and home centers display only a few railing styles and brands—and they have fewer, if any, in stock. Before you order, pin down your retailer about actual delivery times. Check out local deck suppliers as well as online retailers. The cost of shipping may be offset by sales-tax savings.

INSTALLATION INSTRUCTIONS

None of the railings are difficult to install, but detailed instructions, and especially online videos, can help you avoid the pitfalls.

CODE APPROVAL

Make sure that any railing system you consider is code compliant, and then call your local building department to get its OK, too. The building department is the final arbiter.

Mix and Match Components

Railing-system manufacturers package the components of their products in separate boxes, and there are a couple of reasons for this. You may want to buy light-brown rails and black post sleeves, for instance. Or you may like the matching rails and posts from a certain manufacturer but not its balusters. Or maybe you want safety-glass panels between your rails, but your rail company doesn't offer that option.

Fortunately, it's possible to mix and match balusters and rails from different companies. Still, before you assume that the 1-in.-sq. balusters from one company fit the 1-in.-sq. mortises in another company's rails, check the exact specifications, or do a little hands-on research at your supplier. You don't want to have to do on-site modifications on a deck-rail section that was supposed to go together in less than 30 minutes.

Some companies specialize in balusters for use in other rail systems or in site-built wood rails. Deckorators (www.deckorators.com) sells a huge variety of balusters, and Feeney (www.feeneyinc.com) offers horizontal stainless-steel baluster systems.

Along with making sure that the balusters and rails fit together, check for code compliance when you mix parts. You don't want your rails to pass only to have your balusters flunk.

Following is a sample of manufactured railing systems currently on the market.

METAL

AFCO-RAIL (AFCO-IND.COM)

AFCO's low-cost Series 100 aluminum-railing system has the same durable powder-coated finish as its high-priced rails. Rails are available in 36-in. and 42-in. heights and in 48-in. to 120-in. lengths. Support blocks under the bottom rails are required for lengths over 72 in.

The Series 100 rail sections can be mounted post to post or with special 1⅞-in. square posts and rails that mount over the posts for a continuous handrail. Post sleeves are 4x4 or 6x6, and ¾-in. square and round balusters are available. Rails are equipped with spaced baluster-mounting connectors. Tapping the balusters with a rubber hammer fits them into the connectors. Surface-mount posts bolt through decking and site-installed 2x blocking.

Colors
Gloss finishes: White, Clay (beige), and Wicker (light beige). Textured finishes: white, black, bronze, and brown.

Accessories
Welded gates, 3 ft. wide and 36 in. or 42 in. tall with hardware; matching aluminum post wraps to conceal tall underdeck supports; ADA-compliant handrails.

Assembly instructions
Illustrated and available at afco-ind.com.

COMPOSITES

LATITUDES INTREPID™
(WWW.LATITUDESDECK.COM)

Intrepid is the brand name for the substantial railing system that matches Latitudes composite deck boards. There are two rail choices: a plain 2×4 style and an elaborate molded rail. Each top and bottom rail has two pieces: an inner rail that's screwed to the balusters and the post bracket, and a finish top and bottom rail that covers the brackets. The order in which you assemble the rails, brackets, and balusters is not necessarily intuitive; you'll want to spend some time with the instructions before you begin.

Support blocks under the bottom rail are required every 2 ft. Balusters are available for 36-in.- and 42-in.-high railings, which are available only in 6-ft. lengths.

Colors

Walnut, Cedar, Gray, and Redwood.

Accessories

Seven baluster options in glass, metal, or composite materials; 15 different post caps, some with integral lighting; ADA-compliant handrails.

Assembly instructions

Text-heavy instructions are at www.latitudes.com, and an admittedly "abbreviated" installation video on YouTube[SM] cautions viewers to read the printed instructions "so the installation is proper."

TREX TRANSCEND (WWW.TREX.COM)

Trex's top-of-the-line Transcend decking is a capped composite material. Its Transcend railing system, however, is made from a composite with no vinyl-like covering. The rails use a unique mortised baluster collar that snaps into a channel in the top and bottom rails and that fits tight around the balusters and spaces them evenly. The collar also covers the post-to-rail brackets, making for a clean-looking joint.

There are three options for top rails, two for bottom rails, and three for balusters. Post sleeves are 4×4; for a beefier look, Trex also has a 6×6 post sleeve that's shimmed to fit directly over a 4×4 wood post.

Colors

Trex has the dubious distinction of adopting the most cryptic names for color choices: Vintage Lantern (dark brown), Classic White, Fire Pit (rust), Gravel Path (gray), Rope Swing (beige), Tree House (medium brown), and Charcoal Black.

Assembly instructions

For installation videos, search "railing" on TheTrexCo YouTube channel. Instructions in PDF form are at www.trex.com.

Accessories

Dimmable LED lighting for post caps and stairs (can be used with other railing systems as well); ADA-compliant handrails.

MOISTURESHIELD (WWW.MOISTURESHIELD.COM)

Unlike most decking and railing companies, MoistureShield doesn't offer a wide variety of balusters, molded rails, and hidden brackets. Instead, its composite railings are straightforward and rectilinear, with the exception of a simple profile molded into the post collars and caps.

Assembling the railings is similar to putting together a simple site-built wood railing, except that all the parts are made from MoistureShield's composite lumber. Identical top and bottom L-shaped rails, available in 6-ft. lengths, are attached to the 4×4 posts with 2¼-in. #7 stainless-steel finish screws, and the posts are through-bolted and blocked to the deck framing. Square balusters are attached between the rails with similar screws. Nothing fancy, but it's a simple, elegant look.

Colors

Standard colors: Bridle (light brown), Cape Cod Gray, Earthtone (gray-brown), Rustic Cedar (burnt ochre), Seasoned Mahogany. Premium colors have embossed wood grain patterns: Desert Sand (light grayish brown), Tigerwood (chocolate brown with darker grain patterns), and Walnut.

Accessories

None.

Assembly instructions

Illustrated and available at www.moistureshield.com.

CAPSTOCK

**AZEK (WWW.AZEK.COM) AND
TIMBERTECH (TIMBERTECH.COM)**
CPG Building Products owns both Azek
and TimberTech and has recently made
adjustments to both railing systems, making
them more compatible, especially with
regard to installation hardware.

Both Azek Premier and TimberTech
Evolutions railings are made from composite
material with an outer layer of scratch-
resistant polymers. Premier railings use a
single-piece bottom rail and a two-piece
top rail that includes a retaining rail through
which balusters are fastened and
a wider finish rail that covers the fasteners.
A 10-ft.-long rail is available but only in black
and white. Surface-mount posts and 4×4,
5×5, and 6×6 post sleeves are available,
as are post collars and four different post
caps, two of which have LED lights. Square

composite and square or round metal balusters are
offered in four lengths: 29 in., 31 in., 35 in., and 37 in.

Instead of using post caps, TimberTech Evolutions'
flat top rails are installed over the tops of the posts.
Rails are available in 8-ft. lengths. For longer runs, the
rails are butted together at a post. A spokesman for
TimberTech said that a biscuit could be used at the joint
for registering purposes. Surface-mount and 4×4 post
sleeves are available in 36-in. and 42-in. lengths. Square
composite and square or round aluminum balusters are
also available.

Colors
Azek Premier: Brownstone (milk chocolate), Slate Gray,
Kona (dark brown), Black, and White. TimberTech
Evolutions: Black, Walnut, and Brick.

Accessories
Azek Premier: LED cap lights, gate hardware kit, cable-
rail kit, ADA-compliant handrails. TimberTech Premier:
post-mounted LED lights and ADA-compliant handrails.

Assembly instructions
Azek Premier: text and video at www.azek.com.
TimberTech Evolutions: text and video at timbertech.com.

VINYL

FAIRWAY® MASTERS RAILING SYSTEM (FAIRWAYBP.COM)

Fairway Building Products makes many styles of railing in composites and vinyl. Its Masters vinyl rail is considerably larger than other rails and has a grand, formal appearance. The system is composed of aluminum-reinforced 6½-in.-wide top and bottom rails with a heavily molded profile. Two balusters are offered—a 2⅝-in. square and a 3¾ in. with a lathe-turned profile. Post sleeves (8 in. sq.) are available with flat sides or with a recessed-panel profile. The post sleeves can be used over 4×4 or 6×6 wood posts; the instructions show a simple way to build out the post to accommodate the large sleeves. Fairway also sells code-complaint steel posts that can be used on concrete or, when used with a special bracket, bolted to a wood deck frame. Rails are available in 4-ft., 6-ft., 8-ft., 10-ft., and 12-ft. lengths and heights of 36 in. or 42 in. Brackets are available for 22.5° and 45° rail-to-post intersections.

Colors
White.

Accessories
Brackets for mounting Masters railings to Fairway's 8-in. or 10-in. round porch columns; ADA-compliant handrails.

Assembly instructions
Two pages, available at fairwaybp.com.

CERTAINTEED OXFORD (WWW.CERTAINTEED.COM)

The Oxford vinyl-railing system uses aluminum-reinforced rails and offers two different rail-to-post connections depending on whether you use your own 4×4 wood posts and CertainTeed post sleeves, or you use the company's deck-frame-mounted galvanized-steel posts and sleeves. For the steel-post system, posts are bolted to the deck frame. The vinyl post sleeves are mortised to receive the aluminum-reinforced rails that connect to the post inside the post sleeve, providing a completely concealed metal-to-metal connection inside the post (photo at right and below right). The post-sleeve system uses brackets to attach rails to posts (left photo below). Rails come in 6-ft., 8-ft., and 10-ft. lengths. Square, colonial-style, and 4-in.-wide tempered-glass balusters are available.

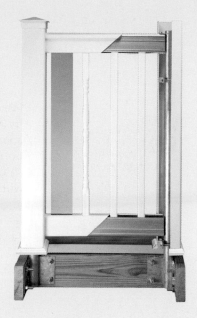

Colors
Almond (beige), Clay (darker beige), and White.

Accessories
Gates, available in kits up to 60 in. wide; decorative and solar-powered lighted post caps; ADA-compliant handrails.

Assembly instructions
Thorough instructions at www.certainteed.com, plus 20 videos at www.youtube.com/ctfreedomofchoice (look for the "Evernew" tab).

Railing Retrofit

BY MIKE GUERTIN

When a home needs repairs, there sometimes is also an opportunity to make significant visual or structural upgrades. Such was the case with this deck. The framing was sound, and the pressure-treated decking could wait a few more years until it had to be replaced. The painted rim and railing, though, were in bad shape.

Besides the peeling paint, the railing wasn't too sturdy. The homeowners could have added some fasteners and hardware to strengthen the railing, then scraped, primed, and repainted it. Instead, they decided to take the opportunity to dress up the deck with new ipé posts and rails, cable infill, and ipé trim around the rim. Their decision not only opened the deck to a better view, but it also transformed the whole exterior.

The original railing posts were mounted inside the deck frame and weren't centered on the structural posts beneath. To improve the deck's appearance from the yard, my crew and I mounted the new posts outside the frame and positioned them above the structural columns, roughly 8 ft. apart. Intermediate cable spacers were needed, so we installed 2x4s on edge between the structural posts. To dress up the painted rim joist, we added layered bands of ipé between the posts and the cable spacers. Because the homeowners have young children, we kept the old railing system in place for as long as possible.

The detail that had the greatest visual impact and took the most planning, however, was the cable-rail system. Thankfully, these systems have come a long way since I started in this business.

FITTINGS TAME DESIGN CHALLENGES

CABLE RAILS ARE SUBJECT TO THE SAME BUILDING CODES AS OTHER DECK-BALUSTER OPTIONS, with an important caveat: Spacing needs to account for how much the cables will flex when a force is applied. Therefore, spacing between cables is typically 3 in., and the distance between structural posts is either reduced or offset with nonstructural cable spacers. The final design considerations are corners and the length of cable runs, both of which make it challenging to take the slack out of the cable.

While there is a dizzying array of cable-rail hardware parts on the market, system basics are pretty common

and straightforward. The cable is typically 1×19 type and ranges from 1/8 in. dia. to 3/16 in. dia. Other cable braid types are more flexible than 1×19 type and spread apart too much under force to be good choices. Fittings for attaching cables to posts come in different styles, including surface mount, lag mount, and through post. These fittings serve two basic functions: to attach the cable to the post and to tension (or tighten) the cable. As seen in the drawing, at least one end of each cable run needs a tensioning device. The hardware shown here is from Atlantis Rail.

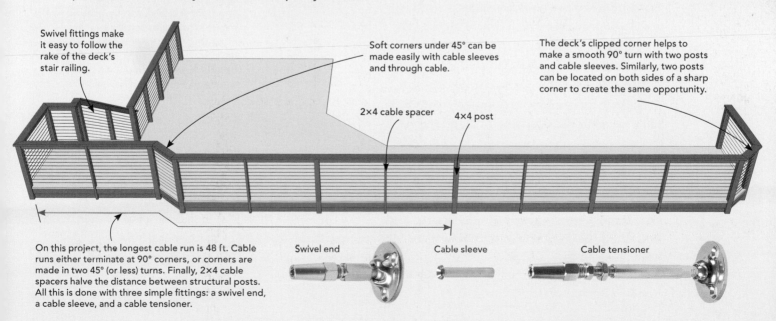

Swivel fittings make it easy to follow the rake of the deck's stair railing.

Soft corners under 45° can be made easily with cable sleeves and through cable.

The deck's clipped corner helps to make a smooth 90° turn with two posts and cable sleeves. Similarly, two posts can be located on both sides of a sharp corner to create the same opportunity.

2×4 cable spacer

4×4 post

On this project, the longest cable run is 48 ft. Cable runs either terminate at 90° corners, or corners are made in two 45° (or less) turns. Finally, 2×4 cable spacers halve the distance between structural posts. All this is done with three simple fittings: a swivel end, a cable sleeve, and a cable tensioner.

Swivel end

Cable sleeve

Cable tensioner

Ideal System for Retrofits

Twenty years ago, I cobbled together a cable-rail system from sailboat-rigging hardware. It was functional, had an airy feel, and opened the deck to the backyard; however, installing the shackles, cleats, and turnbuckles was clunky, to say the least. Today, there are several slick cable-hardware systems either adapted for or specifically designed for deck railings. Some cable systems are integrated with structural metal post-and-rail assemblies; others can be used with site-built wood posts and railings. In most cases, I've found that the material in cable railings costs less than nice wood or manufactured deck railings. Once you learn the basics, the labor to install cable systems is actually less than that for other types of guardrails.

I prefer the versatility of hybrid cable-rail systems—that is, systems that can be used with wood posts and top rails. These systems give you the freedom to design a guardrail suitable to each project, including deck remodels like this one, and to design custom details. These systems rely on sturdy 4x posts and a top rail that can resist the inward tension of the cables. On this project, I used the RailEasy™ system from Atlantis Rail Systems (www.atlantisrail.com). I usually include a subrail in my designs for extra strength. Here, the subrail is a 2x4 installed on edge, but you also can use 1x or 2x stock flat between posts. Sometimes it looks nice to add a bottom rail between structural posts and to position cable spacers between the top rail and bottom rail (more on cable spacers in a bit).

Most cable hardware is pretty straightforward. At one end, the hardware fixes the cable to the post and is generally not adjustable. At the other end, the hardware—called a tensioning device—can be tightened to take the slack out of the cable. Cable-rail hardware mounts in a few different ways, including surface mount, lag mount, and through post. Through-post systems may be difficult to work with after some posts, such as those close to the house, are installed.

POSTS AND TOP RAILS COME FIRST

To create a robust structural support system capable of resisting the cable's tension, the author bolted new 4×4 posts to the deck frame, installed a subrail between the posts, and tied the whole structure together with a continuous top rail. The cables are spaced 3 in. apart and run through holes drilled in the posts and through intermediate cable spacers. It's important to keep the holes aligned precisely and perfectly straight through the posts and spacers. It's easier and faster to bore accurate holes through posts and spacers using a template and a drill press before mounting them to the deck frame.

TEMPLATE SHOWS THE POST LAYOUT. Use a piece of plywood marked with the entire post layout for a template. Top and side stops register the template to the post. Mark the centerline of the post, and drill ⅛-in. holes to identify where cable will run through. The template also can be used to locate pilot holes for hardware mounting screws, which may or may not be necessary, depending on the density of the wood being used and the type of hardware.

Planning Runs and Corners

Cable rails have to meet the same building codes as any other deck balustrade in that the space between them cannot exceed 4 in. Because cables flex, there are limits to how far they can span between

MARK WITH A NAIL SET. Rather than marking posts with a pencil or using the template as a drill guide, use a nail set to dimple each cable location. Dimples are easier to see than pencil marks, and they center the drill bit for precise boring. Some cable-rail companies have layout templates stamped at standard 3-in. centers.

A BIG MACHINE MAKES PERFECT HOLES. For the precision holes required for cable rail, it's worth using a drill press if you have access to one. If you don't, bore holes through the post from each side so that the entry and exit points are aligned and any drift is in the middle of the post. Use drill bits 1/32 in. larger than the cable diameter.

MOUNT THE POSTS TO THE RIM. Earlier, the author used a drill press to bore 9/16-in. pilot holes 2 in. down from the top and 2 in. up from the bottom of the post. In the next step, shown here, he used the straight pilot holes to guide a 9/16-in. drill bit through the framing. He used 1/2-in. hex-head bolts and rim-to-joist hardware mounted inside the frame to resist outward force.

SUBRAIL RESISTS TENSION. The subrail is critical to maintaining cable tension. Without a subrail between posts, the cables would pull the end posts inward. Here, a 2×4 subrail is pocket-screwed on edge between each pair of posts using structural screws. A simple plywood jig is used first to guide pilot holes and later to register the subrail for installation. With the subrail in place, the nonstructural 2×4 cable spacers can be notched to fit around the subrail and fastened to the rim with structural screws.

FLASH FORWARD. When cable enters or exits a post at an angle, sleeves are needed to protect the wood. Rather than oversizing holes for the sleeves during the production boring process, the author drills out the larger holes after the posts are in place. The cable sleeves require a countersink to accept the flare at the end.

CAP RAIL TIES IT ALL TOGETHER. You can use 5/4×6 decking or 2×6 stock attached with screws for a top rail. The resulting T between the cap rail and the subrail forms a strong top-rail system. Joints can land on top of a post or along a subrail span. Use dowels or biscuits to keep the joints tight and cap-rail pieces in plane with one another.

deck posts or spacers. The combination of the cable spacing and the post spacing, along with the cable diameter and the tension, must be balanced to account for the cables spreading apart under force. Manufacturers save us the trouble of making complex calculations by publishing guidelines for cable spacing and support-post spans.

The most common cable spacing recommended by manufacturers is 3 in., and the span limit between structural posts and cable spacers is from 3 ft. to 4 ft. Some manufacturers permit wider post and spacer spans with corresponding reductions in cable spacing. Manufacturer-recommended cable runs between termination fittings range from 50 ft. to 65 ft., depending on whether the cable runs keep straight or turn corners. Here, I used a combination of structural 4x4 posts and intermediate 2x4 cable spacers to keep uninterrupted cable runs less than 50 ft.

Corners can be handled a few different ways depending on whether you want to mount posts inside or outside the deck frame. To turn a 90° corner at a single post mounted inside the frame, the run in each direction has to terminate on that post. Double posts are needed outside the frame to turn a 90° corner if you want the cable run to be continuous. Cable-rail hardware manufacturers offer sleeves to line the holes in posts where a run of cable turns. The sleeves prevent the cable from tearing into the wood. These sleeves also can be used to maintain a continuous cable run through corners under 90°. Sleeves are not needed on straight cable runs.

This project had hard 90° corners, clipped 90° corners, and a soft corner (under 90°). I used a combination of techniques to make the turns, as you can see in the plan (p. 157).

INSTALL CABLE SLEEVES. Swipe the holes bored earlier with a piece of sandpaper to clean off any wood fibers and to allow the sleeve to sit nicely in the post. Gently tap the sleeves into position. There are nuances to working with each manufacturer's hardware, but the general process and tensioning sequence is the same.

MOUNT ALL THE HARDWARE. The surface-mounted swivel fittings and tensioners shown here are mounted to the posts before pulling and cutting the cable. Because of this, you can mount all the hardware at once. Be careful not to snap or strip the stainless-steel screws by driving them too fast into hardwoods like ipé. Bored deep enough, pilot holes save headaches if they prevent even one broken screw.

PULL CABLE. The author buys his cable in economical 500-ft. rolls because the cable is easier to handle if it's unspooled during installation. He sets the outfeed of the roll in line with the cable run so that it's easy to pull the cable straight through the post holes starting with the first post or spacer after a cable-run termination.

ANCHOR CLEAN CABLE ENDS. It's important to have clean end cuts on the cable. If any cable strands are bent or have burrs, clean their ends with a grinder, or recut the cable. Attach one end of the cable to the fixed fittings.

TENSION CABLES IN ORDER. There are two steps to tensioning cable: first by hand and then by tightening the tensioning device. On long runs, hand-tensioning doesn't get the cable tight enough, so the author uses a ratcheting device and a pair of locking pliers to pull and hold the cable tight. Loosen the tensioning device before attaching the cable so that you'll have the greatest adjustment.

TRIM DRESSES UP THE RIM

The final step in upgrading this deck's railing was to install ipé trim between the posts and spacers to conceal the old pressure-treated rim.

STEPPED TRIM, HIDDEN FASTENERS. The trim was attached with Starborn's Pro Plug® system of countersunk wood screws and plugs (starbornindustries.com). Two boards were used to create a shadowline. The top board was padded out with a rip of pressure-treated decking. A new pressure-treated deck board will be fit to overhang the trim by an inch, but that's a temporary solution. The next phase of this deck upgrade will be to replace all the decking.

THERE'S A SEQUENCE. Once all the cables have been finger-tightened, begin the real tensioning. That's generally done by holding the receiver cone immobile while turning the tensioner body. This manufacturer recommends tensioning the center cable first, then alternating the cables above and below until reaching the top rail and decking. Other cable companies specify starting at the top and bottom cables and alternating toward the center.

2 Ideas for Custom Railings

BY DEBRA JUDGE SILBER

While there's no shortage of off-the-shelf railing systems from decking manufacturers, there still can be advantages to building your own system. Cost is one. Craft is another. Still another is the ability to deliver a unique outdoor feature that fits a client's desires—and a deck's design—perfectly. "It's a lot more fun to play with different ideas and to create something that's more than the sum of its parts," says North Carolina builder Michael Chandler, who incorporated agricultural panels and coil stock in the railing shown on p. 167. "There's an alchemy in taking something very prosaic, like galvanized flashing and goat wire, and turning it into something that's high value and more attractive than premade cast-aluminum stuff."

A MIX OF MANUFACTURED AND FABRICATED. The option of using balusters from a manufacturer outweighed the labor cost of fabricating them.

NAUTICAL OPTION

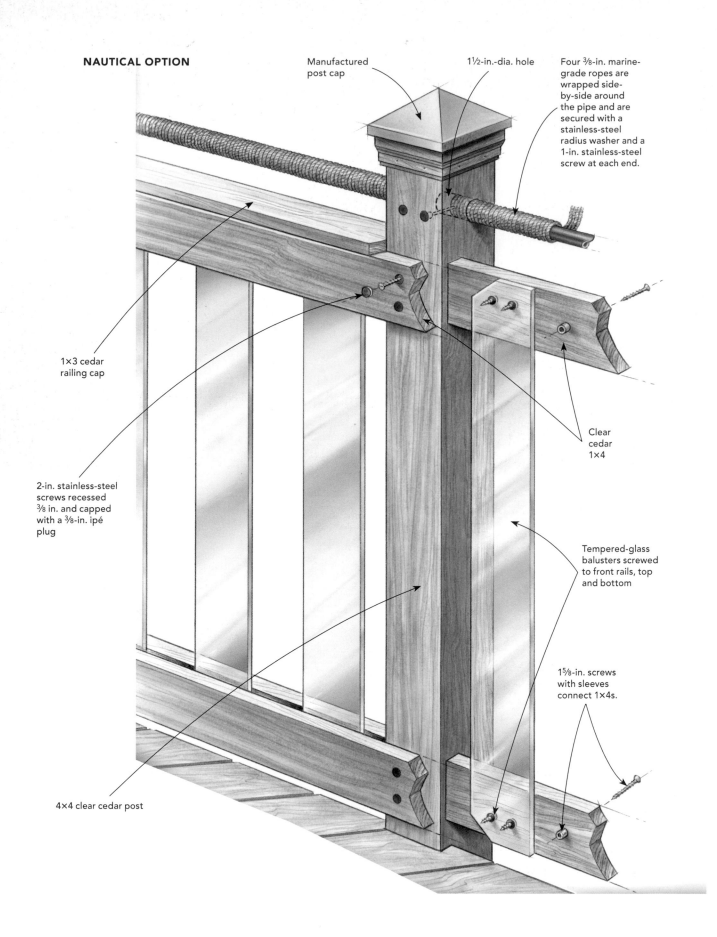

Manufactured post cap

1½-in.-dia. hole

Four ⅜-in. marine-grade ropes are wrapped side-by-side around the pipe and are secured with a stainless-steel radius washer and a 1-in. stainless-steel screw at each end.

1×3 cedar railing cap

2-in. stainless-steel screws recessed ⅜ in. and capped with a ⅜-in. ipé plug

Clear cedar 1×4

Tempered-glass balusters screwed to front rails, top and bottom

1⅝-in. screws with sleeves connect 1×4s.

4×4 clear cedar post

A CREATIVE USE OF MATERIALS. Also known as "feedlot panels," the wire sections used in this railing are available from agricultural suppliers in 16-ft. by 4-ft. sections.

Maryland deck builder Clemens Jellema used two types of manufactured balusters in the railing he designed for a home near the Chesapeake Bay (photo, p. 165), but he supported them in a cedar framework detailed with ipé plugs and a rope-wound top rail. In Jellema's case, with the high labor costs associated with a metropolitan area, it pays to incorporate some ready-made components. Keep in mind that although the railings shown here meet the code requirements for their jurisdictions, regulations vary, so check the codes in your area.

1. Nautical details

This design was produced by Clemens Jellema for a client who wanted a rail with nautical features that wouldn't obscure his view of the nearby woods and river. Jellema achieved the shipshape appearance with a top rail of 1-in. copper pipe wrapped with marine-grade roping. To preserve the view, he chose tempered-glass balusters from Deckorators. For the stair rails and deck sections facing the yard, he used the company's stainless aluminum balusters and connectors. In those sections, a single cedar 2x4 was used for each top and bottom rail.

2. Wire panels for a wide-open view

When budget concerns arose, North Carolina builder Michael Chandler corralled the cost of this 600-sq.-ft. deck project by using agricultural wire—goat panels—for the guardrails rather than the custom metalwork initially planned (photo above). The panels are made of $7/32$-in.-dia. wire in a 4-in. grid pattern that's stiff enough to stand in for traditional balusters. The ends of each panel are inserted in holes drilled into the posts or, along the bottom, in a 1-in.-dia. rigid-steel conduit that serves as the bottom rail. Rope lights tucked under the top rails provide illumination.

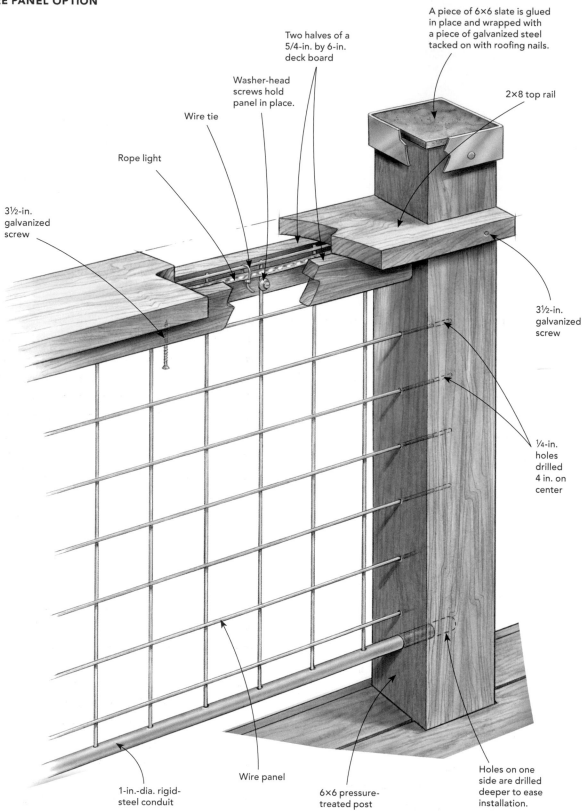

Two halves of a
5/4-in. by 6-in.
deck board

Washer-head
screws hold
panel in place.

A piece of 6×6 slate is glued
in place and wrapped with
a piece of galvanized steel
tacked on with roofing nails.

Wire tie

2×8 top rail

Rope light

3½-in.
galvanized
screw

3½-in.
galvanized
screw

¼-in.
holes
drilled
4 in. on
center

Wire panel

1-in.-dia. rigid-
steel conduit

6×6 pressure-
treated post

Holes on one
side are drilled
deeper to ease
installation.

Mounting Deck Stairs

BY MIKE GUERTIN

On the decks I built in the past, I never gave much thought to how secure the connection was between the stairs and the deck frame. I cobbled together an attachment using whatever was at hand: screws, nails, blocks of wood, and occasionally, angle brackets or field-modified metal hardware. Judging from what I've seen of others' work, I wasn't alone.

I started taking this connection seriously after seeing that a ½-in. gap had developed between the stringers and the frame on an older deck I was examining. Years of use, seasonal expansion and contraction of the wood, and frost heave at the bottom of the stairs had worked the nails out of the stringers' end grain. Now I look at the stringer attachment on every deck I inspect. Rarely are the stairs mounted securely, and many connections are downright scary. Not only is the stringer attachment suspect but so is the capacity of the deck frame where the stringers mount. Most deck frames are designed for uniform loads, such as people and furniture. Impose a concentrated point load such as a stair without additional support, and you are likely overloading the frame.

Granted, the load is minimal when, for example, there are just two steps from grade to deck, and the risk of injury is pretty low should such a stair fail.

But as the distance between the ground and the deck increases, so do the load and the risk. How tall must a set of stairs be before you take the connection seriously? I avoid that question altogether. To ensure that stairs of any size are supported properly, I frame a dedicated support system for the stairs and secure them with hardware specifically designed for stringer attachment. It doesn't take much more time or material to make a solid, durable stair connection than it does to cobble together a risky one, and no one ever complains when you don't cut a corner.

The Case for Independent Stair Support

Design loads for stairs parallel those for decks: generally, a combined live and dead load of 50 lb. per sq. ft. Let's take the example of a set of stairs that's 3 ft. wide, with eight treads that are 10 in. deep and a rise from grade to deck surface of 5 ft. That's 20 sq. ft. and a total load of 1,000 lb. Half of this load is borne by the footing at the bottom, which leaves a 500-lb. load at the top. Adding that load from the stairs to an end joist sized for the deck load only will overload that joist. You might double the joist to handle the load, but what about the ledger, the beam, and the footing? Standard ledger-fastening

SLICK AND QUICK THROUGH BOLT. FastenMaster's ThruLOK requires no wrenches. Drive it most of the way with a drill, thread the special nut on the back side, and finish tightening.

1. CONNECT THE POST. To support the stair as well as the eventual railing, run a 4×4 post from a footing through the frame to the railing height. With posts mounted inside the framing, use through bolts to resist thrust from the stairs. Posts mounted outside the deck frame can be fastened with structural screws since the thrust on the header will push the post against the frame.

details don't allow for concentrated loads such as a double joist. Also, the beam and the footing may not be able to handle the additional load imposed by the double joist supporting the stairs unless specifically designed to do so.

Mounting the stairs to a deck's rim joist invites similar questions: How is the rim joist mounted to the joists, and can that connection handle the concentrated load? Were the beam and the footings sized to account for the stair load?

2. FASTEN THE HEADER. A single 2×8 (or larger) 7 in. wider than the outside of the stairs serves as a header. Secure it to the posts with structural screws.

You can certainly beef up the ledger-to-house connection, the joists, the beam, and the footings to handle stair loads, but since the code doesn't provide a prescriptive solution, that might require an engineer. The alternative is to support the stairs independently with their own posts and footings.

FASTER THAN LAGS. Structural screws such as Fasten-Master's LedgerLoks offer strength similar to ½-in. lags, but they install with a drill or impact driver and require no washers.

Footings and Posts Support the Stairs

There are usually 4x4 posts for railings at the top of stairs anyway, and I just extend these posts down to a pair of independent footings to support the stair load. It doesn't matter if the posts are mounted inside or outside the deck frame. I secure the posts to the footings with metal post bases and anchor bolts.

For most stairs, the footings only need to be 6 in. to 8 in. dia. The maximum code-allowed span for unnotched southern-pine stringers accommodates about 16 10-in.-deep treads. In this scenario, half of the treads are supported by these posts, and half are supported by the landing at the bottom. That's about 40 sq. ft. for a 3-ft.-wide set of stairs, which, multiplied by the 50-lb.-per-sq.-ft. design load,

3. HAMMER IN A JACK. To fully support the header, run 2×4 jacks between it and the footings. Join the jacks to the posts with structural screws.

equals a total design load of 2,000 lb., half of which needs to be carried at the top of the stair. The load on each footing is 500 lb., and 8-in.-dia. footings can handle about 575 lb. based on the code's default soil-bearing capacity of 1,500 lb. per sq. ft. These footings need to be as deep as the other footings for that deck.

Two through-bolts secure each post to the end joist or rim joist. To make an attachment point for the stringers, I bolt a 2x8 or larger board to these posts as a header, then support it further with 2x4 jacks that run to the footings. (The jacks should be treated and rated for ground contact.) To comply with hardware manufacturers' required minimum of 3½ in. between the edge of the stringer and the end of the single-ply header, I make the header at least 7 in. wider than the outside of the stairs.

I attach the stringers to the header with Simpson Strong-Tie's LSC adjustable stair-stringer connectors or USP Structural Connectors' CSH concealed stair hangers. I fasten the angle-shaped hardware to the header with structural-connector screws so that the point where the plumb cut meets the bottom of the stringer will align with the bend point on the hardware. The side tabs on the hardware go on the inner face of the outside stringers so they aren't visible. The stringer is fastened to the hardware with screws through the side-tab holes and with a single screw through the bottom of the hardware.

4. BOLT A 2×4 TO THE LANDING. Wedge anchors drilled into the concrete secure a 2×4 cleat that will connect to the bottoms of the stringers.

EASY CONCRETE ANCHORS. Wedge anchors rely on a cone-shaped bolt head that pulls up as the nut is tightened on the bolt. The bolt head pushes on the inside of a steel sleeve, expanding it inside a hole drilled in the concrete.

I use structural-connector screws because the 2012 IRC says that stairs can't be fastened using nails subject to withdrawal (R311.5.1). Even though the stringer is attached using a metal connector, the connector is commonly fastened with nails driven straight into the header. These nails are subject

to withdrawal and may come loose over time. Mounting the connector with screws reduces the risk of withdrawal. Both Simpson and USP have structural screws for their hardware.

Securing the Bottom of the Stairs

There are no metal connectors made specifically to secure stringers directly to a stair landing or footing. I dig and form a concrete slab to serve as a footing for the stringers, as well as for a landing. The footing portion is directly beneath the bottom cut of the

Stringer hangers provide a reliable connection to the header. For aesthetics, set the end hangers so their flanges are to the inside of the stringers.

stringers and is 12 in. to 16 in. thick, 16 in. deep, and a few inches wider than the stairs. The landing portion is 6 in. to 8 in. thick and extends at least 3 ft. from the finish nosing of the bottom step.

Using wedge anchors, I attach a 2x4 cleat to the slab so it fits between the outer stringers, flush with their fronts. Screws through the outside stringers attach them to the cleat. I notch the middle stringers to fit around the 2x4. A hot-dipped galvanized ½-in.-dia. threaded rod (www.jamestowndistributors.com) and blocking tie the posts to the stair.

CONNECTOR SCREWS DON'T PULL OUT. Connector screws offer much higher withdrawal strengths than nails. Unlike many other kinds of screws, they also offer shear strength similar to nails, which often makes them a superior choice for attaching structural connectors.

STRINGER HANGERS ARE SIMPLY BETTER. Made by both Simpson Strong-Tie and USP Structural Connectors, stringer hangers provide a simple and reliable connection. Fasten them with structural-connector screws by the same manufacturers.

MOUNTING DECK STAIRS   **175**

6. JOIN THE POSTS AND STRINGERS.
Blocking behind the posts reinforces them and the stringers. A threaded rod between the posts pulls them together, sandwiching blocking along the front.

TENSION ROD SQUEEZES OUT A SOLID CONNECTION.
A long, ½-in. bolt joins with a 3-ft. piece of threaded rod and a connector nut to create a tension rod that pulls the rail posts tight against continuous blocking.

PART 6

Complete Deck Guides

A LOW, CURVY DECK 178

A RAISED DECK WITH A 199
CUSTOM RAILING

A GRADE-LEVEL DECK WITH A 220
DECORATIVE BORDER

A Low, Curvy Deck

BY CLEMENS JELLEMA

When I build a deck, I want the result of my design and construction to improve the homeowners' property as well as their lifestyle. In this case, my crew and I were hired to build a replacement for my clients' old deck, a simple 24-ft. by 14-ft. rectangle. They rarely used that deck, even though they loved to entertain outdoors. It was time for a change.

My clients wanted a dining area that wasn't too close to the house and a place to relax where they could grill. They also wanted a hot tub, but they weren't sure if the tub was possible because of space and privacy concerns.

After discussing the project with the homeowners, I made a number of computer-generated drawings and came up with a design they liked: a low, two-level deck that curved along one side. (For 3D renderings, I use a program called Realtime Landscaping Architect by Idea Spectrum.) Several large trees limited the buildable space, but a curve on one side was an ideal way to optimize the space without resorting to a traditional rectangle.

After demolishing the old deck, we started to build the new one. Because the deck was nearly on grade, much of the work was easier than if we had to work from ladders. Our first task was to establish the footing locations, then dig the holes and pour

VINYL IS FIRST. The crew tacks up 14-in.-wide vinyl flashing along the deck's perimeter at the house, making sure to extend it up behind the siding and under the doorways.

ESTABLISH A LEVEL GUIDELINE. The doorsill sets the height of the 2×8 pressure-treated ledger. It's tacked into position and later secured to the house's rim joist with ½-in. by 4½-in. hot-dipped galvanized lag screws.

concrete. At the same time, we formed and poured the hot tub's pad. Framing, decking, stairs, and skirting followed in sequence.

Ledger Installation

A deck needs a ledger-to-house connection for support and extra rigidity. Although the design of this low deck made it a self-supporting structure, I still paid careful attention to the details of the ledger, which would act as a fail-safe support for the deck.

Flashing the ledger protects the house from water damage that could compromise the ledger's connection to the house, as well as the house itself.

Layout

Deck frames high enough to stand under can be built first on temporary posts that then are used to locate the required footings. This deck's height was less than 3 ft., however, so we had to locate, dig, and pour the footings before we could frame. Working from the ledger, we used stringlines and long lengths of framing lumber to extend perpendicular lines, then temporarily braced the lumber plumb and level. We used those references to measure and plumb down for post locations. The post holes for this project were spaced at a maximum of 8 ft.

LEDGER DETAILS

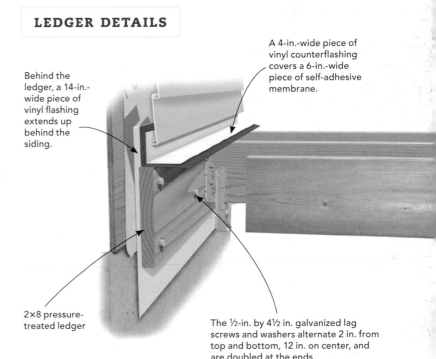

Behind the ledger, a 14-in.-wide piece of vinyl flashing extends up behind the siding.

A 4-in.-wide piece of vinyl counterflashing covers a 6-in.-wide piece of self-adhesive membrane.

2×8 pressure-treated ledger

The ½-in. by 4½ in. galvanized lag screws and washers alternate 2 in. from top and bottom, 12 in. on center, and are doubled at the ends.

Code✓Check

Changes to the International Residential Code (IRC) spell out spacing requirements for ledger bolts and require the installation of additional hardware to increase the strength of the deck-ledger connection. For more information, consult with your local code official to determine how the code applies in your area.

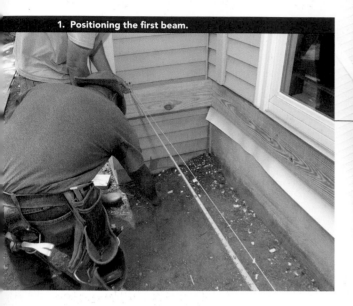

1. Positioning the first beam.

First parallel line

STRING IS EASIEST. To locate the footings that support the beam closest to the house, the crew stretches a string parallel to the foundation and plumbs it down. Footing centers are flagged.

Footings for radius kept at 7 ft. on center

2. Positioning the second beam.

THE LEDGER REFERENCE POINT IS THE SAME. To establish the second beam's footings, the crew tacks a 16-ft. 2×6 to the ledger, then braces it so that it is perpendicular to the foundation and level (above left). Rather than set the layout string high and then use a level to determine the second beam's footings, it's better to position the line lower, just above the footings (above right).

5. Lay out the lower deck.

RUNNING RIGHT ANGLES. For accuracy, the crew does not locate the lower deck's footings until the main deck is framed and the hot-tub pad poured. Instead of using temporary framing, the crew frames the deck perimeter and supports it with temporary posts until the footings are located, dug, and poured.

Line continued from foundation

45°

Second parallel line

Line parallel to 45° angle

Pad

Code✓Check

The number, size, and depth of concrete footings or piers vary with the size of the deck, the regional climate, the soil conditions, and the codes. Consult the IRC and/or local code officials to find the most appropriate methods for your area.

3. Establishing the angle.

4. Marking the curve.

AN IMPORTANT ANGLE. By measuring an equilateral triangle from the corner of the house, workers can set a temporary 2× at a 45° angle. This side of the deck determines the location of the hot-tub pad and the termination of the outside radius.

SWING THE ARC. A tape anchored at the corner of the deck layout establishes the outer radius. A crew member walks it off, marking where it intersects the temporary 2×s. Pieces of 1×3 strapping (photo above right) mark the radius's position and the location of the footings for the beam that will support that side.

Footings

With the footing locations marked, we started to dig. Because we had more than a dozen 18-in.-dia. footings to dig, I went straight to labor-saving devices and rented a power auger. Because the diameter of the power auger's bit was 16 in. and the footing forms were 17½ in., we needed to do some digging by hand to enlarge the holes before setting the forms.

In this county, the code calls for 30-in.-deep footings. We cut the forms 36 in. long so that about 6 in. or so protruded above the hole. To plumb up the forms, we used a short level to check the top in two directions.

HANG ON. Nominally a two-man machine, the aggressive auger sometimes required three operators as it dug into the hard-packed soil. The auger rental saved time and money.

FORM PREP, PRODUCTION STYLE. The easiest way to cut cardboard footing forms to length is to use a circular saw while a helper rotates the form. The cuts should be as square as possible.

PLUMB THE FOOTINGS. A short level held across the top indicates when the form is level and, therefore, plumb. When the forms are plumb, they are backfilled.

DIG, FILL, AND CLEAN UP. As the builder's forms are placed and backfilled, the site is raked to slope away from the house in preparation for a layer of landscape fabric and gravel beneath the deck. The gravel minimizes moisture transpiration and creates a safer working surface.

THE TRUCK WON'T REACH. Due to limited access to the site, the crew has to transfer the concrete from the truck to a wheelbarrow. Plywood pathways make it easier to roll between the truck and the footings.

PREP FOR THE NEXT STEP. Once the footing is poured, a wooden float is used to screed off the excess so that the concrete is flush with the top of the footing form.

THE PAD NEEDS A SOLID BASE. After leveling and staking the pad form into place, a worker compacts the dirt to lessen the chances that the pad will shift after it is poured.

The Hot-Tub Pad

With the concrete truck coming to pour the footings, we had to get the hot-tub pad ready, too. The pad needed to remain crack-free and stable over the long term while supporting a ton or more of water. We used 2x8s to make a square box form, then leveled it, tacking the box's sides to stakes driven into the dirt on the downhill side. Pieces of ½-in. plywood filled the gaps between the form and the sloping grade and were braced with 2x diagonals nailed to stakes.

REINFORCEMENT REQUIRED. After cutting and tying the ½-in. rebar into a grid of approximate 12-in. squares, the crew drops it onto wire supports that keep it in the center of the form.

NO-STICK SPRITZ.
Instead of the traditional oil-based form release, the crew uses common bathroom spray cleaner; its surfactants perform the same function as oil.

FILL AND SCREED. Workers place the concrete carefully in the form so that the rebar isn't knocked off its supports. When the form is filled, they use a straight 2× on edge with a relaxed back-and-forth motion to level the top. They finish the surface with a float.

Framing the Deck

Our default framing method is to cantilever the joists over a carrying beam supported by 6x6 posts. Because this deck is fairly low to the ground, the ledger's support is less critical and serves more as a termination for the joists. We minimized the distance the joists spanned by adding a second beam closer to the house. As when we located the footings, we ran a 16-ft. 2x8 joist out from the ledger and braced it level and square. We then set the height of the outer beam by bracing it beneath the first joist and extending it across to the house just beneath the ledger.

Working backward, we established the inner beam's height by spanning the tops of the outer beam and the underside of the ledger. Because the inner beam was more than 16 ft. long, we made it from four pieces of 2x and arranged the joints so that they landed over post locations.

Once the beams were up, we nailed the joists onto the ledger, 12 in. on center. (Joist hangers are installed after the joists are nailed up to reduce the discrepancies in height from board to board.) To prevent water from collecting between sistered joists, we covered them with strips of self-adhesive membrane. We used W.R. Grace's Vycor®, as we do in most cases.

FRAMING

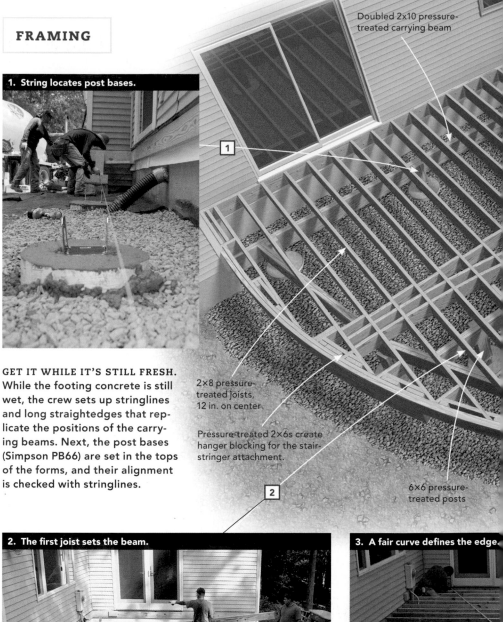

Doubled 2x10 pressure-treated carrying beam

1

2×8 pressure-treated joists, 12 in. on center

Pressure-treated 2×6s create hanger blocking for the stair-stringer attachment.

6×6 pressure-treated posts

1. String locates post bases.

GET IT WHILE IT'S STILL FRESH. While the footing concrete is still wet, the crew sets up stringlines and long straightedges that replicate the positions of the carrying beams. Next, the post bases (Simpson PB66) are set in the tops of the forms, and their alignment is checked with stringlines.

2. The first joist sets the beam.

3. A fair curve defines the edge.

THE OUTER BEAM COMES FIRST. After tacking a long joist to the ledger and bracing it plumb and square, workers position the outer carrying beam beneath it. They cut 6×6 posts to length, bolt them half-lapped to the beam with two ½-in. by 8-in. through bolts, and repeat the process with the inner beam.

Bridging between joists at centerline

Code ✓ Check

At 12 in. on center, the joist spacing on this deck is atypical; normal spacing is 16 in. on center. However, because the decking will be installed on the diagonal, the distance spanned is closer to 16 in., which is the maximum span allowed by many composite-decking manufacturers. Check their span tables and/or installation instructions for specific recommendations.

Pressure-treated 2×8s create hanger blocking for lower-deck rim attachment.

Sistered joists overlap by 4 ft. to extend the length of the middle joists.

3

MARKING THE RADIUS. The joists are run long on the side of the deck that will be curved. The radius is marked on each joist by holding a tape at the inside corner and swinging it across that side of the deck (above left). Angled cuts create the curve. The top marks are carried down across each joist's face, and a reciprocating or circular saw is used to make the cut (above center). The rim joist is curved by cutting ¾-in.-deep sawkerfs every inch or so along the inside face and then nailing it to each joist as it is bent (above right). Blocking between the rim and the joists strengthens the doubled rim (inset).

Decking

The decking is the finish that everyone notices, so the material choice, installation, and design are important. First, it should provide a durable finish for the deck. After years of trial and error, I've decided that capstock composite decking is the best. (Capstock has a thin skin of tough plastic applied to its surface. Capping makes the surface last longer and increases its resistance to staining and fading.) We used Fiberon's Horizon decking on this job, but I also like the capped products made by Trex, Azek, and EverGrain. They cost $1 to $2 per ft. more than regular composite decking.

The Fiberon decking is installed with hidden fasteners, which give the deck a clean look. We screwed and plugged the perimeter and accent boards, which couldn't be securely attached with the hidden fasteners.

The homeowners didn't want to see any field joints in the decking, but that meant board lengths would exceed the 20-ft. pieces available. I decided to use a one-board outer perimeter of a darker color, and then run an accent board bent in the same radius across the center of the deck. The accent board provides a clean break in the decking and lends some flair to the field.

INSTALLING DECKING

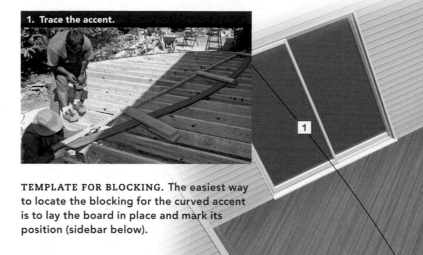

1. Trace the accent.

TEMPLATE FOR BLOCKING. The easiest way to locate the blocking for the curved accent is to lay the board in place and mark its position (sidebar below).

2. Blocking comes next.

PROPER SUPPORT COUNTS. Workers cut and nail blocking on each side of the accent strip to provide a nail base for the decking ends that terminate against the strip.

LOW-TECH BENDING TECHNIQUES

WE COULDN'T KERF THE DECKING as we did the rim because the required bend was across the flat, not the edge. Luckily, we needed to bend only three boards, they were made of plastic, and it was summer. First, I cut a template of the curve from a pair of 2×12s laid end to end. On a hot day, I laid a 16-ft. length of decking on the driveway. After a few hours, the decking was about 120°F and limp as a noodle. I clamped it between both sides of the template, screwing a brace across the top every few feet. I cooled the board with cold water, bringing down the temperature enough to keep the correct radius in place. I reinforced the curve by keeping the board in a brace until I was ready to use it.

3. Decking is laid out.

DIAGONAL LAYOUT STARTS FROM THE CORNER. To add visual interest, the decking is installed at a 45° angle. After snapping a reference line at the deck's midpoint, the crew works toward the house, then back toward the hot-tub deck.

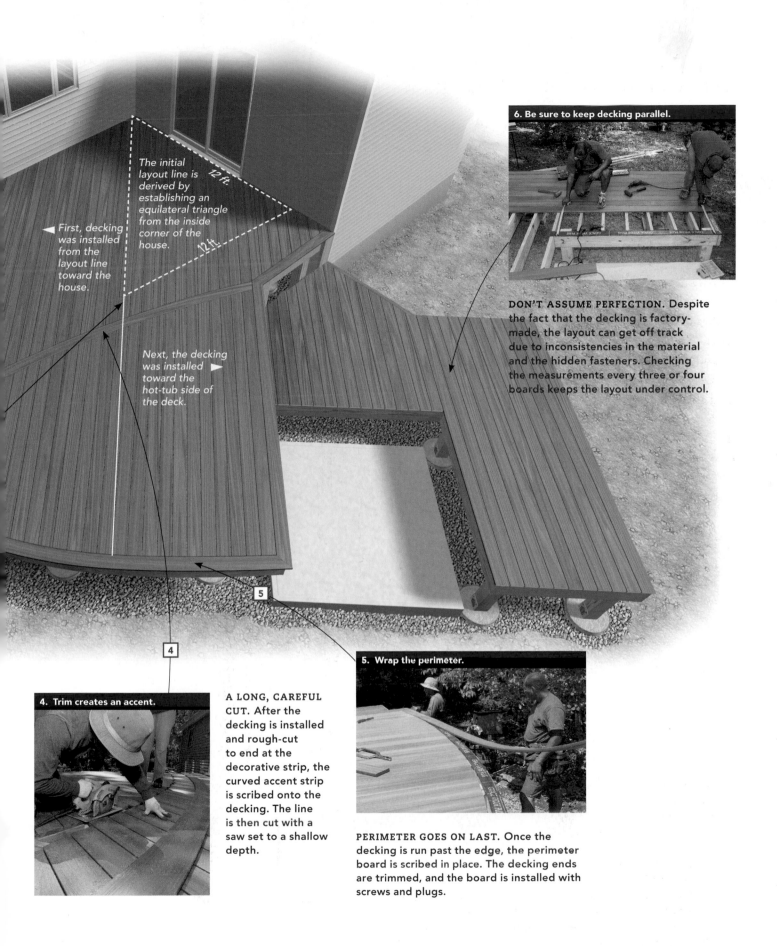

The initial layout line is derived by establishing an equilateral triangle from the inside corner of the house.

12 ft.

12 ft.

First, decking was installed from the layout line toward the house.

Next, the decking was installed toward the hot-tub side of the deck.

6. Be sure to keep decking parallel.

DON'T ASSUME PERFECTION. Despite the fact that the decking is factory-made, the layout can get off track due to inconsistencies in the material and the hidden fasteners. Checking the measurements every three or four boards keeps the layout under control.

5

4

4. Trim creates an accent.

A LONG, CAREFUL CUT. After the decking is installed and rough-cut to end at the decorative strip, the curved accent strip is scribed onto the decking. The line is then cut with a saw set to a shallow depth.

5. Wrap the perimeter.

PERIMETER GOES ON LAST. Once the decking is run past the edge, the perimeter board is scribed in place. The decking ends are trimmed, and the board is installed with screws and plugs.

Main Entrance Stairs

Because this deck is fairly low to the ground, the stairs were relatively simple. The main entrance stairs are on the radiused side of the deck and are wide enough to be inviting without taking over the entire side of the deck. The stringer spacing for composite decking is 12 in., and I installed six stringers cut from 2x12s. Because the deck has a radius on the side where the stairs are built, the stringers flare slightly outward, creating a similar radius on the risers and treads.

Each stringer is secured to the hanger with galvanized hardware (Simpson A35Z).

A 2×8 header is kerfed to bend along the radius and is attached to 2×6 blocking.

To bend the treads, the stock is left long, attached at one end, and levered along the radius as it's fastened.

PVC risers bend along the stringers' curve.

Stringer ends are tied together with a kerfed 2×8.

Code✓Check

The IRC is very specific about stair construction, and it includes guidelines on stringer size and span, riser height, tread width, and overall dimensions. Be sure to consult the code or your local code official before designing stairs.

Skirtboards

To give the deck a more finished look, we usually add a screen of skirtboards below the fascia. Here, we used the same decking boards, attaching them with two screws at each end while maintaining a ¼-in. space between for ventilation. We kept the screws close to the end of each board so that they could be covered with a trim piece later.

At the corner near the hot tub, we created an access point by exposing the fasteners of the last five boards. If there ever is a need to go under the deck, the boards can be removed without dismantling the trim.

LOCATING THE BOTTOM FRAME. The skirt frame consists of a kerfed 2×4, top and bottom. After the top 2×4 is attached to blocking, a plumb bob establishes the position of the bottom half of the frame.

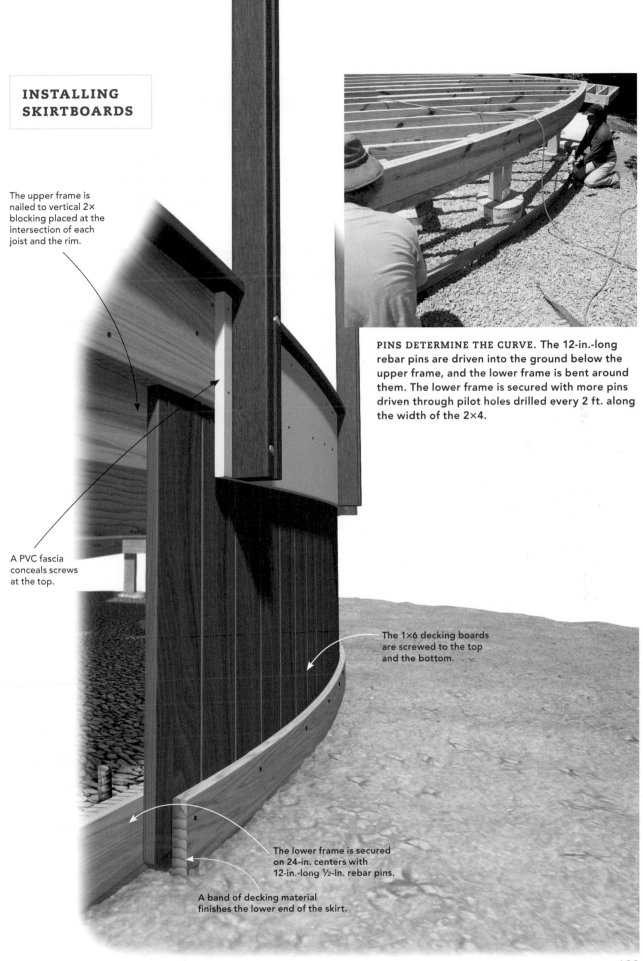

INSTALLING SKIRTBOARDS

The upper frame is nailed to vertical 2× blocking placed at the intersection of each joist and the rim.

A PVC fascia conceals screws at the top.

PINS DETERMINE THE CURVE. The 12-in.-long rebar pins are driven into the ground below the upper frame, and the lower frame is bent around them. The lower frame is secured with more pins driven through pilot holes drilled every 2 ft. along the width of the 2×4.

The 1×6 decking boards are screwed to the top and the bottom.

The lower frame is secured on 24-in. centers with 12-in.-long ½-in. rebar pins.

A band of decking material finishes the lower end of the skirt.

Stairs for the Lower Deck

The three-riser stair that leads from the upper deck down to the hot tub follows the angle of the deck edge so that the transition in height becomes part of the deck. Instead of cutting stringers, we built these stairs as two stacked boxes.

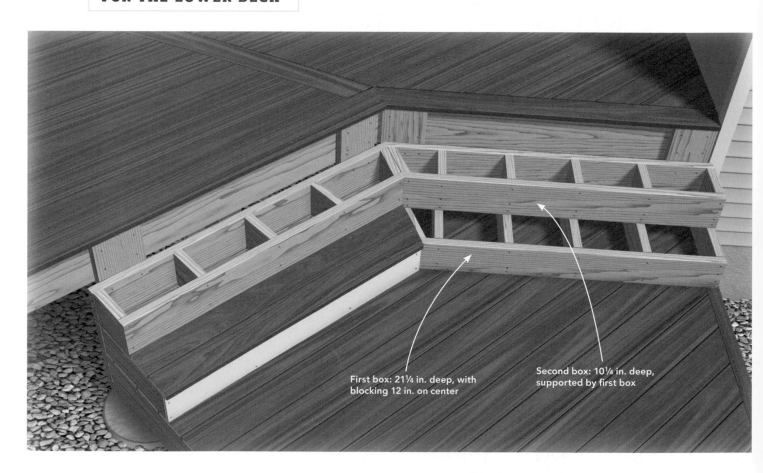

First box: 21¼ in. deep, with blocking 12 in. on center

Second box: 10¼ in. deep, supported by first box

CONCEALED FASTENERS. To attach the treads securely without visible fasteners, the crew drills pilot holes before driving screws. Plugs cut from the decking conceal the screwheads.

SQUARED AWAY. The stairs are a focal point, so it's important to keep the details sharp by aligning the tread ends and miters at the center of the stairs.

A CLEAN FINISH. Once the treads are installed, the risers are covered with PVC trim, and a skirt of the same material is applied over the tread ends.

Handrail

This handrail consists of 4x4 ipé posts, 2x4 rails, and a 2x6 railing cap combined with balusters and railing brackets manufactured by Deckorators. The railing is 36 in. high, and the posts are spaced at a maximum of 5 ft. For structural and aesthetic reasons, my designs usually place the railing posts inside the frame. In this design, however, I decided to install them outside to maximize the deck space and to make the installation on the curved portion much easier.

RAIL-TO-POST CONNECTION. After bolting the posts to the rim, the crew attaches the railing connectors by screwing them to the ends of each rail, then screwing the assembly to the posts.

BALUSTERS GO ON NEXT. After using a template to lay out the correct spacing (less than 4 in. between balusters), the crew screws the curved balusters to the top and bottom railings.

GRAB RAIL SATISFIES CODE. Here, the 2×6 railing cap is structurally sound but larger than code specifies, so the crew installs a smaller 2×2 grab rail by screwing through its mitered return at each end.

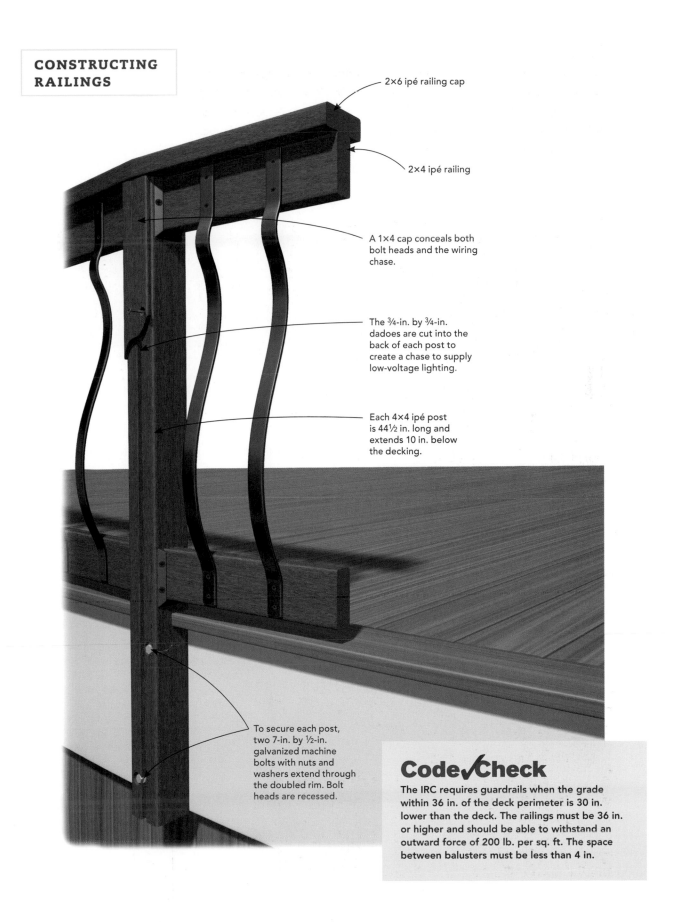

2×6 ipé railing cap

2×4 ipé railing

A 1×4 cap conceals both bolt heads and the wiring chase.

The ¾-in. by ¾-in. dadoes are cut into the back of each post to create a chase to supply low-voltage lighting.

Each 4×4 ipé post is 44½ in. long and extends 10 in. below the decking.

To secure each post, two 7-in. by ½-in. galvanized machine bolts with nuts and washers extend through the doubled rim. Bolt heads are recessed.

Code✓Check

The IRC requires guardrails when the grade within 36 in. of the deck perimeter is 30 in. lower than the deck. The railings must be 36 in. or higher and should be able to withstand an outward force of 200 lb. per sq. ft. The space between balusters must be less than 4 in.

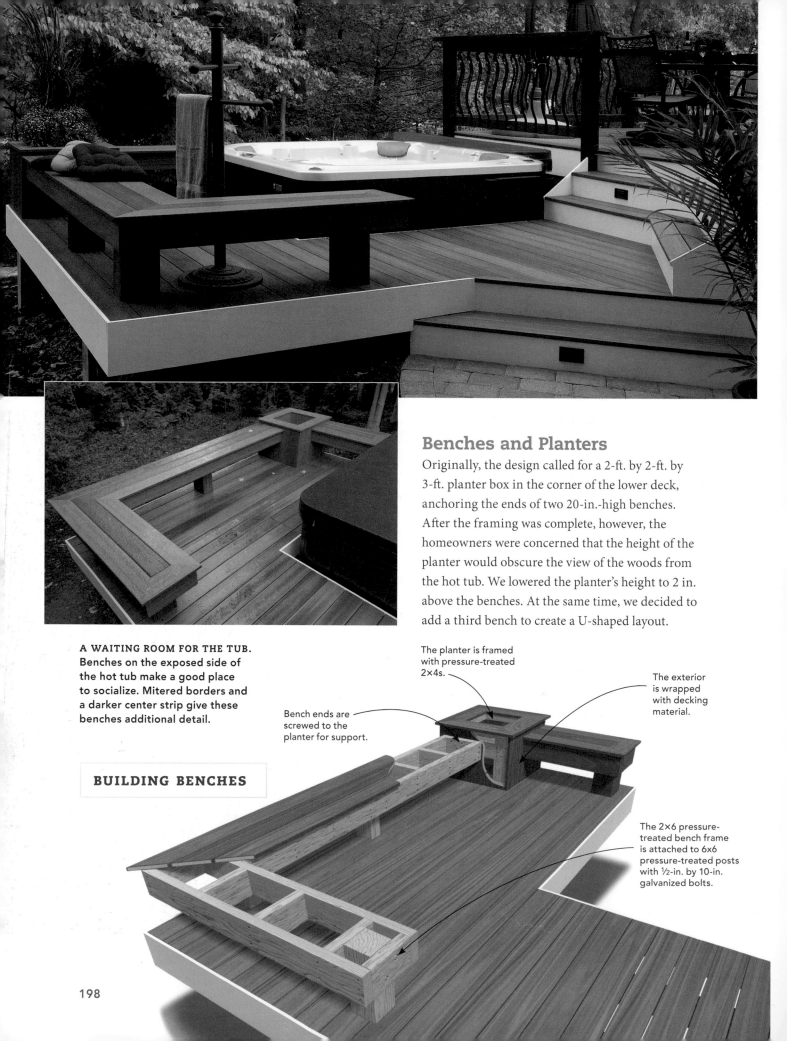

Benches and Planters

Originally, the design called for a 2-ft. by 2-ft. by 3-ft. planter box in the corner of the lower deck, anchoring the ends of two 20-in.-high benches. After the framing was complete, however, the homeowners were concerned that the height of the planter would obscure the view of the woods from the hot tub. We lowered the planter's height to 2 in. above the benches. At the same time, we decided to add a third bench to create a U-shaped layout.

A WAITING ROOM FOR THE TUB. Benches on the exposed side of the hot tub make a good place to socialize. Mitered borders and a darker center strip give these benches additional detail.

The planter is framed with pressure-treated 2×4s.

The exterior is wrapped with decking material.

Bench ends are screwed to the planter for support.

BUILDING BENCHES

The 2×6 pressure-treated bench frame is attached to 6×6 pressure-treated posts with ½-in. by 10-in. galvanized bolts.

A Raised Deck with a Custom Railing

BY BOBBY PARKS

My company designed and built the deck profiled here to replace a relatively new deck whose code violations were too numerous to mention. Our clients, who live in an Atlanta suburb, had asked us to integrate the new deck with an existing grade-level patio and to use materials that would perform well and look good for many years. Because they liked the look of natural wood but wanted to minimize maintenance, we used vertical-grain pressure-treated decking kiln-dried after treatment (KDAT). The frame and railings are pressure-treated as well, and the balusters are aluminum.

A crew of three built this deck. They established the ledger, erected the beam, and then filled in the framing. Decking was installed next, followed by the footings, posts, railings, and stairs. To be efficient, we didn't wait to complete each stage of the process before moving to the next. While one carpenter was starting the layout for one phase, the other two could finish the previous phase.

Attach the Ledger

Because the ledger is connected to the house's framing, it must be flashed to prevent water from getting behind the ledger and into the framing, where it could compromise the attachment points and cause the deck to separate from the house. I use three pieces of vinyl flashing, bending the bottom piece into a Z to fit behind the ledger. For more protection, use self-adhesive membrane as the final piece, which laps over the top (drawing on the facing page).

BEND VINYL WITH A NAIL SET. The easiest way to make precise bends on vinyl flashing is to use a straightedge and to score the bend line with a nail set or a similar tool that won't cut through the material.

PUT THE LEDGER IN PLACE. After you install the Z-flashing and a wide piece of vinyl flashing, tack the 2×12 ledger in place with 16d galvanized nails. Its position is determined by a previously chalked level line and checked with a level during installation.

THE FAST WAY TO LAY OUT BOLTS. My crew typically doesn't drill the holes for the carriage bolts that secure the ledger to the house until the joists are tacked in place temporarily. The wait lets them space the bolts so that they don't interfere with the joist hangers.

ATTACHING THE LEDGER

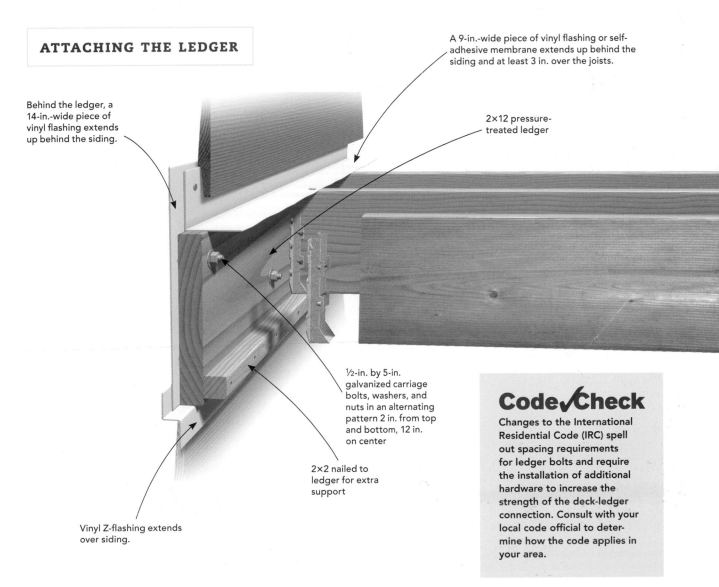

A 9-in.-wide piece of vinyl flashing or self-adhesive membrane extends up behind the siding and at least 3 in. over the joists.

Behind the ledger, a 14-in.-wide piece of vinyl flashing extends up behind the siding.

2×12 pressure-treated ledger

½-in. by 5-in. galvanized carriage bolts, washers, and nuts in an alternating pattern 2 in. from top and bottom, 12 in. on center

2×2 nailed to ledger for extra support

Vinyl Z-flashing extends over siding.

Code Check

Changes to the International Residential Code (IRC) spell out spacing requirements for ledger bolts and require the installation of additional hardware to increase the strength of the deck-ledger connection. Consult with your local code official to determine how the code applies in your area.

Frame the Deck

We use a post-and-beam cantilever method rather than a doubled outer-deck band. Cantilevering deck joists over a carrying beam creates a stronger structure that minimizes the distance the joists have to span. In turn, this increases the deck's live-load capacity, or its ability to carry weight beyond that of the deck itself. This method also makes it easier to include bays and bump-outs in the deck's design without locating a post at every corner.

1

2

3½-in. joist spacing to
capture railing posts

6x6 post (permanent
location)

3

1. Raise carrying beam on temporary posts.

2

RAISE THE BEAM, AND RUN OUT THE SIDES.
After two temporary posts are braced plumb, the doubled 2×12 beam is lifted into place. The perimeter joists are brought out from the ledger and trimmed flush with the outside edge of the beam.

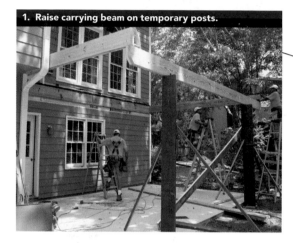

2. Install joists on 12-in. centers.

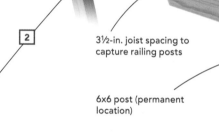

3. Add backing for diagonal decking.

REASONS FOR MORE JOISTS. Locate the joists on 12-in. centers to increase the deck's load capacity and to shorten the distance between decking fasteners created by the diagonal decking pattern planned for this deck.

A PARTING BEAM SUPPORTS THE ENDS OF THE DECKING. To support the diagonal decking detail at the center of the deck, nail together a parting beam. Two 2×10 joists are joined with a full-length 2×4 along the top edge and spaced accordingly with 2×4 blocking underneath.

Blocking stiffens deck framing.

Joists are doubled here for extra support at corners.

Joist hangers Simpson LUS28Z or similar

4. Trim the overhang.

5. Install the perimeter bands.

6. Add the upper stair's landing.

DEFINE THE PERIMETER WITH CHALKLINES. Once the joists are in place, mark the amount of overhang beyond the beam, snap a chalkline, and cut off the excess.

MITER THE CORNERS. After installing the long runs of perimeter bands, miter shorter sections at both ends, and nail them across the corners.

HANG THE UPPER LANDING FROM THE DECK. Strap-hang the two carrying beams from the deck's rim, and support them with temporary posts. Then frame the landing box on top, and brace it square to the deck.

Install Decking on the Diagonal

The decking is the finished skin of the deck, so we put a lot of effort into its visual details and installation. We often use a diagonal decking pattern because it looks good, and we can run single boards out to the perimeter, avoiding butt joints in the field. On this job, we used 2x5 vertical-grain pressure-treated yellow pine that doesn't cup as much as wider decking. We attach the decking with coated deck screws, drilling pilot holes for all screws to reduce splits. For the sake of accuracy, we don't use screw guns with extensions.

INSTALLING DIAGONAL DECKING

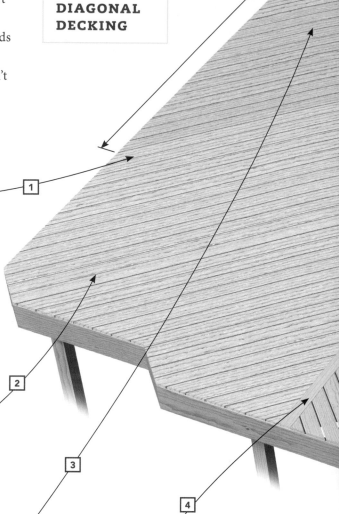

RUN THE FIRST BOARD FROM THE CORNER. The 45° decking angle is established by measuring a right triangle from the intersection of the house and the parting beam, then snapping a chalkline as a reference for the first board.

1. Establish the angle.

COVER THE AREA QUICKLY. For better workflow, lay out the decking from the first board toward the perimeter, leave it long, and tack it into position. Later, someone will go back, drive all the remaining screws, and trim the board ends around the perimeter.

2. Install decking efficiently.

THIS IS THE PLACE FOR PRECISE CUTS. Once the outer portion is filled in, the inner corner can be tackled. Hemmed in by the house, each board must be cut to fit on both ends.

3. Small areas can take more time.

4. Create a space for the parting board.

CHALK THE MIDLINE, AND CUT. When one side of the decking is complete, chalk a line just inside the parting beam, and trim the deckboard ends at the line. Always use blue or white chalk; red is indelible.

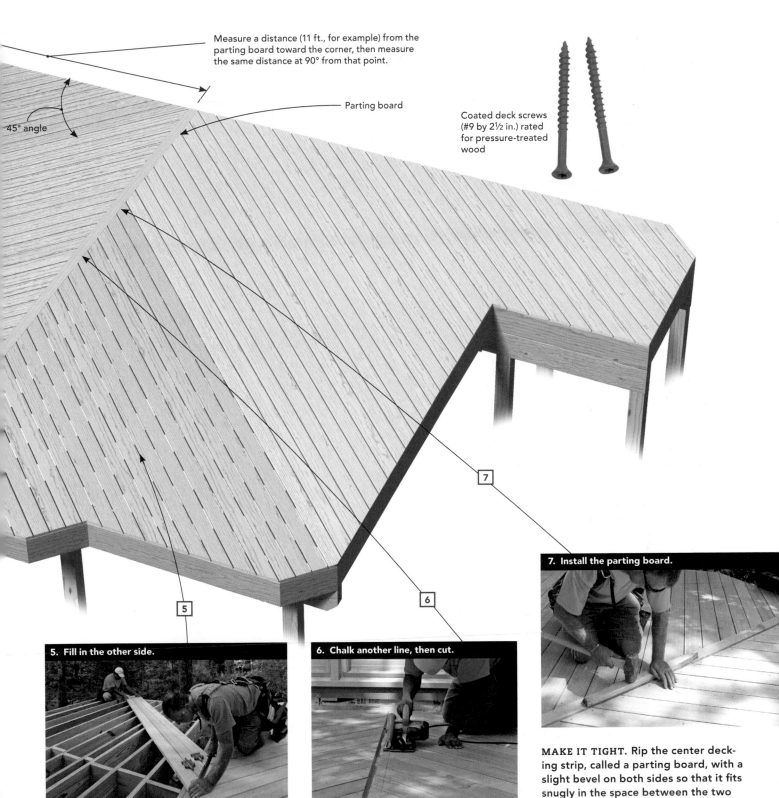

Measure a distance (11 ft., for example) from the parting board toward the corner, then measure the same distance at 90° from that point.

Parting board

45° angle

Coated deck screws (#9 by 2½ in.) rated for pressure-treated wood

5. Fill in the other side.

6. Chalk another line, then cut.

7. Install the parting board.

MAKE IT TIGHT. Rip the center decking strip, called a parting board, with a slight bevel on both sides so that it fits snugly in the space between the two fields of decking. A sledgehammer and block will persuade the fit.

START IN THE MIDDLE. To establish the duplicate angle, install a group of three or four boards, and align them with the opposite side. Starting in the middle reduces the chance of accumulated error. Check the angle, then fill in decking on both sides of the group.

TRIM THE CENTERLINE. Once the decking is completed, snap and cut a line on the parting beam to create the exact space for the parting board. A straight line looks better, so work slowly.

FIND THE CENTER OF THE FOOTING. To locate the footings, plumb down from the beam. You don't need a plumb bob for this; a tape measure is a lot faster. This establishes the center of the footing. From there, mark the hole.

Set Footings and Posts

For this deck, the carrying beam and the beams beneath the stair landings are supported by 6x6 posts. Each post is mechanically fastened to a concrete footing and to the beams. The 6x6 posts are spaced approximately 6½ ft. on center under the carrying beam.

CONNECT FOOTING TO SOIL. Even though this 24-in. by 24-in. by 12-in. footing was dug in highly compacted clay, a grid of ½-in. rebar still ties the concrete to the bottom of the hole.

FLATTEN THE FOOTING. After the concrete is mixed and poured into the footing, trowel the surface smooth.

ANCHOR THE POST BASE. The next day, the concrete should be set but not cured. After checking the precise location of the post, use a hammer-drill and masonry bit to drill a hole for the post base's anchor bolt.

RAISE THE PERMANENT POST. Measure the distance between the post base and the beam above. Notch the 6×6 post at the top, set it into the post base, and plumb it into position.

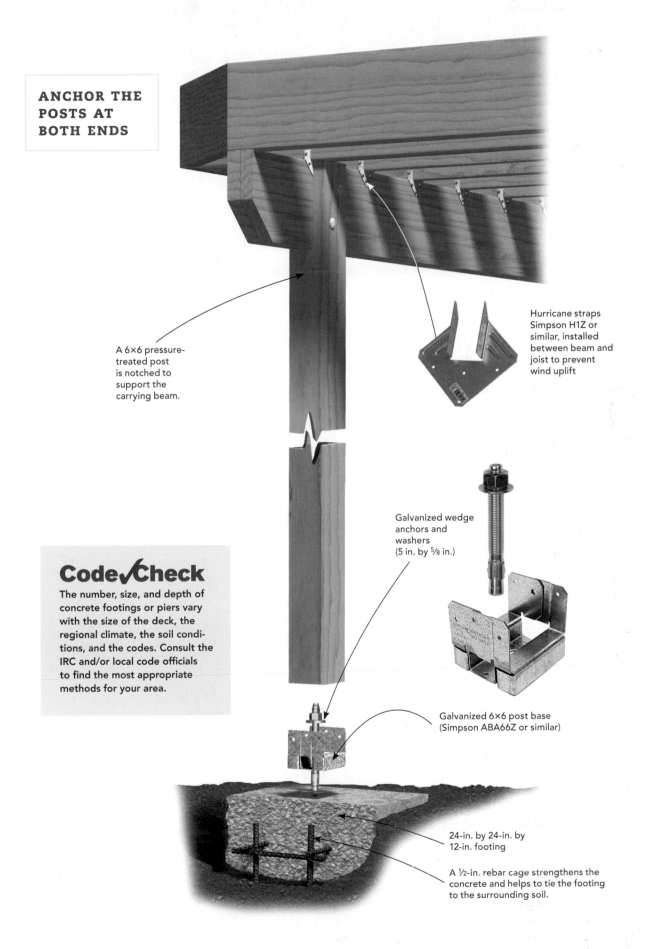

A 6×6 pressure-treated post is notched to support the carrying beam.

Hurricane straps Simpson H1Z or similar, installed between beam and joist to prevent wind uplift

Galvanized wedge anchors and washers (5 in. by ⅝ in.)

Code✓Check

The number, size, and depth of concrete footings or piers vary with the size of the deck, the regional climate, the soil conditions, and the codes. Consult the IRC and/or local code officials to find the most appropriate methods for your area.

Galvanized 6×6 post base (Simpson ABA66Z or similar)

24-in. by 24-in. by 12-in. footing

A ½-in. rebar cage strengthens the concrete and helps to tie the footing to the surrounding soil.

Install Rail Posts and Railings

Spaced at a maximum distance of 6 ft., the 4x4 railing posts are cut to a length of approximately 46¼ in. so that they span the distance between the bottom of the framing and the top of the railing (36 in. above the decking). On this job, the balustrade was made from 2x4s on edge with aluminum balusters (www.solutionsaluminum.com). Baluster cups and end brackets are from Deckorators (www.deckorators.com). A 2x6 railing cap strengthens the railing and adds a higher degree of detail.

MARK THE RAILING POST LOCATIONS. Using a cut-off, trace the post positions onto the deck so that the post will sit just inside the rim.

CUT THE HOLE. Drill pilot holes at the corners of the outline, and cut out the post hole with a jigsaw.

ATTACH THE POSTS. After plumbing up the posts in the hole, tack them in place, and then attach blocking with 6-in. construction screws.

STRENGTHEN RAILING POSTS WITH EXTRA BLOCKING

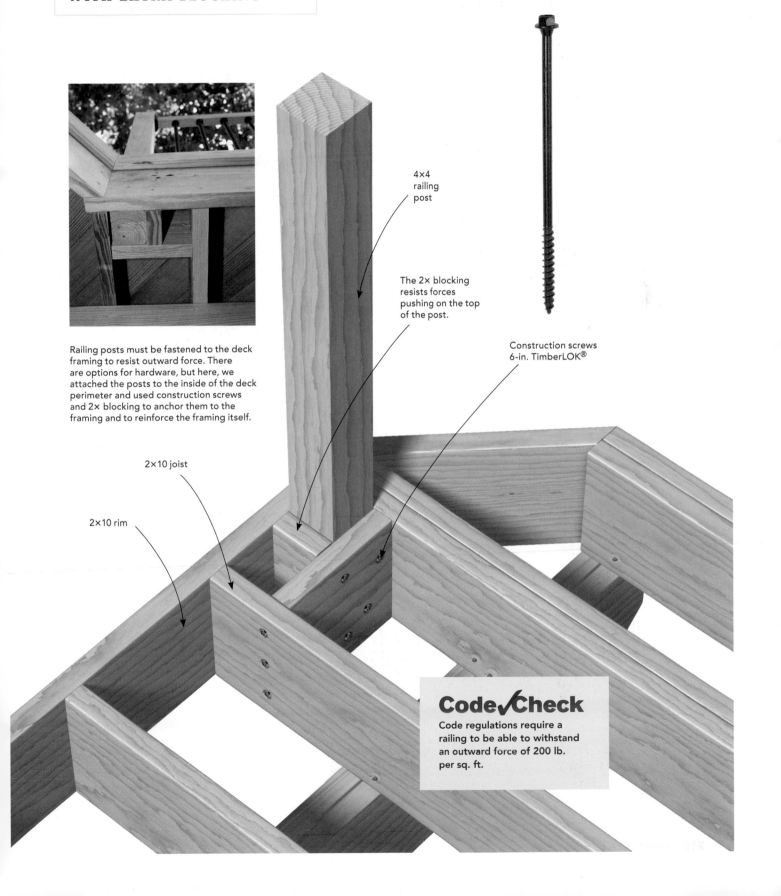

Railing posts must be fastened to the deck framing to resist outward force. There are options for hardware, but here, we attached the posts to the inside of the deck perimeter and used construction screws and 2× blocking to anchor them to the framing and to reinforce the framing itself.

4×4 railing post

The 2× blocking resists forces pushing on the top of the post.

Construction screws 6-in. TimberLOK®

2×10 joist

2×10 rim

Code✓Check
Code regulations require a railing to be able to withstand an outward force of 200 lb. per sq. ft.

COMPLY WITH THE CODE.
The IRC dictates that
guardrails 36 in. or higher be
installed on all decks that are
30 in. or more off the ground
and that the space between
balusters be less than 4 in.

CENTER THE BALUSTER CUPS. Screw down the cups to the rails in pairs so that the balusters have the same spacing on the top and on the bottom.

CONNECT RAILINGS TO POSTS WITH BRACKETS. After the balustrade is assembled, screw brackets onto the railing ends. Then screw the brackets from the opposite side onto the posts to attach the assembly.

TIE EVERYTHING TOGETHER. Railing caps made from 2×6s connect each of the posts and add strength to the balustrade. An ogee profile routed onto the edges gives the rail a finished look.

Frame the Stairs: Upper Section

Deck stairs should be situated so that they create practical traffic and egress patterns. I like to design stair locations so that the foot traffic from the house to the stairs doesn't interfere with the prime deck territory along the outer rail. Placing the stairs at a right angle from the house keeps them from interfering with views from below the deck.

We build stairs from the top down. First, we hang the stringers from the upper landing. After building the lower landing to the correct height, we build the two-tread run that connects the landing to the concrete pad at the base of the stairs. Like framing a deck on temporary posts and then locating the footings, building stairs this way takes some getting used to, but in the long run, it creates fewer errors.

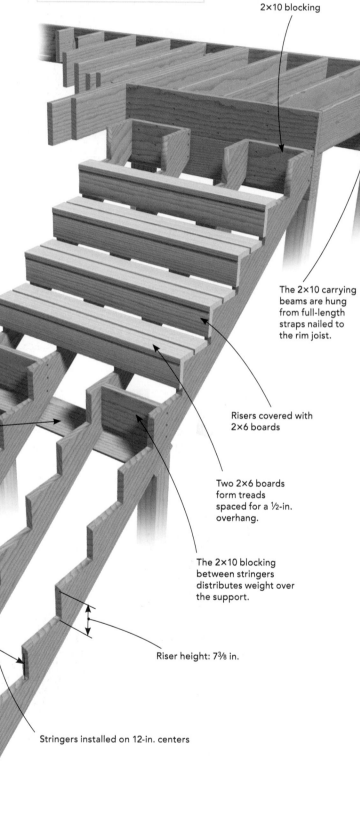

FRAMING THE UPPER STAIRS

2×10 blocking

The 2×10 carrying beams are hung from full-length straps nailed to the rim joist.

Risers covered with 2×6 boards

Two 2×6 boards form treads spaced for a ½-in. overhang.

The 2×10 blocking between stringers distributes weight over the support.

Riser height: 7⅜ in.

Midcarriage support

2×12 stringers

Overall width of staircase: 48 in.

Stringers installed on 12-in. centers

LAY OUT THE FIRST STRINGER. After calculating the rise and run of the top section of stairs, attach brass stair gauges to a framing square. Referenced from the top of the 2×12 stringer stock, the square is repeatedly traced over the length of the run.

Code✓Check

The maximum recommended height for deck-stair risers is 7¾ in., according to the IRC, which dictates other limits as well with regard to deck-stair construction. Be sure to consult the code or your local code official before designing stairs.

USE THE FIRST STRINGER AS A PATTERN. Because the first stringer is used to lay out the remaining stringers, the cuts should be accurate. With a circular saw, cut to the intersection of the tread and riser lines, then finish the cut with a jigsaw or a reciprocating saw.

HANG THE FIRST STRINGER.
After marking a level line on
the upper header, toenail the
first stringer into place, and
tack it to a temporary post
at midspan to keep it at the
correct elevation.

TIE THE LOWER ENDS.
After attaching the two
outside stringers, con-
nect their lower ends
with a 2×8, then add the
middle stringers.
The 2×8 forms
one side of the
lower landing.

**KEEP THINGS IN
PLACE.** Although the
next step is to frame
the lower landing, it's
a good idea to install
a couple of treads and
risers at the bottom
of the run to keep the
stringers from twist-
ing. Note the space
left for decking above
the 2×8 cleat.

Frame the Stairs: Lower Section

When the upper portion of the stairs has been framed and braced, we locate, dig, and pour the lower landing's post footings. Placed on the footings, short 6x6 posts are notched to support doubled 2x8 beams that in turn support the landing's frame. After the landing is framed, we know the exact position and height of the concrete pad that anchors the last stair carriage. Once the pad is set, we can complete the stairs.

ESTABLISH THE LOWER LANDING. When the upper stair run has been leveled and plumbed, locate and pour pads for four 6×6 posts. Notch each pair of posts for a doubled 2×8 carrying beam, which will support the landing frame.

BUILD THE LANDING IN PLACE. With a pair of carrying beams in place, the landing box can be framed. Note the clipped corner detail and 12-in.-on-center framing. Like the deck above, the landings are decked with a diagonal pattern.

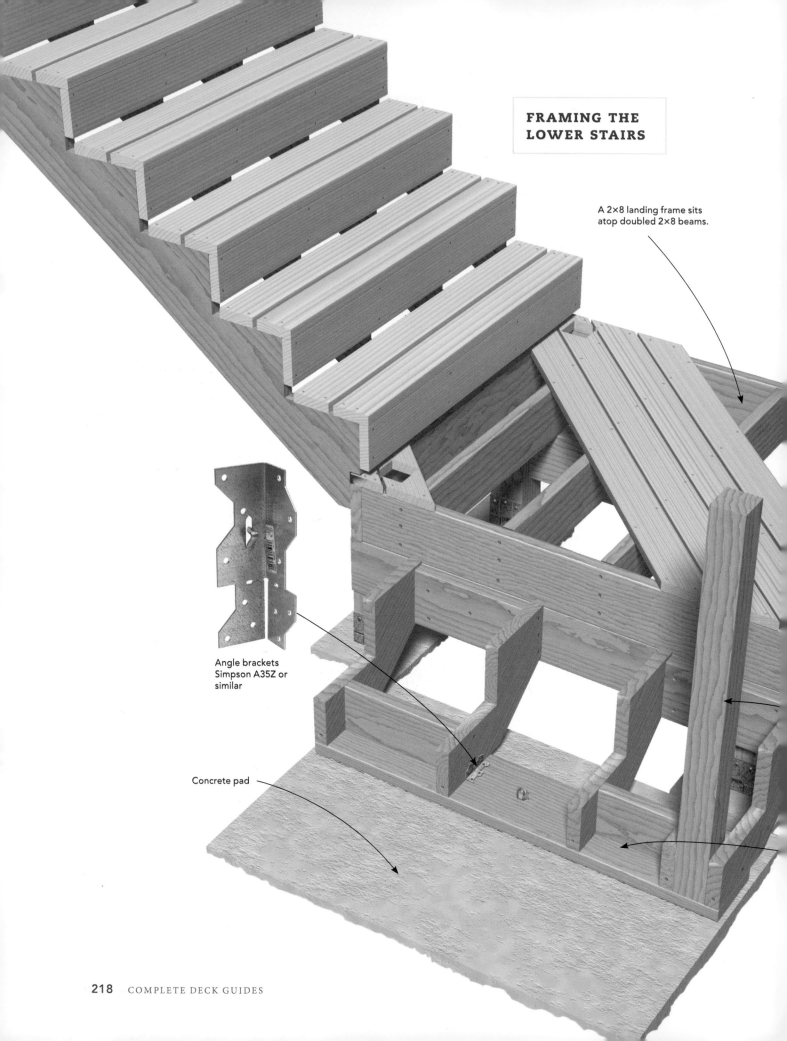

A 2×8 landing frame sits
atop doubled 2×8 beams.

Angle brackets
Simpson A35Z or
similar

Concrete pad

COMPLETE THE BOX. After the lower stair landing's perimeter is complete, it's a good time to install the interior blocking that supports the railing posts at each corner.

6×6 posts notched to support beams

A LEVEL FORM IS CRITICAL. A concrete pad is formed to terminate the two-tread run from the landing above. After setting and filling the form, screed the concrete flush with the top of the form, and trowel it smooth.

The 4×4 railing posts are nailed to stringers and reinforced with angle brackets.

FRAME THE STAIRS. Once the pad has cured, the stairs from the landing can be built. Attach the short stringers to a 2× nailer bolted to the pad. Blocking between the outer stringers supports the posts.

2×6 pressure-treated sleeper

A Grade-Level Deck with a Decorative Border

BY MIKE GUERTIN

For this year's whole-deck project, *Fine Homebuilding* asked me to participate in a cooperative effort to add a new deck to their Project House. Maryland-based contractor Clemens Jellema contributed a design for a compact, grade-level deck (see p. 35). I revised his plans to include some of the details that I wanted for this project, such as an integral rim beam, post-to-frame attachment, and robust ledger flashing.

Built with pressure-treated framing and composite decking, this deck doesn't have a railing (none are required for decks less than 30 in. above grade) but still offers lots of fundamental, code-compliant details that can be applied to other decks. You'll also find plenty of valuable tricks, such as site-made footing forms, improved ledger details, and tips on working with composite decking material.

It took me a day to sketch the details, but extra planning paid off by improving my efficiency on the project. Project House editor Justin Fink provided hands-on assistance.

Adjust the Deck's Width

Every deck, even one with a simple plan, still has plenty of elements that must be worked through before it can be built. Here, the plans show framing

DIAL IN THE DECK WIDTH. The decking width needs to be exact so that the perimeter boards have a consistent overhang. Lay out a series of deck boards, and insert hidden fasteners as spacers between them. Once they're snugged together, measure and extrapolate how many full-width boards will come closest to the target deck width.

dimensions of 16 ft. by 12 ft., but they don't include details for things like decking, perimeter skirting, and trim. The composite decking chosen for the project uses a hidden-fastener system that locks into edge slots on the boards. I had to resize the deck frame slightly so that I could build with full-size decking and trim boards, rather than have to rip everything to size and then screw and plug the ripped boards.

Locate and Dig Footings

To locate the footings that support the outside of the deck, and also the footing for the stairs, I started by locating the ledger on the house. Then I set up a stringline at the location of the deck frame's outermost face. Using the Pythagorean theorem, I created perpendicular lines from the ends of the ledger to the stringline. This established the deck's perimeter, which I needed to lay out and dig the footings.

I calculated the load each footing would carry and determined the necessary size (see "Sizing

LAYING OUT THE DECK

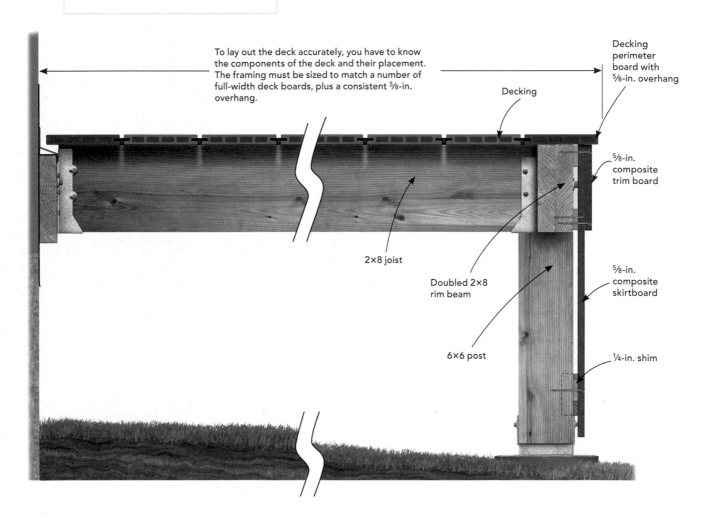

To lay out the deck accurately, you have to know the components of the deck and their placement. The framing must be sized to match a number of full-width deck boards, plus a consistent ⅝-in. overhang.

Decking

Decking perimeter board with ⅝-in. overhang

⅝-in. composite trim board

2×8 joist

Doubled 2×8 rim beam

⅝-in. composite skirtboard

6×6 post

¼-in. shim

Deck Footings," pp. 72–79). However, instead of digging 13-in.-dia. holes for the outboard footings and a 16-in.-dia. hole for the middle (which carries a greater load than the outboard footings), I dug 10-in.-dia. holes and flared the holes' bottoms. Plastic bags attached to cardboard form tubes allowed the concrete to fill the holes and create spread footings. The required footing depth in this jurisdiction is 42 in.

After digging the holes and pouring concrete into our modified footing tubes, we placed the anchor bolts and checked their locations with the stringline. Once everything was set, we graded the soil from the footing holes to establish a positive slope away from the house. This was the last chance to adjust the grade beneath the low deck before we started to erect the frame. After raking the footing spoils smooth, we compacted them with a tamper.

STRINGLINE DEFINES THE OUTSIDE EDGE OF THE DECK. Set a string between batter boards, and adjust it to match the width of the deck. Diagonal measurements pulled from the ends of the ledger location give the precise outside corners, which in turn determine the footing locations.

AN EASY JOB. With only three footings to dig, it doesn't make sense to rent a gas-powered auger. Ten-in.-dia. holes go pretty quickly with post-hole diggers and a digging bar. Widen out the last 12 in. of footing depth to the width of the spread footings.

ECONOMICAL SPREAD-FOOTING. Tape garbage bags to the bottom of 30-in.-long, 10-in.-dia. cardboard footing tubes. When filled with concrete, the bags balloon into the bottom of the holes to a width greater than the tube.

LOCATING THE FOOTINGS

These 12-in.-deep footings support the stairs. They were sized to match the box that frames the bottom steps (p. 233).

THE FOOTINGS MUST BE LOCATED DIRECTLY BELOW THE BEAM. After placing the bags and tubes, pour enough concrete to fill the bags up to the cardboard tubes. Then reset the string, align the tubes to the center of the beam, and backfill around the tubes.

SITE-MIXED CONCRETE. Mix concrete in a wheelbarrow-style mixer, then shovel it directly into each form. When all are filled, reset the string, and place the J-bolts in the wet mix directly below the string.

Length

Diagonal

Width

Concrete footings support the rim beam.

Using the Pythagorean theorem to find the outside corners, make sure the length squared (A^2) plus width squared (B^2) equals the diagonal squared (C^2).

Code✓Check

The number, size, and depth of concrete footings or piers vary with the size of the deck, the regional climate, the soil conditions, and the codes. Consult the IRC and/or local code officials to find the most appropriate methods for your area.

MARK AND DIG THE STAIR FOOTINGS. Use a 2× as a straightedge to mark the position of the stair footing pads. Dig square and flat holes to the dimensions of the stair frame. Form the top with 2× stock for even edges at the precise position of the stairs.

Install the Ledger

Even on a ground-level deck, the ledger is still an important detail that supports the deck at the house. The ledger must be flashed to prevent water from compromising the house structure. On this deck, we used LedgerLok® structural screws to attach the ledger, rather than the ½-in. bolts or lag screws prescribed in the code. The house's unfinished basement allowed for easy access to the floor framing in order to install the code-required lateral-load connectors (p. 235). I poked a screwdriver into the wood to see if there was any rot or insect damage. I also used a moisture meter to inspect the framing. It read 10%, confirming that the lumber was dry.

FLASHING KEEPS THE HOUSE DRY. After establishing a level top reference point, snap a chalkline that extends beyond the ends of the ledger. Apply a layer of self-adhering, self-sealing membrane to the wall before the ledger is attached.

FIND THE FRAMING. Remove a small piece of sheathing to find the exact locations of the mudsill and rim joist. Mark fastener heights on scrap ledger stock, align the bottom row with the middle of the mudsill, and then mark the top edge of the ledger.

ATTACH THE LEDGER. After installing the first layer of flashing, snap a chalkline on it to indicate the top of the ledger. Snap chalklines onto the ledger to indicate screw rows, then mark the screw and joist layouts. Fasten the ledger to the house at the chalkline with structural screws.

COUNTERFLASHING COMPLETES THE WATERPROOFING. After installing the ledger, apply another strip of self-adhering membrane over the top and down the face of the ledger by at least ½ in. To make installation easier, cut the membrane into 3-ft.- to 4-ft.-long pieces. Last, install rigid drip-cap flashing over the ledger.

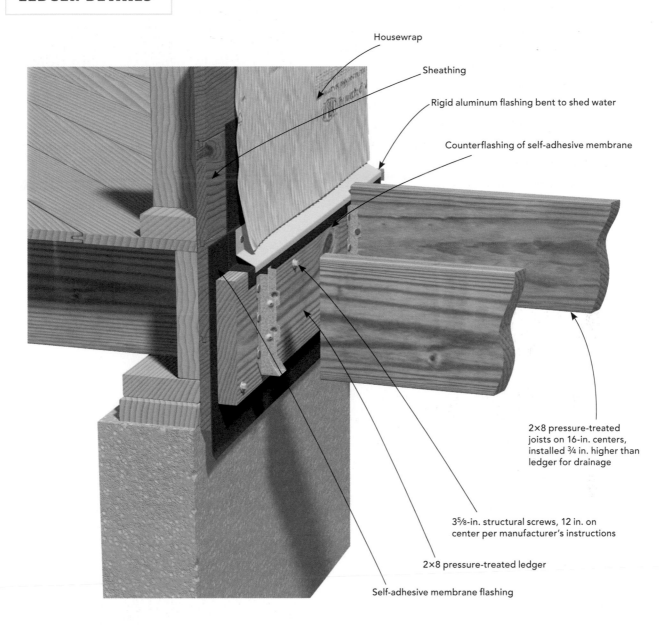

Housewrap

Sheathing

Rigid aluminum flashing bent to shed water

Counterflashing of self-adhesive membrane

2×8 pressure-treated joists on 16-in. centers, installed ¾ in. higher than ledger for drainage

3⅝-in. structural screws, 12 in. on center per manufacturer's instructions

2×8 pressure-treated ledger

Self-adhesive membrane flashing

Code✓Check

The 2012 IRC introduced changes that specify the placement of ½-in. bolts or lag screws through the deck ledger and the house rim joist. One effect of this is that ledgers can't be dropped one step below the house floor, a popular snow-country detail.

Set the Rim Beam

This deck is so close to the ground that a doubled rim beam is a better choice than are cantilevered joists over a beam, which would take up too much room below the deck. Supported by notched 6x6 posts and framed flush with the deck joists, the rim beam allows plenty of clearance between aboveground treated lumber and the soil, and it provides better air circulation. The next step in the framing process is to attach the posts and notch them.

LINE UP THE POST BASES. Once the concrete is set, reattach the layout line to the batter boards, bolt the post bases onto the footings, and align the bases to the stringline.

POST BLANKS MARKED IN PLACE. Cut the 6×6 posts to a long rough length, set them atop the post bases, plumb them up, and mark the beam seat cut precisely using a laser level and a square.

Bracing

AN EFFICIENT NOTCH. After fastening the posts to the bases, crosscut the seat with a circular saw. The plumb cut can be made with a handsaw, but careful use of a chainsaw makes quick work of the job.

Bracing

SET THE INNER RIM BEAM. With the notches cut, the newly exposed wood must be treated with a copper-based wood preservative such as copper napthenate. (Cuts in pressure-treated lumber need to be treated with preservative according to standard M4 of the American Wood Protection Association [AWPA].) Mark the joist layout onto the inner beam, set it on the post notches, and attach it at each post with a clamp (photo at left).

TEMPORARY BRACING. Until the outside joists are attached, it's a good idea to stabilize the beam with lengths of strapping screwed to the ledger and the beam.

Hang the Joists

Unlike larger designs, this deck has a straightforward arrangement of 2x8 joists on 16-in. centers that span between the ledger and the inner rim beam. With the rim in place, we installed the two outer joist hangers and joists, and then squared up the resulting box by comparing the diagonals. When the diagonals were equal, we clamped the rim to the posts. We then installed the joist hangers and joists on the ledger before nailing them to the rim. Each hanger is nailed with pneumatically driven 1½-in.-long joist-hanger nails. Three-in.-long framing-connector nails then are driven diagonally through the hanger and the joist and into the ledger or rim beam using a larger pneumatic nailer. After the joists were installed, we bolted the rim to the posts.

HANGING THE JOISTS

SPECIAL CONNECTORS FOR CORNERS

FLANGED HANGERS AREN'T APPROVED for use on outside corners. Instead, use concealed-flange joist hangers (Simpson LUC26Z or similar) attached with structural screws to the rim or ledger.

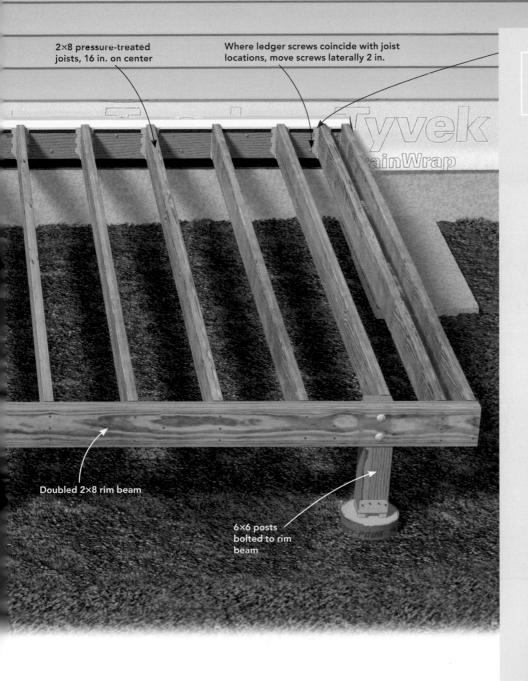

2×8 pressure-treated joists, 16 in. on center

Where ledger screws coincide with joist locations, move screws laterally 2 in.

Doubled 2×8 rim beam

6×6 posts bolted to rim beam

PRODUCTION-STYLE JOIST HANGERS

THE JOISTS' WIDTH VARIED BY LESS THAN 1/8 IN., so all the joist hangers on the ledger were set at the same level using a T-shaped jig. The leg of the jig is the same width as the joists, and the bottom registers the hangers at the same level. Each joist hanger is held onto the jig with a spring-steel clamp (Joist Clip; www.fastcap.com) and nailed to the ledger.

MAKE SURE THE BOX IS SQUARE. After the outermost joists are installed, compare the diagonal measurements. If they aren't equal, unclamp the rim beam, and adjust its position until the measurements are the same.

LOCK THE POSTS INTO PLACE. Once the box is squared, lock it in place with a diagonal piece of strapping screwed to the frame at each end. Next, loosen the clamps, recheck the posts for plumb, and retighten the clamps.

NAIL THE JOISTS IN PLACE. Mark the crowned side of each joist, orient the joist crown up, and drop it into its hanger on the ledger end. On the other end, hold the joists flush to the top of the rim, and through-nail them.

ADD THE SECOND RIM LAYER. After all the joists are nailed, align the second rim flush to the top of the first, and nail it off. Fasten the posts to the doubled rim with ThruLOK® bolts, and install the hangers.

Build the Stairs

With the joists installed, the next phase of framing dealt with stairs, installing blocking for benches and the half-wall, and attaching lateral-load hardware. The main stairs are a focal point of the deck and wrap 5 ft. around one outside corner, so they had to look good. I had two framing options for the stairs: stacked boxes or cut stringers.

Stacked boxes made more sense for this project because they're faster to frame, they're self-supporting, and they provide a more stable and straight base for precise trim. Box frames also make the most sense for short, wide stairs. For more than three risers, box-stair frames aren't as efficient a choice because they use more lumber than cut stringers.

SOLID SUPPORT. The decking manufacturer calls for closer support spacing (12 in. on center) when decking is used for treads. Some manufacturers call for supports to be as close as 8 in. on center.

STACK BOXES FOR STABILITY. Build the bottom box frame twice as wide as the top. Diagonal blocking at the corners provides nailing for the mitered treads. This design locks the boxes together so that the outside corner is less likely to open up over time. Tie the boxes together and to the deck frame with 1× straps that match the thickness of the deck skirt, then push the boxes into place.

BLOCKING AND POSTS FOR BENCH SEATS. Nail 2×8 blocks to support the posts on the deck perimeter. Clamp a jig made from 1x to each post to set it to a consistent height. After tack-nailing the posts to the blocks, check for plumb, and attach the posts with through bolts, such as the FastenMaster® ThruLOK bolts used here.

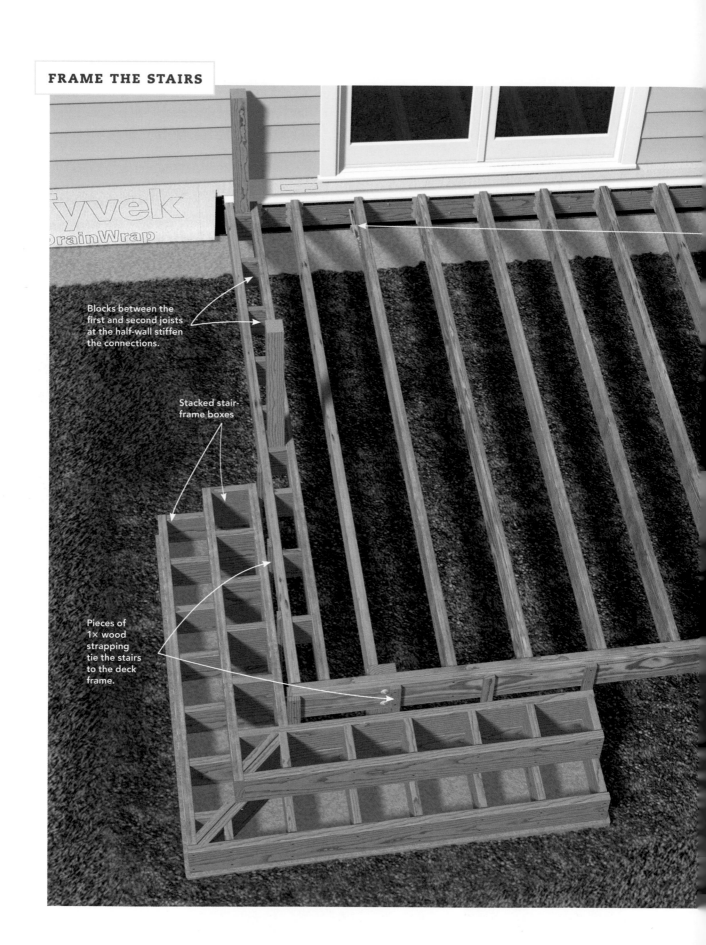

Blocks between the first and second joists at the half-wall stiffen the connections.

Stacked stair-frame boxes

Pieces of 1× wood strapping tie the stairs to the deck frame.

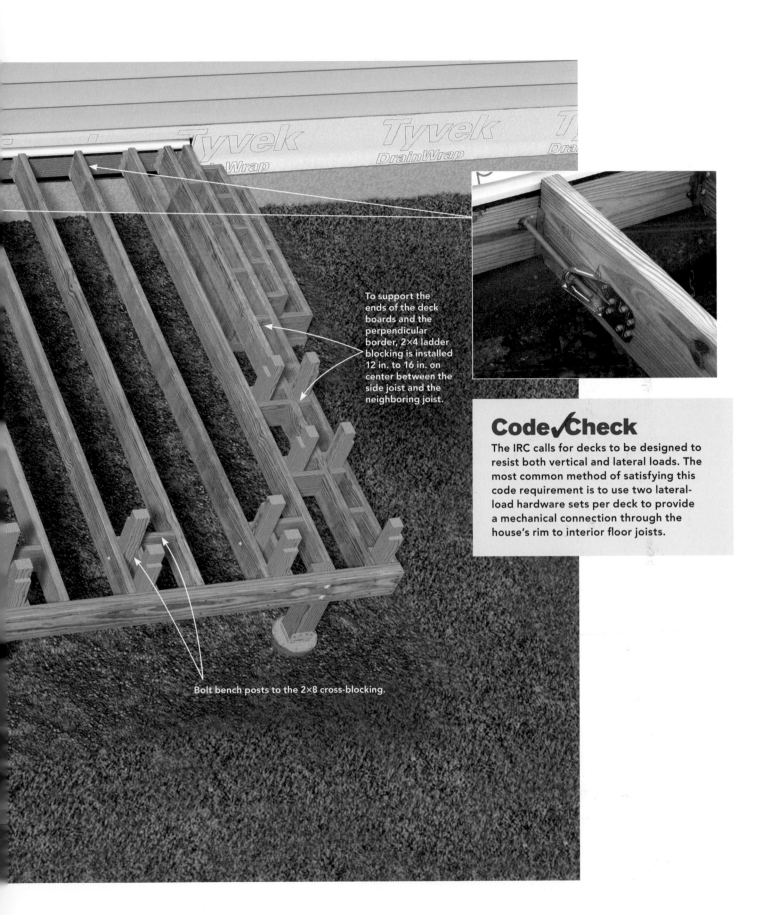

To support the ends of the deck boards and the perpendicular border, 2×4 ladder blocking is installed 12 in. to 16 in. on center between the side joist and the neighboring joist.

Code✓Check

The IRC calls for decks to be designed to resist both vertical and lateral loads. The most common method of satisfying this code requirement is to use two lateral-load hardware sets per deck to provide a mechanical connection through the house's rim to interior floor joists.

Bolt bench posts to the 2×8 cross-blocking.

Install the Decking with Hidden Fasteners

We used composite decking from GeoLam® (www. geolaminc.com) for this job. I generally order decking in lengths that minimize waste for a given deck size. Unfortunately, the deck width of 16 ft. was set before the decking was ordered, and it was only available in 12-ft. lengths. This left us two options: install full-length boards with a 4-ft. piece alternating left and right, or use two 8-ft. pieces cut from full-length boards. To minimize waste, and for looks, we used the former option.

A single-board border encloses the field decking. We installed the border first, then filled in the center. We placed the first board ½ in. away from the house to allow water to drain.

The decking has grooved edges. To avoid showing a groove, we had to rip one edge of the darker boards used along the perimeter. We fastened the field boards with the manufacturer's biscuit-style hidden fastening system, and screwed and plugged the edge boards.

To keep the decking parallel, we measured the distance from the last board to the rim beam every few courses. It's also a good idea to eyeball the decking to keep it straight.

DECKING ANATOMY. This biscuit-style fastener is screwed to the joist and engages the grooves of the adjacent boards. Leave the screws a little loose so that the leading edge of the fasteners easily engages the groove of the next deck board. After the following board is placed, the fastener screws can be tightened. Note the deck board's hollow structure, which adds strength without excess weight.

SLOTTED SCREW HOLES PERMIT MOVEMENT. Drill ⅛-in. pilot holes 16 in. apart along the border decking, then elongate the holes from the underside with a drywall spiral cutter. Cut the slots progressively longer (up to ¼ in.) toward the ends of the boards. Do not slot the center hole on each board.

GAP THE DECKING IN COLD WEATHER

COMPOSITE MATERIAL EXPANDS AND CONTRACTS along the length of the board with temperature changes. To accommodate this seasonal movement, install decking with end gaps according to the manufacturer's instructions. Here, we left ¼-in. gaps at butts, around posts, and at miters. In warm weather, install without gaps.

CAP THE JOISTS FOR LONG-TERM PERFORMANCE. To shed water, cap all single joists with 3-in. staple-on plastic tape, and the doubled rim beam with a 6-in. tape. This reduces the amount of water that can wick into splits in the wood where preservative may not have penetrated or be as fully concentrated.

THE OTHER HIDDEN FASTENER. Unlike the field decking, the border can't be attached with hidden fasteners and must be face-screwed through pilot holes that are then plugged.

Dress Up the Perimeter

Our design called for the perimeter of the deck to be enclosed by a skirt made from ⅝-in.-thick composite trim boards installed vertically. To create nailing for the skirt, blocking hangs from the side joist.

SKIRT INSTALLATION AT SIDE OF DECK

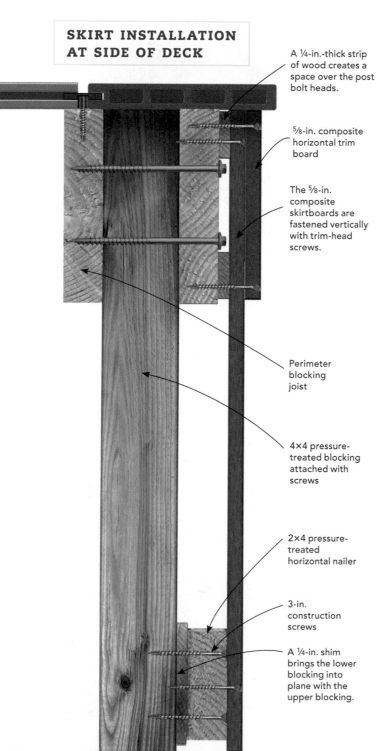

A ¼-in.-thick strip of wood creates a space over the post bolt heads.

⅝-in. composite horizontal trim board

The ⅝-in. composite skirtboards are fastened vertically with trim-head screws.

Perimeter blocking joist

4×4 pressure-treated blocking attached with screws

2×4 pressure-treated horizontal nailer

3-in. construction screws

A ¼-in. shim brings the lower blocking into plane with the upper blocking.

APPEARANCES MATTER HERE. To keep a consistent gap between each board, use a trim-head screw as a spacer at the top and bottom. Cut the skirtboards to reach from the top of the deck frame to grade, which can vary around the deck.

Finish the Stairs

The horizontal trim board that runs across the top of the skirt also serves as the top stair riser, so this was a good time to install the stair risers and treads, which feature the same border treatment as the main deck.

TRIM BOARD HIDES TOP SCREWS. The skirt's top screws are covered by the horizontal trim board, which becomes the top riser at the stairs. The seamless transition results from the vertical 1× used to hang the stair boxes, which is on the same plane as the skirtboards.

KEEPING FASTENERS HIDDEN. Install the tread boards with the same attention to movement as with the deck boards. At the riser, special half-clips anchor the inboard side of the tread.

NEATNESS COUNTS. Drill screw holes 16 in. on center along the length of the outer boards. Leaving outside miters open ¼ in. permits the boards to expand in summer heat.

Build a Bench

Built-in seating on a deck not only defines the perimeter of the deck, but it also provides a great place for folks to relax. We used the same decking, trim materials, and border pattern so that the bench would blend in with the rest of the deck.

A DECK BENCH

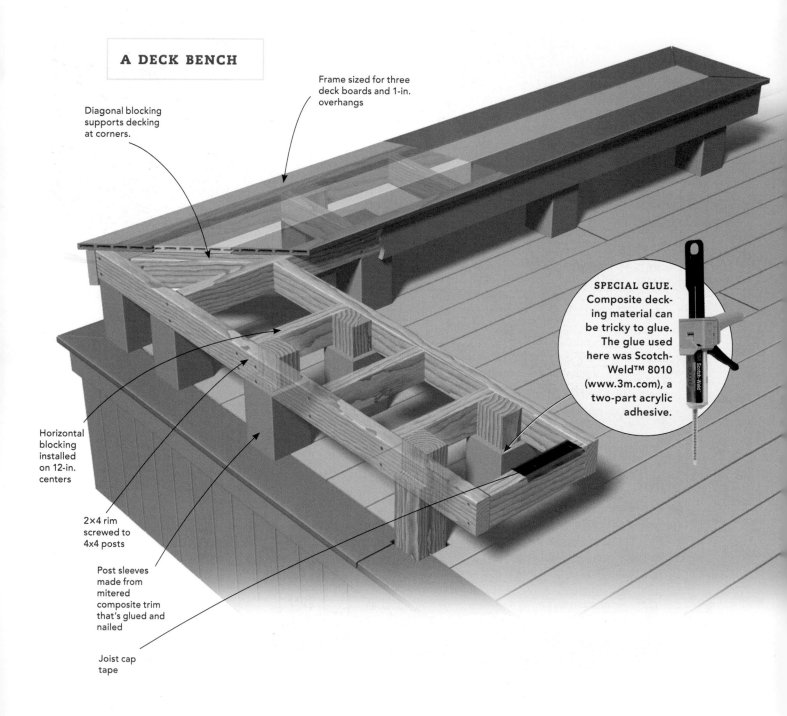

Frame sized for three deck boards and 1-in. overhangs

Diagonal blocking supports decking at corners.

Horizontal blocking installed on 12-in. centers

2×4 rim screwed to 4x4 posts

Post sleeves made from mitered composite trim that's glued and nailed

Joist cap tape

SPECIAL GLUE. Composite decking material can be tricky to glue. The glue used here was Scotch-Weld™ 8010 (www.3m.com), a two-part acrylic adhesive.

PLACE POST SLEEVES BEFORE INSTALLING THE BENCH FRAME. Rip trim stock with a 45° bevel, then assemble sleeves with two-part acrylic adhesive and stainless-steel micropins.

USE PLACEHOLDERS. To locate the first board on the seat, space all three boards with loose deck clips to produce the appropriate overhang. Set the clips, drill pilot holes along the outside, drive in the screws, and plug the holes.

TRIM THE EDGES. Cover the edge of the 2×4 frame with trim ripped to 4 in. wide and fastened with color-matched trim-head screws.

Raise the Half-Wall

A half-wall creates privacy off the deck for a grill, recycling bin, or hose reel. Drill pilot holes before screwing together the 2x2 frame. After attaching ½-in. pressure-treated plywood on one side, apply joist tape where the joints for the vertical boards will be. Space boards ⅛ in. apart, and fasten with color-matched stainless-steel screws.

A SIMPLE BASE. Size a 2×2 frame to fit between the two trimmed-out posts, but make it 3 in. shorter than the post height to create a gap at the bottom.

BUILD A HALF-WALL

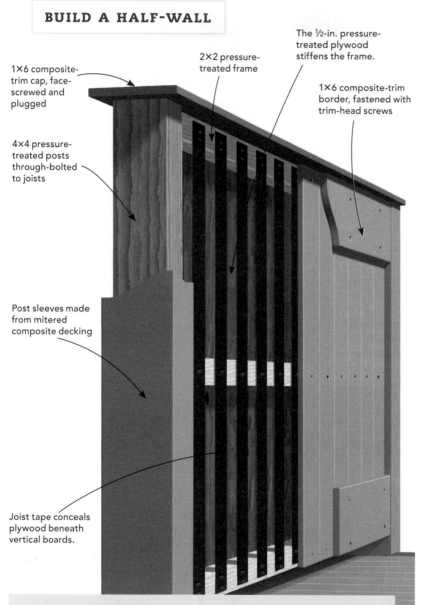

1×6 composite-trim cap, face-screwed and plugged

4×4 pressure-treated posts through-bolted to joists

Post sleeves made from mitered composite decking

Joist tape conceals plywood beneath vertical boards.

2×2 pressure-treated frame

The ½-in. pressure-treated plywood stiffens the frame.

1×6 composite-trim border, fastened with trim-head screws

SCREW THE PANEL TO THE POSTS. Raise the half-clad panel on top of 3-in. spacer blocks, and align it ½ in. from the post cover edges. Drive screws through the 2×2s into the posts to secure the panel. Cover the unclad side with black tape, and install vertical trim boards.

FINISH WITH TRIM. Screw the same trim material used to clad the wall to the top and bottom of the panel. For contrast, cap the top with one of the darker trim boards.

Code✓Check

Decks that are higher than 30 in. off the ground must have guardrails with a top rail at least 36 in. high. Some jurisdictions measure the guard height from the surface of built-in seating; others measure off the deck surface. Check to see how your local building department applies the code.

Add a Garden to the Deck with Planters

Custom-built planter boxes are easy to make from leftover materials. Our boxes were designed to sit on each end of the bench seats, but they could be placed anywhere. Rather than build them into the structure, we built them freestanding so they could be moved off the deck for periodic cleaning and filling. Lined with a waterproof membrane, the planters feature a drain that prevents root rot.

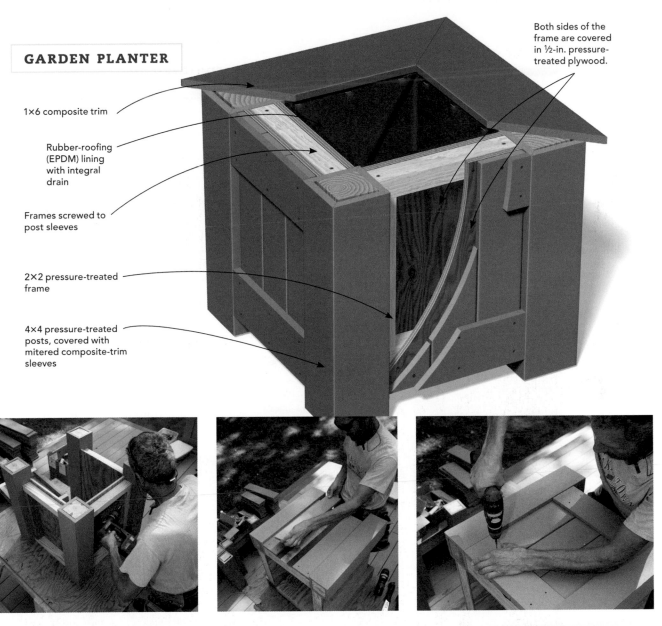

GARDEN PLANTER

Both sides of the frame are covered in ½-in. pressure-treated plywood.

1×6 composite trim

Rubber-roofing (EPDM) lining with integral drain

Frames screwed to post sleeves

2×2 pressure-treated frame

4×4 pressure-treated posts, covered with mitered composite-trim sleeves

A SOLID FRAMEWORK. As a smaller version of the half-wall construction, the first stage of the planters is built with panels made from 2×2s and plywood that are screwed to corner posts. After assembling the box, add a second layer of plywood to the outside of the frame.

FIRST LAYER OF TRIM. Clad the exterior of each panel with trim boards backed with strips of joist tape at gap locations. Fasten the boards with trim-head screws.

BOX THE PANEL. Apply horizontal trim boards across the top and bottom of each panel. The horizontals and the post sides are in the same plane and complete the frame.

IT'S A ONE-PIECE LINER. Made from rubber roofing material (EPDM), the liner is folded into the planter's interior. Measure and mark the membrane carefully so that there's coverage top to bottom.

RUBBER ORIGAMI. Fold the membrane in half, then push it down into the planter.

FOLD THE CORNERS. With the membrane covering the bottom, fold the corners so that the membrane forms a bucket shape.

ATTACH THE CORNERS. While holding each corner fold, tack it to the top of the panel's interior with staples or cap staples.

TRIM THE TOP. When all four corners are fixed in place, use a sharp knife to cut away excess material along the top edge.

INSTALL THE DRAIN. Drill a hole into the plywood bottom just enough to mark the membrane. From the inside, cut a small hole in the membrane and push a length of vinyl tubing through it. From the other side, pull it out so that a ¼-in. stub remains exposed inside on the planter floor.

Chris Ahrens is a custom carpenter in Osterville, Mass.

Paul DeGroot (www.degrootarchitect.com) is an architect who designs custom homes and additions in Austin, Texas.

Justin Fink is the *Fine Homebuilding* Project House Editor.

Scott Gibson, a contributing writer to *Fine Homebuilding*, lives in southern Maine. He also contributed to the "Choosing the Best Deck Finish" chapter.

David Grandpré, P.E., SECB, is a structural engineer with CA Pretzer Associates in Cranston, R.I. He specializes in investigating damaged buildings.

Jim Grant is an outdoor wood-finishing expert from San Diego.

Mike Guertin, the editorial adviser to *Fine Homebuilding*, is a builder and remodeler in East Greenwich, R.I.

Russell Hamlet is a principal at Studio Hamlet Architects (www.studiohamlet.com), an innovative and environmentally focused architecture firm based on Bainbridge Island, Wash.

Clemens Jellema is president of Fine Decks Inc. in Calvert County, Md.

Kim Katwijk is president of Deck Builders Inc. (www.artistryindecks.com) in Olympia, Wash. He and his wife, Linda, write frequently on construction topics.

Jefferson Kolle is a freelance writer living in Bethel, Conn.

Michael Maines (www.michaelmaines.com) is a residential designer in Palermo, Maine.

Glenn Mathewson is a former tradesman/contractor who has served Westminster, Colo., as an inspector and plan reviewer for over ten years. He is a professional speaker on building codes and has authored over 60 articles as well as the book *Deck Construction* based on the 2009 IRC, published by ICC. He is an advisor to the North American Deck and Railing Association and the president of BuildingCodeCollege.com.

Patrick McCombe is a *Fine Homebuilding* associate editor.

Charles Miller, an editor at large for *Fine Homebuilding*, lives in California.

Bobby Parks is the founder and former owner of Peachtree Decks and Porches in Alpharetta, Ga. He now owns BP Consulting and Design LLC (bpconsultinganddesign.com).

Robert Shaw owns Colorado Decks and Framing in Colorado Springs, Colo. (www.mysteeldeck.com).

Debra Judge Silber is the *Fine Homebuilding* design editor.

Emanuel A. Silva owns Silva Lightning Builders in North Andover, Mass.

CREDITS

All photos are courtesy of *Fine Home-building* magazine © The Taunton Press, Inc., except as noted below.

The articles in this book appeared in the following issues of *Fine Home-building*:

pp. 5–13: Buyers Guide: A Plank for Every Deck by Scott Gibson, Decks & Outdoor Projects issue (Spring 2014). Photos by Rodney Diaz, except for photo p. 6 courtesy of Advantage Lumber, photo p. 7 by JohnClemmer.net, photo p. 8 courtesy of Royal Building Products, photo p. 10 courtesy of Trex, top photo p. 12 courtesy of NyloBoard, and bottom photo p. 12 courtesy of Nexan Building Products.

pp. 14–20: Buyer's Guide to Deck Hardware by Patrick McCombe, Decks & Outdoor Projects issue (Spring 2013). Photos by Rodney Diaz and Dan Thornton. Drawings by Christopher Mills.

pp. 21-25: Choosing the Best Deck Finish by Justin Fink, issue 228. Photos by Rodney Diaz, except for photo p. 21 courtesy of PPG.

pp. 27–30: Design a Better Deck by Charles Miller, issue 229. Photos courtesy of www.artistryindecks.com, except for photo p. 28 by Brian Pontolilo.

pp. 31–34: Drawing Board: Improve Your Deck's View by Russell Hamlet, issue 212. Drawings by Russell Hamlet.

pp. 35–38: Drawing Board: Designing a Small but Elegant Deck by Clemens Jellema, issue 242. Drawings by Clemens Jellema.

pp. 39–41: Drawing Board: A Porch with a Roof Deck by Michael Maines, issue 246. Drawings by Michael Maines.

pp. 42–50: Bending Decking for Decorative Inlays by Kim Katwijk, issue 220. Photos courtesy of Kim Katwijk, except for photos pp. 45–47, and photo p. 49 courtesy of Heatcon Inc., Seattle. Drawings courtesy of Kim Katwijk.

pp. 51–56: Bright Ideas for a Well-Lit Deck by Glenn Mathewson, Decks & Outdoor Projects issue (Spring 2014). Left photo p. 51 by Anice Hoachlander, center photo p. 51 and right photo p. 53 courtesy of Hayneedle.com, right photo p. 51 courtesy of Fiberon, left photo p. 52 and top photo p. 55 courtesy of Hinkley Lighting, right photo p. 52 and left photo p. 54 courtesy of Trex, left photo p. 53 courtesy of Kichler Lighting, right photo p. 54 courtesy of the Outdoor Great Room Company, bottom photo p. 55 courtesy of Glenn Mathewson,

top photo p. 56 courtesy of Deckorators, and bottom photo p. 56 courtesy of CertainTeed. Drawings by John Hartman.

pp. 57–64: A Homeowner's Guide to Deck Permits by Glenn Mathewson, Decks & Outdoor Projects issue (Spring 2015). Drawings by Jacqueline Rogers.

pp. 66–68: Deck Loads by David Granpre, issue 228. Drawings by Christopher Mills.

pp. 69–71: Frost Heave by Deb Silber, issue 233. Drawings by Christopher Mills, except for the inset drawing p. 70 courtesy of Acta Materialia.

pp. 72–79: Sizing Deck Footings by Mike Guertin, issue 245. Photos by Dan Thornton, except for photo p. 72 by John Ross, photo of flat-form p. 77 by Scott Phillips, center hardware photos p. 77 courtesy of Hilti, top photo p. 79 by Mike Guertin, center photo p. 79 courtesy of Pin Foundations, and bottom photo p. 79 courtesy of Greg DiBernardo. Drawings by Christopher Mills.

pp. 80–82: Deck Footings Done Right by Mike Guertin, issue 236. Photos by Dan Thornton. Drawings by Don Mannes.

pp. 83–90: Framing a Grade-Level Deck by Chris Ahrens, issue 249. Photos by Charles Bickford, except for top photo p. 84 by Nat Rea. Drawings by Vince Babak.

pp. 91–100: Framing a Deck with Steel by Robert Shaw, issue 244. Photos by Andy Engel, except for the photo p. 91 by Ron Ruscio. Drawings by Trevor Johnston.

pp. 101–108: Top 10 Deck-Building Mistakes by Glenn Mathewson, issue 230. Photos by Glenn Mathewson, except for photo p. 101 courtesy of Woody Roberts and left photo p. 106 and left photo p. 107 by Brian Pontolilo. Drawings by Dan Thornton.

pp. 109–116: Make an Old Deck Safe by Mike Guertin, issue 238. Photos by Charles Bickford, except for the photo p. 109 by Mike Guertin. Drawing by Dan Thornton.

pp. 118–125: Decks That Stand Up to Wildfire by Paul DeGroot, Decks & Outdoor Projects issue (Spring 2014). Photo p. 119 AP/Wide World Photos. Photo p. 120 courtesy of Stephen Quarles. Drawings by Don Mannes.

pp. 126–129: Master Carpenter: Site-built deck drainage by Mike Guertin, issue 220. Photos by Charles Bickford, except for photo p. 126, bottom photo p. 128, and photos p. 129 by Mike Guertin.

pp. 130–137: Decking over a Roof by Emanuel Silva, issue 246. Photos by Andy Engel. Drawings by John Hartman.

pp. 138–145: Deck Refinishing by Jim Grant, issue 237. Photos by Patrick McCombe.

pp. 147–155: Manufactured Railing Systems by Jefferson Kolle, Decks & Outdoor Projects issue (Spring 2014). Photos courtesy of the manufacturers.

pp. 156–163: Railing Retrofit by Mike Guertin, issue 234. Photos courtesy of Mike Guertin, except for bottom photos p. 157 by Rodney Diaz. Drawings by Rodney Diaz.

pp. 164–168: 2 Ideas for Custom Railings by Debra Silber, issue 221. Left photo p. 164 and photo p. 165 courtesy of Clemens Jellema. Right photo p. 164 and photo p. 167 by Michael Sanford. Drawings by Don Mannes.

pp. 169–176: Mounting Deck Stairs by Mike Guertin, Decks & Outdoor Projects issue (Spring 2014). Process photos by Andy Engel. Product photos by Dan Thornton.

pp. 178–198: Complete Deck Guide by Clemens Jellema, Decks & Outdoor Projects issue (Spring 2013). Photos by Charles Bickford, except for photo p. 178 and top photo p. 198 by Anice Hoachlander, bottom right photo p. 188 and photo p. 191 by Justin Fink, photos p. 189, photo p. 190, photos pp. 194-196, and bottom photo p. 198 by Clemens Jellema. Drawings by Toby Welles, WowHouse.

pp. 199–219: Complete Deck Guide by Bobby Parks, Decks & Outdoor Projects issue (Summer 2012). Photos by Charles Bickford, except for photo p. 199 by JohnClemmer.net and bottom right photo p. 213 and bottom photo p. 219 by Bobby Parks. Product photos by Dan Thornton. Drawings by Toby Welles/WowHouse.

pp. 220–244: Complete Deck Guide by Mike Guertin, Decks & Outdoor Projects issue (Spring 2014). Photos by Charles Bickford, except for the product photos p. 236, and the product photo p. 240, by Dan Thornton and bottom inset photo p. 236 by Rodney Diaz. Drawings by Toby Welles, WowHouse.

INDEX

A

Aluminum decking, 12, 13, 122–23
Aluminum railings, 147–48, 149, 167, 199, 210
Aluminum-reinforced vinyl, 153, 154

B

Basement windows
  egress clearance, 105
  ledger placement and, 87, 105
Beams
  choosing, 73
  connectors, 17
  grade-level decks, 89, 186
  porch-rooftop deck, 39
  post connection precaution, 102–03
  project installations, 186, 202, 228–29
  sizes and spans, 73
  splice precaution, 108
  steel, 92, 95
  upgrading posts to support, 111
Benches and planters
  benches, 198, 233, 240–41
  design ideas, 27, 28, 33, 35, 36, 37, 38
  planters, 198, 243–44
Bending boards, 42–45, 49, 188. *See also* Inlays, bending decking for
Blocking, between joists
  for bent decking/inlays, 44, 45
  at half-wall, 234
  for steel joists, 96
  Border, decorative. *See* Complete deck guide: Grade-level deck/ decorative border

C

Cable railings. *See* Railings, retrofitting with cable
Cedar, 6, 120, 122, 166, 167

Cleaning deck, 138–43
Clearances, access and, 105
Codes and permits, 57–64
  about: overview of, 57–58
  code types, 59
  getting permits, 60–62, 63
  importance of, 30, 58
  inspections for, 62–64
  IRC, DCA 6 codes, 59
  permit functions, 58
  project code checks, 179, 181, 191, 197, 201, 203, 209, 211, 215, 225, 227, 235, 242
  railing systems, 148
  responsibility for, 60
  when permits required, 58–60
  wildland settings, 118–19
Columns, 39, 40
Complete deck guide: Grade-level deck/ decorative border, 221–44
  about: overview of, 221
  adjusting width, 221–22
  bench, 240–41
  code checks, 225, 227, 235, 242
  decking/border installation, 236–37
  footings, 222–25
  half-wall, 242
  hanging joists, 230–33
  laying out, 222
  ledger installation, 226–27
  planters, 243
  setting rim beam, 228–29
  skirtboards, 238, 239
  stairs, 233–34, 239
Complete deck guide: Low, curvy deck, 178–98
  about: overview of, 178–79
  beam/footing positions, 180–81

benches and planters, 198
bending boards for, 188
code checks, 179, 181, 191, 197
decking installation, 188–89
footings, 182–83
framing, 186–87
handrail, 196–97
kerfed rim joist, 187
layout, 179–81
ledger installation, 179
skirtboards, 192–93
stairs, 190–91, 194–95
Complete deck guide: Raised deck/custom railing, 199–219
  about: overview of, 199
  code checks, 201, 203, 209, 211, 215
  decking installation, 204–05
  footings and posts, 206, 207–09
  framing, 202–03
  hanging upper landing, 203
  ledger installation, 200–201
  mitering corners, 203
  rail posts and railings, 210–13
  stairs, 214–20
Composites
  allowing for expansion/contraction, 236
  gluing, 240
  nonwood decking, 11–12, 13
  railing systems, 150–53
  wood-plastic decking, 10–11, 13
Concrete. *See also* Footings; Piers
  anchors, 77, 174
  attaching ledger to, 84–86, 87
  hot-tub pad, 184–85
  pad/footing for stairs, 174–75, 217, 218–19
  post connection hardware, 16, 77

Connectors. *See* Fasteners; Hardware

Curvy deck. *See* Complete deck guide: Low, curvy deck

D

Decking installation
   on the diagonal, 204–05
   with hidden fasteners, 188, 236–37
   project installations, 188–89, 204–05, 236–37

Decking materials. *See also* Aluminum decking; Synthetic decking; Wood, pressure-treated; Wood decking
   fastening to steel, 98–99 (*see also* Framing, with steel)
   flame-spread ratings, 120
   hidden fasteners for, 5, 99, 236–37
   overspanning precaution, 103–04

Designing decks, 27–41. *See also* Inlays, bending decking for; Lighting
   about: overview of, 27–28
   codes and, 30
   focal point with patterns/railings, 33
   narrow decks, 34
   optimizing views, 27, 31–34
   on porch rooftop, 39–41
   railings, 29, 30, 32–33
   room concept, 28
   scale and, 31, 32, 34
   small but elegant, 35–38
   sun control, 29–30
   traffic paths, 29
   wind and, 29, 30

Diagonal, installing decking on, 204–05

Dining, lighting for, 53

Drainage, underdeck, 126–29

F

Fascia material
   hiding sleepers, 41
   steel decking and, 99

Fasteners
   biscuit-style, 99, 236
   coated, for pressure-treated wood, 205
   correct, importance of using, 102
   for decking on steel joists, 98
   hidden, 5, 99, 188, 236–37
   ledger to rim joist, 15, 86
   plugs covering, 48, 163, 195, 237
   rust prevention during deck cleaning, 143
   rusty, fixing, 144

Finishes, 21–25
   about: overview of, 21
   applying, 142, 143–45
   cleaning deck before reapplying, 138–43
   formulations (oil-based, water-based, hybrid), 23–24
   options, 23–25
   pigment options, 24–25
   price, 25
   refinishing decks, 138–45
   sunlight, water and, 22
   VOCs and, 24

Fire pits, 36, 37, 54, 64

Fires, decks and. *See* Wildfire, decks standing up to

Flashing
   below-deck protection, 125, 129
   counterflashing, 226, 227
   joist tape cap, 237, 240
   leaky, fixing, 113
   ledger, 58, 85, 99, 113, 179, 200, 201, 226, 227
   metal, 99, 117, 120, 121, 123, 124, 129, 179
   posts, 134
   rubber, 134
   seams between lumber, 89
   tape, 99
   vinyl, 99, 129, 179, 200, 201

Footings, 72–82. *See also* Piers
   about: overview of, 72
   alternative, 79
   beam selection and, 73
   code checks, 181, 225
   concrete strength, 82
   done right, 80–82
   form options, 74, 77, 79
   frost heave/lines and, 69–71, 76
   helical piles, 79
   holes and concrete, 80–82
   loads and, 74–75, 76, 79, 221–23
   pin, 79
   post connection hardware, 16, 77
   project installations, 182–83, 206, 207–09, 222–25
   shallow, correcting, 110, 111
   sizing, 72–78
   soil types and, 69, 76, 78, 180
   stair posts and, 172–74
   weight of, 78

Framing. *See also* Beams; Footings; Joists; Posts, framing support

complete deck guide projects, 186–87, 202–03, 228–32
   frost heave and, 69–71
   grade-level. *See* Framing, grade-level deck
   loads and. *See* Loads
   steel. *See* Framing, with steel

Framing, grade-level deck, 83–90
   about: overview of, 83–84
   avoiding ground contact, 90
   beam placement, 89
   ledger challenges, 84–86, 87
   piers for, 86–90, 106–07
   pre-joist-install check, 90

Framing, with steel, 91–100
   about: overview of, 91–93
   avoiding rust, 93, 94, 99
   beams, 92, 95
   blocking joists, 96–97
   building department hurdle, 93–94
   connectors, 96, 99, 100
   cutting and notching, 94
   dimensions and configurations, 92
   fascia material, 99
   finding supplier, buying steel, 98–99
   galvanization levels, 98–99
   hurdles to overcome, 93–99
   joists, 92, 95–98
   ledgers, 93–94
   nearly-fireproof deck, 124–25
   rim to joists, 97
   screwing down decking, 98–99
   stairs and railing posts, 100

Frost heave, 69–71

G

Gluing composite decking, 240

Grade-level decks. *See* Complete deck guide: Grade-level deck/ decorative border; Framing, grade-level deck

Guardrails. *See* Railings

H

Half-walls, 36, 38, 234, 242

Hardware, 14–20. *See also* Fasteners
   concrete anchors, 174
   deck to house, 19
   hurricane straps, 209
   joists to ledger/beams, 17, 203, 209, 230, 231
   lateral load connectors, 12
   locations, illustrated, 14

posts to footing/framing, 16, 77, 209
protection, 20
railing posts to framing, 18, 100
stairs stringer brackets, 218
stairs to header, 19, 120, 175
Header
 fastening, 172
 stair connectors, 19, 120, 175
 supporting, 173
Helical piles, 79
Hot tubs
 lighting, 53–54
 load considerations, 66–68, 203
 pad for, 179, 181, 184–85, 189
 stairs to/benches around, 194, 198
Hurricane straps, 209

I

Inlays, bending decking for, 42–50
 about: overview of, 42
 best boards to bend, 46–50
 blocking for, 44, 45
 design ideas, 43
 installing boards, 47–48
 methods for, 42–45, 46
 warranty issues, 45–46
Inspections, 62–64. *See also* Codes and
 permits
Ipé wood, 6, 156, 163, 166, 167, 196–97

J

Joists
 blocking, 96–97
 capping for long-term performance,
  237
 connectors, 17, 203, 209, 230, 231
 installing, 186–87, 202–03, 230–32
 on-center measurements (12" or 16"),
  202, 227, 230
 radius deck, 186–87
 steel, tracks, beams and, 92, 95–98
 tape cap, 237, 240

K

Kitchen, outdoor, 29, 53

L

Ledgers
 attaching, 15, 84–86, 87, 105–06, 179,
  200–201, 226–27
 basement windows and, 87, 105
 code checks, 201, 227
 connectors, 15, 17, 86

fastening by code, 86
flashing, 58, 85, 99, 113, 179, 200, 201,
 226, 227
out-of-square corners and, 87
precaution, 105–06
steel, 93–94
unsecured, correcting, 112
wavy walls and, 87
Lighting, 51–56
 about: overview of, 51
 ambient, 51, 54
 designing, 30
 essential (stairs/doors), 51, 52
 line vs. low voltage, 55
 living spaces, 54
 solar, 56
 sources, 56
 stairs, 52
 targeted (food prep/dining/hot tubs),
  51, 53–54
Loads, 66–68
 cantilevering joists for, 202
 code check, 235
 dead, 72, 74, 78, 169
 footings and, 74–75, 76, 79, 221–23
  (*see also* Footings)
 gravity (vertical), 66–68, 71, 235
 guardrails and, 107–08
 hot-tub pad, 184–85
 lateral, 66, 68, 235
 lateral connectors for, 112
 live, 66–68, 72, 74, 202
 post/beam connections and, 102–04
 shifting, 71
 stairs and, 169–73, 233

M

Maintenance and repairs
 making old deck safe, 109–16
 refinishing decks, 138–45
 retrofitting railing, 156–63
Mistakes to avoid, 101–08
Mitering composite materials, 236, 239
Mitering deck corners, 203

N

Nailers, 17

P

Patterns
 basket weave, 34
 bending decking for inlays, 42–50
 border boards, 34

creating focal point with, 33
diamond, 34
options, 34
short orientation, 34
PC Decking, 13
Permits. *See* Codes and permits
Piers, 70, 71, 86–90, 106–07
Pilasters, 40
Planters. *See* Benches and planters
Pools, 53–54, 67, 68. *See also* Hot tubs
Porches
 decks vs., 29
 designing rooftop deck on, 39–41
 lighting, 55
Posts, framing support
 beam connection precaution, 102–03
 connectors, 16, 77, 209
 existing, upgrading for beam support,
  111
 fasteners for, 171, 172
 for porch-rooftop deck, 40
 project installations, 208–09
Posts, railing
 connection precaution, 107–08
 connectors, 18, 100
 with extra blocking, 211
 project installations, 210–11

R

Railings
 about: overview of options, 147–48
 blocking wind, not view, 29, 30
 broken balusters, fixing, 114
 cable. *See* Railings, retrofitting with
  cable
 capstock, 153
 choosing system, 148
 code approval, 148
 composites, 150–53
 continuous, on stairs, 101–02
 custom options, 164–68
 designing, 29, 30, 32–33
 height requirements, 212, 242
 lighting, 54–56
 manufactured systems, 147–55
 matching to view, 32–33
 metal balusters with wood, 196–97,
  210–13
 metal systems, 149
 mixing and matching components,
  148
 nautical custom option, 165, 166, 167
 for porch-rooftop deck, 41

post connection hardware, 18, 100

post connection precaution, 107–08

project installations, 196–97, 210–13

for safety, sociability, 30

steel stairs and posts, 100

vinyl, 154–55

wire-panel option, 167–68

Railings, retrofitting with cable, 156–63, 157

about: overview of, 156

advantages of, 158

fittings for, 157

installation, illustrated, 158–60, 161–64

planning runs and corners, 158–61

post layout, 158

pulling, adjusting cable, 162–63

spacings and specs, 157

trim, 163

Redwood, 6, 120

Refinishing decks, 138–45

Repairs. See Maintenance and repairs

Rim joist

attaching ledger to, 15, 84–86, 105–06

attaching stairs and, 171, 173, 214

guardrail precaution, 107

insufficient, reinforcing, 111

ledger to, fasteners, 15

steel, covering, 99

Roof, decking over, 131–37

about: overview of, 131

edge drip protection, 133

flashing posts, 134–35

framing the roof, 131–33

gluing down EPDM roofing, 133–35

sleepers and decking, 135–37

substrate detail, 130

underlayment, 130, 131, 133, 134

Rust

fixing fasteners with, 144

preventing on steel framing, 93, 94, 99

preventing when cleaning deck, 143

S

Safety

guardrails for. See Railings

making old deck safe, 109–16

mistakes to avoid, 101–08

Scale, 31, 32, 34

Skirtboards, 192–93, 222, 238, 239

Slotted screw holes, 236

Small decks, 35–38. See also Designing decks

Soil

disturbed, setting piers in, 106–07

frost heave, 69–71

sizing footings and, 75, 76, 78, 180

types of, 69, 76, 78

Solar lighting, 56

Sources

deck-drainage systems, 129

decking manufacturers, 13

lighting, 56

Stairs. See also Railings

connection hardware, 19, 175, 218

continuous railing importance, 101–02

on curved deck, 190–91

footings and posts for, 172–74

framing, 214–19

hiding fasteners, 239

independent support for, 169–72

joining posts and stringers, 176

kerfed stringers for, 191

landings, 86, 174–75, 203, 214, 216, 217, 218, 219

lighting, 52

mounting, 169–76

project installations, 190–91, 194–95, 214–20, 233–34, 239

riser height, 104, 215

securing bottom of, 174–75

stacked-box, 194, 233, 234

steel, 100

unsafe handrail repair, 115

weak, strengthening, 116

Steel framing. See Framing, with steel

Sun

controlling, 29–30

trellises for, 29, 32, 53

Synthetic decking

about: overview of, 9

all-plastic decking, 9–10, 13

fasteners for. See Fasteners

manufacturers, 13

nonwood composites, 11–12, 13

overspanning precaution, 103–04

wood vs., 5

wood-plastic composites, 10–11, 13

T

Tension rod, 176

Trellises, 29, 32, 53

U

Underdeck, drainage system, 126–29

Underdeck, wildfire protection, 125

Underlayment, for over-roof decking, 130, 131, 133, 134

V

Vents, 125

Views, optimizing, 27, 31–34

Vinyl flashing, 99, 129, 179, 200, 201

Vinyl railing systems, 154–55

W

Wildfire, decks standing up to, 118–25

about: overview of, 118

below-deck protection, 125

code requirements, 118–19

flame-spread ratings, 120

nearly-fireproof deck, 124–25

surrounding area and, 122

traditionally-framed class-1/class-2 decks, 122–23

upgraded class-3 deck, 120–21

Wind, deck and, 29, 30

Wood, pressure-treated, 6–8

advantages of, 5, 6

alternative preservatives vs., 8–9

color-infused, 8

ground contact and, 90

KDAT, deck built with, 199–219

purchasing, 60

railing systems, 147

treating, 6, 135

twisting and checking, 6, 60, 91

Wood decking

acetylated, 8

advantages of, 5

alternative preservatives, 8–9, 135

cleaning, 138–43

naturally resistant, durable, 6

refinishing, 138–45

thermally modified, 8–9

If you like this book, you'll love *Fine Homebuilding*.